THE LAST BOSS OF BRIGHTON

ALSO BY DOUGLAS CENTURY

*Hunting El Chapo: The Inside Story of the American Lawman Who
Captured the World's Most-Wanted Drug Lord*

*Brotherhood of Warriors: Behind Enemy Lines with a Commando
in One of the World's Most Elite Counterterrorism Units*

Barney Ross: The Life of a Jewish Fighter

*Under and Alone: The True Story of the Undercover Agent Who
Infiltrated America's Most Violent Outlaw Motorcycle Gang*

Takedown: The Fall of the Last Mafia Empire

Street Kingdom: Five Years Inside the Franklin Avenue Posse

THE LAST BOSS OF BRIGHTON

BORIS "BIBA" NAYFELD
AND THE RISE OF THE
RUSSIAN MOB IN AMERICA

DOUGLAS CENTURY

WM

WILLIAM MORROW
An Imprint of HarperCollinsPublishers

Grateful acknowledgment is made to the following for the use of the photographs that appear in the art insert: Courtesy of the Nayfeld family (pages 1–5; page 6, top left and right; page 7, bottom; and page 8, bottom); Photograph by Timothy Fadek for the *Washington Post* via Getty Images (page 6, bottom); Photograph by Frederick Kelly/The New York Historical Society via Getty Images (page 7, top); Photograph by Seth Wenig for the Associated Press/AP Images (page 8, top); and Photograph by Alexey Yurenev for the *New York Times* (page 8, middle).

The names and identifying characteristics of some individuals have been changed.

HarperCollins books may be purchased for educational, business, or sales promotional use. For information, please email the Special Markets Department at SPsales@harpercollins.com.

FIRST EDITION

Designed by Nancy Singer
Map by Jeffrey L. Ward

Library of Congress Cataloging-in-Publication Data has been applied for.

ISBN 978-0-06-301495-4 (hardcover)

ISBN 978-0-06-325218-9 (international edition)

22 23 24 25 26   LSC   10 9 8 7 6 5 4 3 2 1

For Marcia and Lena

POWER IS GIVEN ONLY TO THE ONE WHO
DARES TO BEND DOWN AND PICK IT UP.
THERE'S ONLY ONE THING THAT MATTERS,
ONLY ONE: TO BE ABLE TO DARE!

—RASKOLNIKOV IN FYODOR DOSTOEVSKY'S *CRIME AND PUNISHMENT*

THE BASIC CREED OF THE GANGSTER, AND
FOR THAT MATTER OF ANY OTHER TYPE OF
CRIMINAL, IS THAT WHATEVER A MAN HAS
IS HIS ONLY SO LONG AS HE CAN KEEP IT,
AND THAT THE ONE WHO TAKES IT AWAY
FROM HIM HAS NOT DONE ANYTHING WRONG
BUT HAS MERELY DEMONSTRATED HIS
SMARTNESS.

—HERBERT ASBURY, *THE GANGS OF NEW YORK*

CONTENTS

BORIS NAYFELD'S
EUROPE

0 Miles 600
0 Kilometers 600

Arctic Ocean

to Norilsk

FINLAND

NORWAY

Stockholm

Leningrad, a.k.a. St. Petersburg

*North
Sea*

SWEDEN

Moscow

to Siberia and
Sakhalin Island

UNITED
KINGDOM

DENMARK

Baltic Sea

USSR

IRELAND

NETHERLANDS

Babruysk

London

Amsterdam   Berlin   Warsaw   Gomel

*Atlantic
Ocean*

Antwerp

Brussels   EAST
GER.   POLAND   Kiev

BELGIUM
LUXEMBOURG   WEST
GERMANY   CZECHOSLOVAKIA

FRANCE   Zurich   Munich

SWITZERLAND   Vienna
AUSTRIA   HUNGARY   Odessa

Geneva

ITALY   ROMANIA

Monte Carlo

Black Sea

PORTUGAL

SPAIN   YUGOSLAVIA

Rome   BULGARIA

ALBANIA

Mediterranean Sea

GREECE   TURKEY

MOROCCO

TUNISIA   SYRIA

CYPRUS
LEBANON

ALGERIA

Tel Aviv — Jerusalem
ISRAEL   JORDAN

AFRICA

SAUDI
ARABIA

to Freetown, Sierra Leone

LIBYA   EGYPT   *Red Sea*

© 2022 Jeffrey L. Ward

MIDTOWN:
The Diamond District on West Forty-Seventh Street in Manhattan, where Boris Nayfeld and his crew pulled off numerous lucrative gem thefts.

NEW JERSEY

N

0   1   2
Miles

LIBERTY ISLAND:
The Statue of Liberty

BOROUGH PARK:
The apartment on Ocean Parkway and Church Avenue where Evsei Agron lived with his second wife, the popular émigré chanteuse Maya Rozova.

BENSONHURST:
Where Boris Nayfeld met with many powerful Cosa Nostra mobsters like Anthony "Gaspipe" Casso, underboss of the Lucchese crime family.

STATEN ISLAND:
Where Boris Nayfeld and his family lived on a block near the nature preserve, surrounded by many high-ranking Italian American mobsters.

BENSONHURST:
Passage Palace, where Boris had his lavish sixtieth birthday gala, under surveillance by the DEA and FBI.

STATEN ISLAND

SEAGATE:
The first apartment of Boris Nayfeld and his family in New York City was in the housing projects of Coney Island— near Seagate, Neptune Avenue, and Thirty-Sixth Street— after emigrating from the USSR in 1979.

© 2022 Jeffrey L. Ward

Hudson River

East River

Midtown

MANHATTAN

Green

East Village

Williamsburg Bridge

Manhattan Bridge

Brooklyn Bridge

Williams

DUMBO

Battery Tunnel

Brooklyn Heights

Cobble Hill

Carroll Gardens

Red Hook

Prospe Height

Park Slope

Prospect Park

Pro Le Gar

Upper New York Bay

Sunset Park

Fla

Kensington

Dyker Heights

Borough Park

Bensonhurst

Verrazzano-Narrows Bridge

Fort Hamilton

Gravesend

Lower New York Bay

Seagate

Brigh Bea

BORIS NAYFELD'S BROOKLYN

QUEENS

Bushwick

Bedford-Stuyvesant

Ocean Hill

East New York

BROOKLYN

East Flatbush

Flatlands

Marine Park

Mill Basin

Jamaica Bay

Floyd Bennett Field

Sheepshead Bay

Atlantic Ocean

EAST VILLAGE:
The Russian and Turkish Baths on East Tenth Street in Manhattan, where Boris Nayfeld, Evsei Agron, and their friends would regularly go for a weekly session in the *banya*.

MILL BASIN:
El Caribe country club, the large catering hall where Boris Nayfeld, his cousin, and Evsei Agron built a fitness center and where they would meet with leading Italian American mobsters.

SHEEPSHEAD BAY:
The office of the Platenum Energy Company—the gasoline distribution company owned by Boris Nayfeld and his cousin—was in this quiet residential neighborhood.

BRIGHTON BEACH:
The heart of the Soviet-Jewish émigré community in the United States. By 1980, this was home to an estimated forty thousand Russian-speaking immigrants. Numerous popular restaurants and nightclubs—such as Sadko, Odessa, the National, Paradise, and Metropol—flourished on Brighton Beach Avenue and Emmons Avenue.

AUTHOR'S NOTE

When I embarked on this project by asking Boris Nayfeld to tell me the story of his life, I found him to be frank and forthcoming: he possesses a sharp memory for details and can vividly re-create conversations from decades past.

I was also aware that he can, at times, have quite a selective memory as a storyteller. To that end, I've conducted numerous interviews with his family, his friends, other mobsters, and members of law enforcement; I've read hundreds of pages of court documents in order to verify or, in places, correct Boris's account.

On occasion, I've noted my own opinion in the text. In general, though, I've allowed Boris to relay his version of events, trusting that readers will come to their own conclusions.

Working with an experienced Russian-language expert—himself a Soviet-Jewish émigré—I've done considerable research into the nature of life for Jews in the Soviet Union and during the first wave of emigration to the West in the 1970s, in order to provide broader historic and cultural context to Boris Nayfeld's stories.

Over the course of the past four years, I've interviewed Boris extensively in both English and with the assistance of my translator. Boris's

English remains rudimentary—barely comprehensible to an outsider. In Russian he is a chameleon: by turns erudite and earthy, his conversations filled with criminal slang (known as *fenya*) as well as literary allusions, Russian proverbs, Yiddish idioms, and his own neologisms. All his quotations in the book have been professionally translated from Russian and slightly edited for clarity.

In places, when uniquely colorful and evocative, I've gone with the original Russian word or phrase in the text; readers will find an extensive glossary at the end of the book to help them navigate this richly complex linguistic terrain.

A note on the use of the word *Russian* to describe this era of Soviet émigré organized crime: The term is inexact, since many of the criminals described in this book hailed from Ukraine, Moldova, Georgia, Armenia, or—in Boris Nayfeld's case—the Byelorussian republic of the USSR. Before its collapse in 1991, the Soviet Union was made up of fifteen republics, with more than a hundred ethnic groups and many distinct national languages; Russian was the official, unifying language of the vast State.

Almost all the Soviet émigré criminals who came to the West were described both by the media and law enforcement as *Russians*. As used in this book, then, the terms *Russian mob* or *Russian organized crime* refer to the fact that these émigrés were primarily Russian *speakers,* or identified most closely with Soviet Russian *culture,* regardless of their precise place of origin.

THE LAST BOSS OF BRIGHTON

PRELUDE

NaN*New York Times*

One Is Killed and Two Wounded by
Gunmen at a Brooklyn Office

FEB. 4, 1986

By Michael Norman

Two men fired automatic weapons through the side door of a wholesale gasoline company in Brooklyn yesterday, killing one man and wounding two others, the police said.

The shootings took place at 12:15 P.M. at the offices of the Platenum Energy Company at Avenue U and Batchelder Street in the Sheepshead Bay section.

Last night, the police were sorting out the incident and interviewing witnesses and the wounded.

According to the police, the office workers spoke Russian, and the authorities said last night that they were trying to determine if there was a link between the shootings and a Russian crime group.

Alice T. McGillion, the deputy police commissioner for public information, said there were "a small number of people involved in crime with a Russian background, and we're looking to see if it's connected to that . . ."

Asked about the assailants' use of automatic weapons, one of which was identified as a 9-millimeter submachine gun, she said:

"A machine gun is not normally what we see."

Five people were in the office of the red brick building when the gunmen knocked on the side door. They exchanged words in Russian with two employees inside, then fired through the door into the office and fled on foot down Avenue U, the police said. . . .

The police identified the dead man as Elia Zeltser, 34 years old, of 2387 Ocean Avenue in Sheepshead Bay. He was pronounced dead at Coney Island Hospital.

The wounded, who were also taken to Coney Island Hospital, were identified as Boris Nayfeld, 38, of 161 Nevada Avenue in Egbertville, Staten Island, and Michael Vax, 27, of the Brighton Beach section of Brooklyn. Mr. Nayfeld was wounded in the right hand and was listed in good condition. Mr. Vax was wounded in the chest and forearm and was in stable condition.

—

On February 4, 1986, as Boris Mikhailovich Nayfeld—the most notorious Soviet-Jewish émigré mobster then active in the United States—lay in the ER of Coney Island Hospital, recovering from the 9 mm bullet wound to his right hand, he spoke in heated tones, solely in Russian, to the assembled members of his *brigada,* or "crime crew."

Boris had clearly seen the face of the gunman who'd burst through his office door brandishing an Uzi 9 mm submachine gun; he knew exactly who'd shot him through the hand and murdered his best friend, Ilya Zeltzer—known as "Zelya." Boris had been standing only feet away as one of the Uzi's bullets had blown Zelya's right eye out of his head.

There in his hospital bed, Boris laid out his plan to track down the shooter—a fellow Soviet-Jewish émigré gangster, originally from Kiev.

The killer was, in fact, a former friend of Boris Nayfeld's—a well-known criminal in Brighton Beach and a man who, like Boris, had done hard time in a Soviet prison camp before emigrating to Brooklyn.

The conversation was overheard by someone who understood Russian, and two NYPD homicide detectives promptly came to interview Boris at his bedside, demanding that he give a witness statement, revealing the identity of the suspected murderer.

Boris repeatedly denied all knowledge.

He flat-out refused to cooperate with the open investigation.

"Look, the cops kept pressuring me, but I wasn't going to tell them a word. I stuck to my story. Didn't see a face. Didn't know who might have done it. Didn't see *shit*. Why would I tell the *musors* a fucking thing? That's not our way," Boris tells me today, thirty-six years after the brazen daytime attack inside his office on Avenue U and Batchelder Street.

"Why talk to them? Of course, I knew who shot us—I'd seen his face clearly—and, believe me, I didn't want the cops to catch him. I had every intention of tracking down this motherfucker and killing him myself!"

INTRODUCTION

I shouldn't be alive today."

That was one of the first things Boris Nayfeld told me when I met him four years ago.

On a sweltering Saturday in late June 2018, we sat outdoors at Tatiana Grill, a popular restaurant on the Brighton Beach boardwalk, tossing back shots of Russian vodka chased by the warm salty Atlantic breeze, surrounded by young women from St. Petersburg and Kiev and Odessa who wore more makeup than clothes.

Known to his friends and family as "Biba" and described in the New York tabloids as "the last boss of the original Russian Mafia in America," Boris had every right to marvel at the fact that he was alive and smiling and talking into my digital recorder. He'd survived multiple assassination attempts—shot point-blank by that Uzi submachine gun in 1986; he also escaped unscathed in 1991 when a grenade planted under his Lincoln Town Car failed to detonate. At age eighteen, he served three years of hard labor in a Soviet prison camp; after emigration to the United States, he spent a substantial portion of his life in various federal penitentiaries.

Now seventy-four, Boris is still an imposing figure with a shaved head, piercing blue eyes, and a burly physique covered in prison-inked tattoos. Four macabre skulls. A menacing tail-rattling scorpion. A massively hooded king cobra. A Star of David inset with a Hebrew Bible topped by an elaborate crown. To initiates in the world of Russian organized crime, the blue ink on his upper body can be read like a pictorial storybook, rendering Nayfeld's entire résumé as a professional criminal: it's a rap sheet that includes convictions as a racketeer, a heroin trafficker, a money launderer, and an extortionist. He's also been suspected of orchestrating several high-profile gangland murders, though he was never charged or indicted and has—of course—repeatedly denied complicity.

Few of his contemporaries from the Soviet émigré underworld in Brighton Beach made it to his advanced age. Many, though not all, died public and violent deaths. Boris is virtually the last mobster of his generation standing.

The ultimate survivor.

His life story offers us a window into a singular moment in modern history—when a wave of Jews fleeing Soviet oppression in the 1970s arrived in the United States and, following in the footsteps of a previous generation of young hoodlums like Meyer Lansky, Benjamin "Bugsy" Siegel, and Louis "Lepke" Buchalter, applied both brains and brawn to making their fortunes as outlaws in America.

But that wave of Soviet émigré criminals in the 1970s and '80s was unlike any that had come before. They were cosmopolitan, sophisticated, often university-educated men who'd survived for years in the Soviet Union by applying their ingenuity and daring to bilk the corrupted state. They settled in the decaying South Brooklyn neighborhood of Brighton Beach, for generations a haven for immigrant Jews, and refashioned it as their own "Little Odessa."

Almost immediately, criminals like Boris Nayfeld distinguished themselves for their fearlessness. They partnered with, but were never cowed by, the Italian American Mafia. They joked about how easy it was to steal in America. They scoffed at the cushiness of U.S. penitentiaries in comparison to the starvation conditions in the forced labor camps they'd experienced in the Soviet Union. They displayed a ruthlessness and casual use of violence that shocked even jaded members of U.S. law enforcement. In contrast to more established organized crime groups—as Boris never fails to remind me—their power lay in the fact that they felt they had fuck all to lose.

Yes, they were tough, but their intellect, creativity, and global ambitions truly distinguished them among the ranks of American gangsters. The schemes concocted by Boris and his fellow criminals from the Soviet Union seem, even today, remarkable for their ingenuity and brazenness. These were guys who'd survived in a totalitarian state that normalized illegal activity, one that viewed crime as a form of anti-communist rebellion and even elevated it to an art form.

In the United States, their illicit ventures escalated from audacious and theatrical jewelry swindles to the most sophisticated financial fraud, stock manipulation, and international money laundering. In a few short years, the Brighton Beach mob's tentacles stretched over to Antwerp and Berlin, from Bangkok to Sierra Leone. As you'll read, Boris Nayfeld and his partners were among the first to spot and exploit the untold fortunes to be made in the economic chaos after the Berlin Wall fell and the Soviet Union began its inexorable collapse.

They also targeted many routine aspects of daily life that we all take for granted in the United States—from putting gas in our cars to the credit cards we use to pay for it. Soviet-born criminals, and their Italian American mob partners, stole *billions* of dollars in gasoline excise taxes through daisy-chain schemes that have become the stuff of underworld lore. And it took FBI and IRS agents years to figure out how they were doing it. They pioneered and perfected new forms of bank fraud and myriad health insurance scams; they counterfeited everything from hundred-dollar bills to Marlboro cigarettes.

Their criminal genius lay in exploiting the unseen weaknesses within the economic system right under our noses.

When I met Boris Nayfeld, he was seventy years old and on parole for his final felony conviction—a bizarre murder-for-hire plot turned into an extortion scheme that was splashed all over the tabloids for weeks; at the sentencing hearing in the Southern District of New York in July 2016, the prosecutor described Boris as "an extremely complicated person with a rich criminal history" who'd spent "most of his adult life in Russian organized crime."

"Extremely complicated" is an understatement.

In the four years I've known Boris—interviewing him at his home, hanging out in noisy Brooklyn restaurants and scorching *banyas*—his personality remains a conundrum. He's at once chilling and charming; cunning and street-smart, and, somehow, remarkably naïve.

I've watched him describe with utter detachment scenes of extraordinary violence committed to him, around him, by him. I've also listened to him talk with passion and sophistication about reading Dostoevsky's novels while locked up for eight straight months of solitary confinement in the notorious Special Housing Unit (or "Shoe") at the Metropolitan Correctional Facility in Lower Manhattan.

Boris has said repeatedly that he has no regrets for anything he's done in his life. Yet across his stomach, tattooed in massive blue Hebrew letters, are the words "God Forgive Me."

It's hard to reconcile many of these internal contradictions; but this duality is, I believe, what makes Boris Nayfeld a uniquely fascinating character.

His story provides the first authentic insider's perspective on the birth of modern Russian organized crime and its continuing ramifications in our contemporary world. Vladimir Putin's Russia has often been described as a virtual mafia state; the criminal career of Boris Nayfeld, a man roughly the same age as Putin, offers us a unique, granular insight into how the former Soviet Union became the largest kleptocracy in history.

On one level, this is a classic immigrant story: in the early 1950s, Boris Mikhailovich Nayfeld was just some abandoned Jewish kid in a backwater city in the Byelorussian Republic of the USSR. In 1979, he managed to escape to the West, and by the early 1990s he'd become a Bentley-driving multimillionaire who'd clawed his way to a top perch in the New York City underworld.

—

Almost from the first moment I met Boris Nayfeld, he fascinated me. In part, this could be because our family roots are so similar. Though one of my grandfathers hailed from Warsaw—before the Holocaust the largest Jewish community in the world, outside of New York—my other three grandparents came to the United States from Bialystok, then a predominantly Jewish city within the Russian Empire, located approximately four hundred miles to the west of Boris's hometown of Gomel.

White Russia.

That's the literal translation of "Byelorussia"—today's independent Republic of Belarus.

Though the borders were constantly shifting, in my grandparents' era, the Jews of White Russia lived within the Grodno Governorate, a far western province of Czar Nicholas II's empire, abutting on Poland and home to some of the largest cities—Bialystok, Grodno, Minsk, Brest—in which Jews were allowed to live and work under the restrictive laws of the "Pale of Settlement."

Unlike Boris's family, my grandparents were lucky to get out of Russia in time.

Still teenagers, traveling alone, sometimes lying in the official paperwork about their ages, they escaped the pogroms and the Czarist
conscription of World War I and, later, the scorched-earth devastation of
the Nazi invasion of the USSR, the Shoah that took the lives of almost
all their older siblings and their families—landing in Ellis Island several
years before the 1917 Revolution.

The Nayfelds were the ones who stayed behind.

Citizens of the USSR, they were subject to the incomprehensible collective sacrifice of the Great Patriotic War against Hitler. Boris's grandparents survived the Nazi invasion only by escaping into the interior of
the Soviet Union—settling in Kazakhstan. After the war, returning to
Gomel, they lived through the decades of official antisemitism under
the repressive Stalinist state.

My grandparents, on the other hand, like many working-class
Russian Jewish immigrants, had their youthful values shaped in the
cauldron of the Pale of Settlement; even before the Bolshevik Revolution,
they embraced the utopian ideals of Marx and Engels. Well into their
golden years, in retirement in Chicago and Miami Beach, I remember
them reading *Der Morgen Freiheit* ("The Morning Freedom"), the far-
left Yiddish-language newspaper published daily in New York City.

Lifelong progressive idealists they may have been, and Yiddish was
always the *mama loshen*—the "mother tongue"—yet they all became
proud American citizens.

Throughout the last century, the immigrant experience bred a wide
variety of tough Jewish types. It produced infamous gunmen, gangsters, and labor racketeers. Also: anonymous hardworking men like my
maternal grandfather, Willie Smith—born Velvel Schmid—who'd fled
from Bialystok in 1914 to avoid the Czar's draft at the start of the First
World War. Even as a teenager, he was highly politicized, considering
himself an anarchist (*not* a communist); he was a short, powerfully built
guy with an explosive temper who often had to use his fists to fend off

antisemitic insults when he arrived for the morning "shape-up" as a longshoreman on the Brooklyn waterfront during the Great Depression.

After leaving Russia, he and my grandmother settled in a small apartment on West Twenty-First Street, Coney Island—that was where my mother was born in 1930—a short walk from where Boris Nayfeld and his family, a half century later, would find their first modest American home, in the housing projects, on Neptune Avenue and Thirty-Sixth Street, near Seagate.

—

One morning in 2019, while staying at Boris's sprawling house in Staten Island, I awoke to find him whipping up some scrambled eggs and lox and blini. He's a very good cook; when I asked, he explained that he'd spent a few semesters at a culinary school in Gomel in his early twenties.

But before breakfast, we both needed to swallow our morning levothyroxine pills on empty stomachs—we learned, with mild amusement, that we shared the autoimmune disease of hypothyroidism, and we had the exact same dosage of medication prescribed to correct it.

In the brilliantly sunlit kitchen, Boris smiled and offered me a glass of hot tea.

It reminded me of how my Grandpa Willie drank his tea.

Black. In a water glass. Not a mug.

I remembered how he, too, had been able to read Tolstoy and Dostoevsky and Babel in the original Russian. How he, too, loved to play cards and gamble with his Yiddish- and Russian-speaking friends, though their game of choice was pinochle and Boris's game is clabber.

Of course, none of my grandparents were convicted criminals—let alone headline-making heroin traffickers, money launderers, or suspected murderers. But in the years that I've been hanging out with Boris Nayfeld, I've often wondered what my grandparents would have made of him. Would they have regarded him with revulsion—as a *shtarker*, a gonif who made a fortune preying on his fellow Jews? Or would they—if even begrudgingly—have recognized a familiar character in Boris Mikailovich Nayfeld: The Jew with the indomitable spirit? The Jew whom absolutely *nothing* could break?

For me, Boris represents a throwback: a walking reminder of the hardscrabble origins of Russian Jewry in America—the world that produced a cohort of muscular, savvy, steely-eyed men, men for whom survival often meant doing the things that were *necessary*—difficult, unsavory, oftentimes outside the law.

—

Over the past four years, I've listened to Boris describing mind-boggling tales of greed and violence and betrayal.

Breathless accounts of daylight shootings in Brooklyn. Audacious heists in the diamond districts of Manhattan and Antwerp. Mountains of pure China White heroin smuggled from Thailand through Warsaw into JFK Airport. Suitcases stuffed with millions in counterfeit U.S. currency. Marathons of high-stakes gambling over cards in West African beach resorts. Escapades with young call girls in Moscow casinos and onboard the yachts of oligarchs in the Black Sea.

I'd only been talking to Boris for a few hours that first afternoon at Tatiana in Brighton Beach when I jotted down a phrase in one of my spiral notebooks that seems, in hindsight, as appropriate an introduction as any to this book:

"Welcome to the dark side of the American dream."

PART ONE

CHAPTER 1

THE INTERNAT

I remember that first beating like it was yesterday," Boris Nayfeld says. "I was nine years old and already a pretty strong kid when I got to the internat. I knew how to fight, but I couldn't handle four or five of the bigger guys at once. One night in the dormitory building, they jumped me. The first punch split my lower lip. The second one dropped me. Then they stood over me, kicking the shit out of me with their shiny boots."

In the first week of September 1957, Boris arrived at the Internat of Gomel, one of the Soviet Union's new boarding schools designed to house the millions of orphaned and abandoned children left behind in the aftermath of the Great Patriotic War. In the cold, dark dormitory, he resolved that he'd never give anyone the satisfaction of seeing him break.

One thing I learned in that place—I could take a beating and keep my fucking mouth shut. Even while they were kicking the shit out of me, I never cried. The whole time, I was taking mental notes, memorizing their faces. Lying there in my bed, I made plans to get revenge on each one of them.

Decades later, in the Soviet-Jewish émigré community in New York, violent retribution would become Boris Nayfeld's stock-in-trade; by the early 1980s, he made his name as one of the most terrifying enforcers in the Brooklyn underworld.

"At what age did you know you were going to be a gangster?" I asked him during one of our earliest meetings in Brighton Beach.

"No one's born a criminal, of course," Boris told me. "You become one. It all depends on your family, your opportunities, your environment. When I was born, two years after the end of the war, it was a hard time in the Soviet Union. There was a famine in 1946 and 1947, widespread food shortages, and many people like my dad were doing anything they could to survive."

In fact, when Boris was born, on October 4, 1947, his father was nearly seven thousand kilometers to the east doing time in a Soviet gulag for black marketeering. Home for the Nayfelds was Gomel, a midsized city in the Byelorussian Republic, and Boris's father, Mikhail, was imprisoned on Sakhalin Island in the Pacific Ocean, north of Japan. By 1950, Boris's mother, Ekaterina, vanished from his life, leaving Boris and his brother Gennady—only eleven months his senior—in the care of their paternal grandparents.

"My mother abandoned us when I was so small—three years old," Boris recalls.

I never loved her. To be honest, I'm only grateful for one thing: she didn't have an abortion. While my dad was in prison, she met another man, fell in love, got remarried, and went off to live with him, leaving me and my brother, Gena, in Gomel. My grandparents raised us on their own. I always called my grandmother "Mama." To me, she was my real mother. She did everything for us—my brother and me.

My father served in the Soviet Navy during the war, and afterward, he did what a lot of guys did to survive. He started traveling back and forth between Belarus and Sakhalin Island, selling things like clothes and watches at a profit. Today, that's no crime—it's called business. But in the Soviet Union it was outlawed. "Speculation." When he got caught, he was sentenced to seven years of hard labor.

Boris's brother was born on Sakhalin Island, in 1946, just before their father was sentenced.

"I didn't even meet my dad until I was five years old," Boris says.

After Stalin died in 1953 there were many amnesties, so my father got out of prison two years early. When he showed up at my grandparents' house in Gomel for the first time, I didn't know who the hell he was. Right away, he and my grandfather got into a huge argument. You have to understand, my grandparents kept a Jewish home. Wasn't easy in the Soviet Union at that time. Practicing Judaism was basically forbidden. But my grandparents were proud Jews. They preferred to speak Yiddish with each other, not Russian. They tried hard to keep up the traditions.

Boris's grandfather, Yosef, worked as a *zakroischik*—a cutter in a garment factory. Though small and soft-spoken, Yosef was also a man of indomitable will.

I was a young kid, but I remember this day so clearly. My father shows up and my *zeyda* tells him, "You need to find a Jewish woman to help you take care of your sons. We gave you permission the first time you took a shiksa. She gave you two children, then she abandoned them. Mikhail, now find a Jewish girl to help you raise these boys."

My grandfather could see that my father wasn't taking him seriously. He says, "If you go with another Russian girl, forget this house. Forget me, forget your mother—you're gone." What does my father do? He goes right out and starts dating non-Jewish girls. And

my grandfather keeps his word. Just like that, for him, my dad stops
existing. My grandfather ripped his coat and sat shiva—from that day
on, his son was dead to him. My dad couldn't set foot in the house. We
didn't mention him.

For the rest of Boris's life, he had virtually no contact with his father.

The last time I saw my dad was in 2004, after my release from my
first term in federal prison in the U.S. I went to Tyumen in Siberia to
visit a friend and my father came to meet me. By then I was in my late
fifties. He was an old sick man—didn't have much longer to live. I felt
nothing when I saw him. No anger, no emotion at all. He had other
children with other women and—who knows?—maybe he loved them
and treated them well. But as for my brother and me, he never helped
out. During his entire life my father never even bought us a fucking
pair of socks.

FOR BORIS AND GENA, there were a few brief years of stability in the
mid-1950s, but things began to fall apart when their grandfather fell ill
with lung cancer and could no longer work.

The disease spread fast. He didn't last more than a month. Maybe two.
Word got to my father that my *zeyda* was near death. My father tried
to see him. But my grandfather refused. He shouted, "No!" He did not
want to see his own son, even though he only had weeks to live. That's
how tough the old man was.

Yosef died at age fifty-seven and was buried in a small Jewish cemetery in Gomel. After the funeral, the boys were left in the care of their
now physically fragile grandmother.

Mama was doing her best, but we had practically no money. She was surviving on a pension of twenty-four rubles a month. That's about seven U.S. dollars. It was difficult for her. She had to rent out rooms in our house to boarders just to be able to feed us. We were never starving, but we were extremely poor. In my memory, there was only one time a year that we ate well—on Passover. Mama would save up her kopeks all year long for a proper Pesach meal.

Despite the official antisemitism of the Soviet Union—synagogues were shuttered; kosher slaughter outlawed—Boris recalls his grand-mother doing her best to keep an observant home.

There was a small house in the neighborhood where someone baked matzoh in secret. It was one street over from our house. On Pesach, we'd go get the matzoh and bring it home in pillowcases. Also, there was a rabbi secretly working as a butcher—you could bring a live chicken, and for fifteen kopeks, he'd slaughter it by the kosher ritual. The houses were constantly moving to stay ahead of the Soviet authorities. As poor as we were, my grandmother saved up all year to make gefilte fish, kneidlach, kugel, gribenes—all the Jewish delicacies. I'll never forget how secretive we had to be about Passover. Anything having to do with Judaism needed to be kept hidden in the Soviet Union. Imagine, risking arrest for baking matzoh?

SINCE INFANCY, BORIS NAYFELD HAS been known as "Biba"—a nick-name given to him due to his round cheeks, bright blue eyes, and cheru-bic appearance. When he was two years old, his family said he resembled a toy doll. But from a young age, it became evident to most adults, if not yet the Soviet authorities, that Biba's personality was inherently transgressive.

Our neighbor had a house with a couple of apple trees in the back. I'd go steal the apples at night, climb the fence, mess up the trees—his dogs would start howling—and we'd grab as many apples as we could carry. It was a thrill trying to get away with it. Sometimes I'd go alone, usually with my buddies on the street. We'd hop the fence, steal the apples, eat some, and sell the rest at the farmers market the next day.

My neighbor was frustrated by the mess we'd make of his place. He'd open the gate in the daytime and shout: "Biba, take whatever apples you want! Just don't come damage the trees in the nighttime. The dogs bark and wake everyone up!"

In the middle of the night I'd go back to the neighbor's place. We'd steal his apples again. Same story—breaking tree branches, dogs howling. I can't explain it: at midnight, they had a different taste. His apples didn't interest me in the daytime. I didn't want them if I didn't steal them.

When my grandfather died, I was finishing Class 3.* I was an okay student: some good grades, some bad. Some good behavior, some bad. It was only after my grandfather died that I started skipping school and getting into real trouble. After he died, I was constantly fighting, stealing—no one could control me. I was too much for my grandmother to handle.

The Soviet authorities had these parents' committees to keep tabs on poor families, to collect money to buy footwear and coats—you know, help out the kids who weren't being cared for. The committee saw that my grandmother couldn't afford to feed us and clothe us properly. They advised her to place me in an orphanage. Right around this time, many of the older orphanages were being shut down and transitioned into internats.

---

* Class 3 is the equivalent of fourth grade in the United States. In the Soviet Union, children started primary education with Class 1 at age seven and finished upper secondary education with Class 11 at eighteen.

"SCHOOLS OF THE FUTURE." That's what Nikita Khrushchev called the new internats at the 20th Congress of the Communist Party of the Soviet Union in 1956. Largely due to the catastrophic impact of the Great Patriotic War, there were millions of homeless and parentless children in the USSR, and for years they had either been living in the streets or warehoused in squalid institutions known as detdoms.

By the mid-1950s, the Soviet Union developed a new mixed boarding school system for orphans, blending education and vocational training, with the intention of molding vulnerable children into patriotic proletarians.

In fact, most children classified as "orphans" were like Boris Nayfeld: they had living parents but were sent to internats due to abandonment, neglect, abuse, or poverty.

My grandmother was getting sicker by the day. She had high blood pressure, asthma, then she developed an abdominal tumor. We didn't know what was wrong at the time—eventually she had to travel to Moscow to have a hysterectomy. Anyway, she got completely overwhelmed.

She went to see the proper department at the Gorispolkom* and told them she was too poor and sick and couldn't handle me. She said she could manage my brother, Gena—he had some health issues, but he wasn't giving her disciplinary problems. She says, "I have one grandson, Boris, who doesn't respond to normal teaching. His teachers can't get him to behave. I can't get him to behave. The way things are going, I'm afraid he'll end up at a juvenile colony."

A brand-new internat was opening up that year in Gomel. The

Gorispolkom sent me to live there for the start of Class 4. It was large four-story school building, had a canteen on premises, and we slept in a separate three-story dormitory building nearby. We were issued clean new uniforms, two pairs of shiny boots, and a Sunday suit. All the subjects were taught in Byelorussian, except for Math, English, and Russian Literature. It created problems for me because my previous neighborhood school was all in Russian.

When I started in Class 4, the oldest students were Class 8. Meaning, I was nine and they were thirteen or fourteen. The bigger kids, if they liked something you had—the candy or cookies we'd get for afternoon snacks—they'd simply grab it from us younger kids. Sometimes they'd give you a smack, too. It was an orphanage—these bigger guys had been in the detdoms. Some had been living on the streets, so they were rough.

Thievery in that place was *constant*. Food was always getting stolen from the canteen—a head of cheese, butter, anything that wasn't nailed down. The internat wouldn't even call in the *militsiya*—the administration tried not to publicize the thefts because the school was being monitored by the Gorispolkom's Department of Education.

Then one by one, our Sunday best suits started to disappear from the dormitory. It was the first proper suit I'd ever owned—a real treasure—because my grandmother was too poor to buy us such nice clothes. This one older kid, his last name was Samsonov—I remember it clear as day—came up to me eating candy, and he shared some with me. He said he'd got it from the stolen suits. They had a small four-person crew, ripping off the Sunday suits and selling them. I didn't steal with them, but I tagged along when they'd go buy ice cream or

---

* In the Soviet Union, all police forces were known as *militisya*. After the October 1917 Revolution, the Bolsheviks disbanded the czarist police forces and formed "All-proletarian Workers' and Peasants' Militsiya." The word "police," associated with corruption, was replaced in everyday speech by *militsiya*.

candy. The little racket didn't last too long, though. They got caught
and could easily have been sent to juvenile colonies. But, again, it was
all covered up. The principal didn't want the Gorispolkom thinking that
the city's model internat was filled with little bandits!

Throughout the school day, the Communist indoctrination was
constant, Boris remembers, and especially intense during that first summer when he was inducted into the ranks of the Vladimir Lenin All-
Union Pioneer Organization—or "Young Pioneers."

The internat had a summer camp for three months—a so-called pioneer
camp. We were taken outside the city to live in large tents. We camped
in a forest, near a river, went fishing, built bonfires.

   We wore clean white shirts with bright red neck scarves. And we all
took a pledge: to love and cherish the Motherland, to live as the great
Lenin taught us to live, to be good and devoted Young Pioneers and—you
know, all the usual Communist nonsense. At nighttime, around the bonfire
we used to recite patriotic poems and act out plays about the Young
Pioneer heroes like Pavlik Morozov—the good little Soviet informant.

Pavel Trofimovich Morozov was a martyred schoolboy praised for
decades in the Communist press, viewed as the idealized symbol of
Soviet patriotism. In 1932—or so the official story goes—Pavlik was
a fourteen-year-old who lived in a tiny Siberian village, who loved and
cherished the Motherland so much that he denounced his own father
for using forged documents. His father was declared an "enemy of the
People," sentenced to a labor camp, and subsequently executed. When
Pavlik's vengeful relatives found out, they crept up on him as he was
picking berries in the woods and stabbed him to death.

   The legend of Pavlik the boy-martyr was taught to tens of millions
of schoolchildren throughout the Soviet Union. "Pioneer Hero Number

One," he was called. An entire cult sprang up around him: Pavlik was celebrated in songs, books, poems, and plays. Maksim Gorky lauded him at the Soviet Writers' Congress in 1934; Sergei Eisenstein made a film about him in 1937. This cult of Pavlik left a huge imprint on generations of children who were encouraged to inform on their parents.

Since the collapse of the Soviet Union in 1991, evidence has emerged that the official propaganda version of Pavlik's story is almost wholly fictitious. Yuri Druzhnikov, a dissident author, performed an exhaustive investigation and published an exposé, *Informer 001: The Myth of Pavlik Morozov*. The real Pavel was a malnourished Siberian boy, most likely murdered by a Soviet GPU officer. He was not even a Young Pioneer.

"That kind of brainwashing never ended in the Soviet Union," Boris says.

"Follow the example of Pavlik. Turn in your parents if they're not being good communists!" Imagine the conflict—the confusion—especially if you come from a Jewish home, where you're taught from an early age the importance of family. *Mischpocha*. To the Soviets, every little kid was supposed to be a snitch for the good of the State. In the internat, they wanted us to believe that the Soviet Union *was* your family, your real family—more than your own flesh and blood.

In class the teachers might have stressed the exemplary behavior of Soviet heroes like Pavlik Morozov, but after school hours, in those dark dormitory halls of the internat, Boris saw a grimmer reality. Many of the older boys could be merciless. Beatings and physical abuse were constant, he says, and few wanted to follow Pavlik's example and be branded a snitch.

We were brawling all the time in the internat. By the time I was ten or eleven, no one wanted to fight me one-on-one. It was always a group of four or five of the bigger kids. Yes, I took a few bad beatings. But I'd always wait for the right moment when their little pack broke up. You know teenagers—they'll argue over a girl or some other foolishness—and as soon there wasn't a gang of four or five of them, I could catch each guy alone. I was a real grudge holder as a kid—I could bide my time, wait months and months. Sooner or later, I made sure I got payback. I caught each one of them and beat the living shit out of him.

Boris's penchant for violence became such problem that after he passed his final exam in Class 7, the principal called him in and said, "Nayfeld, you can no longer remain here. You don't know how to behave. You're always in fights. You must leave the internat immediately. You're a *khuligan*!"*

That was fine by me—I was sick of the fucking place. Twenty-four hours a day, wearing uniforms, following all kinds of rules. I came home and saw my grandmother.

"Mama," I said, "I've been told to leave the internat."

"Why?" she said.

"The principal says I'm a *khuligan*."

---

* *Khuligan:* as far back as czarist times, the Russian language appropriated the Anglo-Irish word "hooligan"—pronounced *khoo-li-GAHN*—to refer to street toughs and members of youth gangs. By the mid-1950s, it was codified as a criminal offense.

CHAPTER 2

KHULIGANS

Actually, a few weekends earlier, just before they kicked me out of the internat for good, I came home for a visit and got the biggest shock of my life," Boris recalls.

I saw this strange woman sitting in the yard. I greeted her with a nod as I walked by and I asked my grandmother, "Mama, who's that sitting there?" She was an attractive woman, blond, blue eyes, very well dressed, had gold rings and earrings—I'd never seen a woman so elegant and stylish.

"Boris, this is your mother."

I stood there, staring back and forth between them. "What do you mean, this is my mother?" The woman was a stranger. I had no memory of ever seeing her before—not in real life, not in a photo. Mama told me this was Ekaterina Petrovna, my biological mother, and that everyone called her Katya.

Mama told me, "Boris, go over and say hello to your mother."

I wanted to say, "That's not my mother—*you* are!" But I came over to her and said, "Good day."

She goes, "Oh, Sonny. My Sonny, how are you? I haven't seen you. How I've missed you! I love you boys so much!"

I looked at her coldly. "If you love your kids," I said, "you don't abandon them."

You have to understand, all I'd ever heard about this woman Ekaterina Petrovna was that she left us, never sent money for child support, never offered to help. And no matter what she said now—no, I couldn't say that I loved her. What kind of love could we share after she abandoned me and Gena when we were three and four years old? My brother wouldn't even talk to her—Gena ran away when she called him over to her. She said that now that she'd found us again, she was going to be helping out. She left us money. We went to the Detsky Mir* where she bought us some decent clothes.

Then Ekaterina Petrovna—the woman who'd given birth to me— vanished. I had no idea if I'd ever see her again. Her second husband was named Valentin Mironov, and they lived in the far north, above the Arctic Circle, in a city called Norilsk.

FOR A SHORT TIME, Boris channeled his natural aggression and pent-up rage into sports. When he wasn't throwing punches in the streets, he started grappling in the gym. "This older guy from the block, who was a

---

* Detsky Mir—or Children's World—was a chain of popular department stores for children in the Soviet Union; the first and most famous one was opened in 1957 in the center of Moscow at Dzerzhinsky Square—today's Lubyanka Square.

Master of Sports* in wrestling, took me and my brother to his club called Spartak. Everyone in the USSR, at least most boys with some athletic ability, saw sports as a path to a university degree. Succeeding at sports meant maybe earning a bit more money than some factory worker."

Boris and Gena were both quick and aggressive, and picked up the techniques fast. They soon began to wrestle competitively. "There were gyms like Spartak throughout the Soviet Union, almost like a YMCA in America, free for kids. We were so poor, had no money for the bus so we'd walk forty minutes in each direction. The gym was next to the only river in Gomel, the River Sozh."

No matter how foul the weather—a blizzard and twenty below zero, a wind whipping off the frozen river—Boris and Gena walked to Spartak and back without complaint. "Honestly, I wasn't that interested in the sport itself, but in what techniques I could take from wrestling and use in a street fight. It was a high-quality wrestling program. We probably would have continued to compete, but our trainer at Spartak got arrested for black market activity."

Then, at age fourteen, Boris had his own first run-in with the law.

I'd been gambling. Playing cards. I won ten rubles from one of the neighbors. He didn't have cash, so he told me he'd pay his debt with a bicycle—he went off and brought me back a nice sports bike. A couple hours later this local *militsiya* detective named Slavin shows up—he already knew me; he was assigned to deal with underaged offenders—and says, "Biba, come here! Let me have a look at that bike!" Turns out the bike had been reported stolen.

This Slavin already has all these reports about me fighting, skipping school, and now he catches me red-handed, in possession of

---

* A prestigious rating in the Soviet Union. An athlete ranked "Master of Sports" could compete at a national championship level.

stolen property, so my grandmother gets called into the Gorispolkom's Department of Children. They tell her they're starting the paperwork to send me to a juvenile colony. My grandmother pleaded with them, "Please don't send him there! I'll call his mother to come and take him away to Norilsk." Immediately, she contacted my mother and said, "Katya, you need to come and get Biba, otherwise he will be sent to a juvenile colony."

The Soviets had special penal colonies for inmates under eighteen years of age. If you were sixteen and got a term of, let's say, ten years, you'd start there and serve the rest of your sentence in an adult prison camp. Normally, once a kid had been in a Soviet juvenile labor camp, that was it—a one-way ticket to a life of crime.

I can see now that my grandmother and mother were trying their best to prevent me going down that path. When she got word, my mother came straight down from the far north. She said, "Sonny, pack your stuff, I'm taking you with me to Norilsk." I quickly packed a bag, and we flew to Moscow, and then up to Norilsk, and she said, "I'm going to register you at school under a different last name, not Nayfeld." When she married my stepfather, she took his last name—Mironov.

I started Class 8 with a new name—no one called me Biba. Or Nayfeld. I was a completely new guy named Boris Mironov. Everyone in school would say, "Hi, Miron!" Everyone thought this guy—who I'd only just met—this ex-military flyer, Valentin Vasilievich Mironov, was my father. I didn't give a shit, actually. I didn't feel like telling the whole story about my real father not being in my life.

Boris had never realized it until he came to live in Norilsk, but his mother held extremely privileged status within the USSR.

She was a Communist Party member, and she was moving up the ladder. She had high aspirations within her trade industry. In the end

she became a restaurant manager just outside Moscow. At the time
I lived with her in Norilsk she was the manager of a large workers'
canteen. They were making good money. My mother made almost eight
hundred rubles per month, and my stepfather about a thousand. North
of the Arctic Circle, people received big bonuses for working in a polar
region.

Norilsk was a closed city. You needed special permission just
to travel there. Since the 1920s and 1930s they've been mining
nickel, gold, rare metals. The city was built by gulag inmates. Tens of
thousands of inmates starved or froze to death or were shot during an
uprising. People used to tell me, "The streets of Norilsk are built on the
bones of the gulag laborers."

Norilsk is the world's northernmost city with a population of more
than one hundred thousand. The prison camp Boris is referring to was
known as Norillag. In the summer of 1953, it was the scene of a major prisoner rebellion, the longest uprising in the history of the gulag
system.

Most of the population was made up of people who'd served out their
sentences in the gulag and then remained in Norilsk. I'd say that fifty
or sixty percent of the population were ex-convicts and their families.
Those were my new classmates, kids whose parents were convicted
criminals or political prisoners. Let's just say it was a city steeped in
crime.

I hated being there, way up inside the Arctic Circle. I had no
relationship at all with my stepfather. Like I said, I felt no sense
of love between my mother and myself. It was just a one-bedroom
apartment, so I slept in the living area. School was a fucking disaster.
I was almost immediately failing all my subjects and the kids teased

me for my Byelorussian dialect. Most days, honestly, I skipped school. My stepfather and mother would leave for work and especially when it was cold—minus forty or minus fifty—I'd stay in the apartment and watch TV.

Lacking money or a plan, Boris made several attempts to run away, escaping Norilsk across the permafrost. In the dark of winter, this was an act of pure madness, especially since he had no means of transportation other than his feet. Norilsk is 3,432 kilometers from Gomel and 2,878 kilometers from Moscow; even the ninety-kilometer walk to Dudinka—a tiny town on the Yenisei River—would likely prove fatal. During one such ill-planned escape, Boris nearly froze to death in a blizzard, before being captured by a pair of sharp-eyed Soviet authorities passing by in a truck.

Whenever I'd run away, I'd get placed in a juvenile detention home—temporary holding facilities for runaways while they waited for your guardians to be notified so you could be released.

Then one afternoon when I was skipping school, I started a fire in our apartment building. I got the idea from a movie I saw on TV. It was this comedy called *The Seven Nannies*. The movie was about this kid—same age as me—who comes out of a juvenile colony and the adults keep trying to rehabilitate him, but he ends up setting his neighbor's door on fire. I thought that was a fantastic idea! We had neighbors who I didn't get along with, so I also lit their door on fire. The local *militsiya* were called but I think only my mother's status in the Party prevented me getting arrested and going to a juvenile colony for arson.

I failed all my subjects and was going to have to repeat the same grade, but that summer my mother decided to send me to Krasnoyarsk, where I lived at an apiary.* She had connections at this apiary—you know, where beekeepers produce honey. All I did during the day was go hunting and spend time wandering around in the taiga. I realize now my mother shipped me out of Norilsk so I wouldn't keep embarrassing her, doing things that were detrimental to her career. But I made some new friends there in Krasnoyarsk, three young *khuligan* guys. One night they robbed a kiosk, got arrested, and ended up getting sent to a juvenile colony. I wasn't with them during the robbery, but I could easily have been arrested, too.

When my mother learned about it, she called me up and said, "Boris, it's time for you to go back to Gomel. I'll be sending you money. You're creating big problems for me. I'm a Party member and I cannot have you creating such problems for me."

She sent money to me in Krasnoyarsk. I packed my bag, got on a plane and flew to Moscow, then back to Gomel. I was sixteen, been left back a grade, didn't want to study anymore. I just wanted to be in the streets—running wild, living as half a criminal. All I wanted to be was a *khuligan.*

A COROLLARY TO THE MASSIVE NUMBERS of orphans left behind in the wake of the Great Patriotic War were the gangs of *khuligans* appearing in many cities by the 1950s and 1960s, as those same impoverished or neglected children hit adolescence and young adulthood. In his early to midteens, Russian president Vladimir Putin was a member of a *khuligan* gang in 1960s Leningrad. Putin has proudly recalled it as being time well spent in a "street university."

---

* Krasnoyarsk is a city in eastern Siberia, known for its aluminum mines and stunning nature landscapes; Anton Chekhov considered Krasnoyarsk the most beautiful city in Siberia.

For Boris Nayfeld, completing the formalities of education was an afterthought: when he got back to Gomel, Boris and another *khuligan* buddy forged documents, skipping over several grades and enrolling straight in their final year of upper secondary education, Class 11 at the School for Working Youth—a high school program for teenagers who already had full-time jobs.

"We forged the papers and actually, no one in the school administration gave a shit," Boris says.

Hardly anyone from these Schools for Working Youth went on to study in universities or technical schools. Most guys simply continued working—as mechanics, truck drivers, running a lathe in a factory. The only thing the teachers and the principal cared about was being able to officially report that they were "eliminating illiteracy among the working youth." We showed up for class sometimes, most often not, but if the cops stopped us for something, since we didn't have jobs, we could at least prove we were enrolled at the School for Working Youth.

The name of the institution was highly ironic given that looking for gainful employment was the furthest thing from Boris Nayfeld's mind. By age sixteen, he was now fully immersed in the seductive and violent world of the Soviet Union's *khuligan* subculture.

I'd been doing competitive sports—lifting weights, wrestling, boxing, and I was known throughout my city as an audacious *khuligan*. I always carried a homemade knife. I often used it in fights. At that time, my city was overrun with *khuligans*. Guys just like me, between the ages of fourteen and eighteen—joined up into street gangs, basically just protecting our turf.

I lived in the Central District. We held an important section of Gomel, because our area also included the open-air market we called the "bazaar." We were fighting constantly with the teenagers from the other nearby sections, the Railway District, Monastyrsky District, and Zabeg District.

If a guy from another district ended up on our turf, just coming to see a girl, he'd get the shit kicked out of him. When we'd cross over to their districts, we'd only go in groups of five or six. You never went there alone because the same rules applied: you could get beaten up or stabbed.

At that time, there was an open-air dance called Chudilnik in our park. Teenagers from all over Gomel came, lots of good-looking girls, so the gangs would all congregate. There was always fighting—fists and knives—around that dance.

Besides fighting over turf, we were always looking for ways to make easy money. In the warm months in Gomel, there was a small beach on the river where we'd target swimmers. It was one of the few places for working people to enjoy themselves—a small sandy beach and a meat-grilling stand. There was no bridge, so to get there, you had to hire a rowboat for five kopeks. We'd pay to get ferried over to the beach, and then start looking for people who were decently dressed. It was rare to see a high-quality pair of shoes or a polo shirt in the Soviet times. People would arrive, undress in an orderly manner, fold their clothes on the shore, and go for a swim. They'd often leave their wallets, cash, watches.

We'd walk along the beach, trying to look inconspicuous. As soon as the guy swims far away, we grab the clothes and valuables and take off. For young dudes just starting out, learning about the criminal life, we thought it was good payday.

In time, we combined forces—the Central District joined up with the neighboring Monastyrsky District and we became the biggest *khuligan* gang in the city. Some of my friends, slightly older guys, escalated to robbing stores and kiosks.

The first time I tasted wine, I was at the outdoor dance and this one Monastyrsky guy says: "Biba, come with me. A couple of our guys robbed a kiosk." They stole bottles of wine, chocolates, raisins, all sorts of sweets. I didn't do the stealing, but it was my first time participating in a robbery as an accomplice. I helped them stash all the stuff at a cemetery, then we came back later in the middle of the night. Three in the morning, we started passing around the bottle. That was the first time in my life I ever drank alcohol, in the dark of that cemetery with my *khuligan* friends who robbed the kiosk.

Eating stolen chocolate, drinking stolen wine. Ripping off watches and wallets at the beach. Small-time stuff. When you're sixteen or seventeen, you don't really give a shit about money. It's all about the thrill, isn't it? Like when I used to steal apples from the neighbor's trees. What you're really chasing is the adrenaline rush. And you form up into gangs, because you want to be part of something bigger than yourself—something that feels like a family.

A couple of Boris's *khuligan* friends had already done time in the juvenile penal camps that Boris had so narrowly escaped. For *khuligans* throughout the USSR, doing time in a juvenile penal camp was a true sign of status—a criminal badge of honor.

The thing is, in my day, kids really learned survival in those juvenile camps, because they have the harshest rules among the inmates—I'd say even stricter than at an adult camp. For example, you could never use red-colored soap to wash because red was the color of the Communists. Everything red was forbidden. In terms of criminal etiquette, the purest ones were the juveniles, because they were reared on the principles of what's allowed and what's not within the underworld.

The rising tide of teenage crime in the USSR was serious enough that after 1956, Communist officials began a crackdown, aiming to curb the "deviant" behavior of Soviet youth and making more arrests for the broadly defined offense of *khuliganstvo*. Under Article 206 of the Soviet Union's 1960s criminal code, *khuliganstvo*—hooliganism—included "all intentional acts which grossly violate the public order, and which demonstrate an obvious lack of respect towards society."

"One by one all my *khuligan* buddies started to fall by the wayside," Boris recalls.

My friend Tolik Plotkin was the leader of a robbery crew—they were a bit older than me, and serious bandits, stealing cars and motorcycles, burglarizing apartments. Tolik got arrested and was sentenced to ten years. The rest of his robbery crew got five to six years.

That was my *khuligan* galaxy. Almost all the guys I knew ended up in prisons. Some didn't make it past their midtwenties. One of my closest friends stabbed a guy in a fight, and back in the Soviet times, the law was "an eye for an eye"—the punishment for murder was almost always execution by shooting. We all knew the score. For most of us, choosing the *khuligan* life meant doing time in a labor camp. And for a few—well, more than a few—their last steps were taken in front of the firing squad.

CHAPTER 3
THE ZONE

In the winter of 1965, when Boris Nayfeld was seventeen, he found a
fleeting moment of respectability: he appeared in the local Belarus
newspapers as a model Soviet citizen and youth sports champion.

I had a good friend named Victor Varava who competed in rowing. He
needed a partner for racing the two-man canoe. I was thinking about
getting back into competitive wrestling, but so many of my friends
who'd been wrestling had cauliflower ears. I didn't want to do a sport
that would leave me looking so fucking messed up.

Victor knew I was strong. He says, "Boris, come on, forget about
wrestling. I'll teach you about the canoe." He brought me to the sports
school to have a look and I liked the canoe.

We rowed the two-man canoe on the River Sozh. We worked well
together and were champions of the Byelorussian Republic in 1965.
First at the youth level, then we were the junior division champions.
We rowed in one national competition and placed second. I earned the
ranking of Master of Sports and was in the newspaper in 1965.

The yellowed clipping is from *Gomelskaya Pravda,* the black-and-white photo depicting two baby-faced teenagers waxing their cross-country skis. The caption in Byelorussian reads:

> The river has frozen over. However, the Republic's youth row-
> ing champions Boris Nayfeld and [Victor] Varava don't stop
> training, all they do is swap oars for ski poles. They have the
> same results in this sport as well—they are ski comrades. And
> although the field hasn't yet been covered by the snow com-
> pletely, they already have everything ready to make the first
> track.*

"At this time in the Soviet Union, rowing was kind of a big deal," Boris says. "Any sport where you could potentially go to the Olympic Games and win medals for the Soviet Union—there was some prestige to it."

Boris saw there was another benefit to being a sports champion, beyond prestige. The date of his compulsory conscription in the Soviet Army was fast approaching—all young men in the USSR not enrolled in university or a technical school by eighteen were required to serve for three years—and Boris viewed his athletic achievements as a way to land a posting to a cushy military unit.

When they called me up for conscription at eighteen, I was planning to go into a sports unit. Many guys who played hockey, boxed, or wrestled did their military service as sportsmen. They had uniforms, but all they really did was train all day and compete in their sports. As a junior level champion, with that Master of Sports ranking, I figured I could

---

* Though Boris's rowing mate went by the name of Victor, his real first name—listed in the caption—was Vitali.

get into one of the military sports units and those three years wouldn't be so bad.

But living that life of "half a criminal" proved untenable—straddling the two worlds of a champion athlete and a *khuligan*—and Boris wound up spending the next three years someplace much less pleasant than a sports unit of the peacetime Red Army. "I got busted by the *militsiya,* thrown into the Gomel jail, and instead of an army athletic unit I found myself going to the penal colony."

In November 1965, having just turned eighteen, Boris was convicted of the criminal offense of *khuliganstvo.* He was sentenced to serve three years of hard labor in Penal Colony Number 2 at Bobruisk, a grim prison camp located 157 kilometers to the west of Gomel.

It's almost impossible to describe what was going on inside the Soviet penitentiary system in the nineteen sixties. Everything about the zone was harsh.* The harshest part had to do with our living conditions. The monthly food budget was eleven rubles and fifty kopeks per month— that translates to about fifteen bucks per inmate. In the zone you always woke up hungry and went to bed hungry. You were constantly thinking of where you could find something to eat.

The hunger was so intense, many guys would lose all self-respect, they'd resort to scavenging for scraps at the garbage dump.

The sanitary conditions were unspeakable. When I got there, it was winter, the toilets were located outside—five-person latrines, no privacy. Can you imagine? It's minus thirty, minus forty, and you need to go outside to use the bathroom? The toilets would be all caked in

---

* In the Soviet Union, inmates generally referred to any prison camp as a *zona*— or zone.

ice—so much ice it was actually impossible to squat down to relieve yourself.

Boris immediately started off his stint in Bobruisk by getting into a fistfight. The altercation was entirely calculated: he knew he had to set down a marker immediately, to establish a reputation inside the zone.

I'm entering the barracks, and the place is crowded. I'm only eighteen, but I already know enough about the rules of the zone. First thing I need to do is get a lower bunk. In every prison—this is universal; it was true when I did time in U.S. prisons, as well—the lower bunk is more desirable than the upper one.

Now, all the other inmates are looking at me without looking at me—you know, watching me out of the corner of their eyes. Normally, they try to figure out who is this new guy? Let's test him, see whether he's got a strong spirit or if he's someone who'll break. I'm looking for a bed and there's a big red-headed guy flopping there on the lower bunk.

He says, "Hey, you should take an upper bunk."

I tell him, "I'm going to take this lower one—get off it."

He tells me "no," and stands up in my face.

Straightaway, I start punching him. I land a few good shots to his face and ribs. For that first fight I get sent into solitary for fifteen days.

The cell in solitary was tiny. There was no bed. Instead, there was a ten-centimeter-wide plank nailed to the wall. You were supposed to sleep sitting upright while keeping your legs locked straight in front of you. Because if you bent your knees, you'd fall straight onto the cement floor. It was the middle of winter and there was frost on the walls. The radiator was barely working. When the guards were leading me away to solitary, I put on a padded jacket, warm pants, and my hat. But when I got to the cell, the guard took away my jacket and my hat. He left me wearing nothing but pants and a shirt. If there was ice on the walls, you can imagine the temperature inside solitary. I could see the clouds of my breath.

For most of the day I'd squat on the floor and lean against the radiator that was barely giving off heat. You got half rations in solitary—a meal every other day. On the first day you'd only get bread and very weak tea; the second day you'd get oatmeal, *shchi*—a soup made from pickled cabbage—and a piece of canned herring on bread. Then back to bread and weak tea. Looking back on it now, I have no idea how I managed to keep from freezing to death.

To compare the conditions in a Soviet zone in the 1960s to an American prison, where I later did many years, well, how can I put this? It's hell versus paradise. Obviously, you've got to know how to behave, how to make a name for yourself inside an American prison—but it was much, much harder to do in a Soviet prison. If you didn't have a strong spirit already, you better develop one quickly, to make your name known, so that people could see you survived in the zone as a man.

During the Soviet times, you weren't worried about doing your time as much as you were thinking about simply staying alive. Not starving to death, not freezing to death, not getting shot by the guards.

Six A.M. we have a small breakfast. I still remember exactly what they gave us: two hundred fifty grams of bread, fifteen grams sugar, oatmeal or millet gruel mixed with flour, and a glass of tea of the lowest possible quality. By seven A.M. our entire work detachment is ordered to report outside, line up for a roll call. To get to work, we've got to walk five kilometers in the middle of a field. If it's snowing or raining, you're soaking wet by the time you got to the work zone. There's about two hundred of us most days, broken into units of five—the whole way there, we're surrounded by guards with machine guns and dogs.

Once we got to the work zone, we have to line up again for another roll call. The labor was intense: hours of digging with shovels or using sledgehammers. The work zone was surrounded by watchtowers with machine gunners on top. You were not allowed to approach a tower or the perimeter fence; there was a marker warning you that if you step outside that line, you'll be shot.

As hard as the labor was, being in the work zone offered the prisoners one benefit—the chance to engage in covert smuggling. Savvy inmates showed Boris how to arrange for food to be stashed by someone on the outside who'd come to the zone before the work started.

Boris's brother, Gena, would take the train from Gomel to Bobruisk and arrive at the labor zone in the predawn darkness, long before the inmates, and toss a package wrapped in plastic over the fence.

That was one of the tricks you learned in order to survive the hunger. Many of us would have a prearranged spot where something might be smuggled. My brother would get to the labor zone ahead of the inmates and leave me a stash of *salo*.* That was a lifesaver. Other times he'd hide candy, sugar, any high-calorie food he could get over the fence. All I really wanted inside the zone was enough calories to feel like I was not going to starve to death.

When you find your stashed food, you've got to carefully smuggle it back to the living zone. The guards need to do the *shmon*—that's criminal slang for a body search—coming in and going out of the labor zone. Many inmates bribe the guards to look the other way. The more experienced guys knew how to smuggle all sorts of food, alcohol, cigarettes. The controlling officer would only pretend to do the *shmon*. Whenever a holiday like New Year's was coming up, the inmates tried to smuggle in alcohol from the work zone. It was clever. They used hot-water bags. They'd fill the bag with vodka, cognac—even homemade

* Cured pork fat.

moonshine—close the screw, then tie the bag under their pants to minimize the chance of detection.

If you don't have a bribed guard, the method is to tie it around your crotch. The officers doing the *shmon* always try not to touch the penis, because if they do, they can be accused of homosexuality.

In a Soviet prison, that's completely taboo: if a guard doing the *shmon* touches your penis, an inmate like me would feel totally free to punch the guard in the face. You'd immediately be sent for fifteen days in solitary confinement. But none of the guards ever did it. That was an unwritten rule. They knew not to check around the penis. In the zone we had many such unwritten rules.

THE STRICT CODE OF BEHAVIOR inside Soviet penal colonies largely grew out of the traditions of the *vory v zakone* ("thieves in law"), an elite criminal brotherhood with roots in the brutal gulags of Stalin's regime in the 1930s. The thieves in law called their society the *vorovskoy mir* ("thieves' world"), a distinct subculture with its own mores, regulations, and language and in stark opposition to legitimate society.

The *vory v zakone* swore to resist the Communist system and its authorities; they saw themselves as upholding the ways of a pre-Revolution criminal society; over time, the *vory v zakone* evolved into a kind of alternative law of the prisons as well as of the underworld in the cities of the Soviet Union.

Though the word-for-word translation from Russian is "thieves in law," the term *vory v zakone* can perhaps best be understood to mean "legalized thieves" or "thieves operating within the code."

Like the Sicilian Mafia, the *vory v zakone* are sworn to uphold this code upon pain of death: they are forbidden from working at legitimate jobs, fighting in the military, and cooperating with police or prison guards. They vow not to marry or have children. All *vory* must contribute a portion of their criminal earnings to a communal fund called an *obshchak*. They reject and resist the norms of the law-abiding world. When a new *vor v zakone* is admitted—or "crowned"—his body is often marked with specific tattoos—a pair of eight-pointed stars on the shoulders or knees—indicating his elevated position within the hierarchy.

The tradition of a criminal brotherhood in opposition to corrupt authority predates the Bolshevik Revolution. The nineteenth-century anarchist Mikhail Bakunin writes about the self-contained "indivisible" world of thieves and outlaws—or "brigands" in this translation—as the purest form of resistance throughout the czarist empire:

> In Russia, the brigand is the only true revolutionary. He is a revolutionary without phrases, without bookish rhetoric . . . the brigands of the forests, towns and villages, scattered throughout Russia, together with the brigands confined in the innumerable prisons of the empire—these constitute a single, indivisible, tight-knit world, and in it alone, there has always been revolutionary conspiracy. Anyone in Russia who seriously wants to conspire, anyone who wants a people's revolution, must go into this world.

In the USSR, the ultimate act of resistance carried out by thieves in law and other professional criminals was to refuse all orders to work.

"In Soviet prisons, work was *all* the authorities cared about," Boris says.

But some inmates, like the thieves in law, simply refuse to obey. The code forbids work. There's this ritual process when a *vor* is imprisoned in a zone. He goes to enormous lengths to resist. At first, you're kept in solitary. That can last anywhere from fifteen days to two months. After that comes the *bur*. You can stay in the *bur* for six months. If you violate the daily routine again and refuse to work again, then you get the *krytka*.*

A thief in law, or any inmate refusing to work on principle, will follow this entire procedure over and over. But the thing is, for the authorities in the zone, all that matters is the quota. If a crew contains one *blatnoy*† the entire crew must work extra hard to cover his quota.

This professional criminal class—*vory v zakone* and *blatnye*—sat at the top of the prison caste system. The majority of a prison camp's population were *muzhiki* ("common prisoners"), inmates who'd committed crimes but were serving their sentences, working as ordered, counting down the days until their release. A separate caste informed on the other prisoners and openly cooperated with the camp administration—they were known as *kozly* ("goats"). At the bottom were the *opushchenny* ("the fallen"), including those forced to become *petukhi* ("roosters"), or "passive homosexuals," victims of prison rape, and others degraded to the lowest level of prison society—a kind of untouchable caste.

Many people don't survive. There are many normal guys who commit crimes—businessmen, engineers, educated people—who find themselves in the zone and can't stand up for themselves, can't fight

---

* *Bur*—acronym for *Barak Usilennogo Rezhima*—a reinforced high-security barracks; *krytka*—meaning "lid"—a self-contained prison reserved for the most incorrigible inmates who systemically violate rules. Prisoners are locked in their cells all day, with no common area for eating or socializing.

† *Blatnoy*—literally a "connected guy"—in this context, Boris means a professional criminal.

back. A guy like that can be easily turned into one of the *opushchenny.*
He quickly becomes a *shestyorka*† for the more powerful prisoners.

Over generations, the *blatnye* developed their own language known as
fenya, from which slang terms like *shestyorka* sprang. With origins in the
nineteenth century, deeply influenced by the cosmopolitan port city of
Odessa, fenya was originally a secret language with many loan words from
Yiddish, though over time some of the vocabulary seeped into everyday
Russian speech. There are thousands of unique terms and expressions,
as well as a rich tradition of criminal ballads, known as *blatnaya pesnya,*
sung entirely in fenya.

"In the zone we had a fenya word or expression for everything,"
Boris says. "It made our conversations almost impossible for outsiders to
understand. The camp commander is the *khozyain*—the 'owner.' The
head inmate is the *koom*—the 'godfather.' The guards walking us to
and from work with machine guns and dogs are *pastukhi*—'shepherds.'"

And the nuances of everyday speech in the zone were potentially
deadly.

That's another thing about surviving inside—you learned to watch your
tongue.

You might have a fight over every single word uttered. One careless
word could lead to a beating, stabbing, murder. For example, the
informants, the inmates who cooperate with the camp administration,
they refer to themselves as *kozly*. Goats. But that word is *only* for

---

* From the verb *opoostit'*—to "lower down"—it has many connotations, but the
most common within the context of prison is rape. Once raped the inmate's status
falls to that of the lowest caste in the camp.

† *Shestyorka*—a "little six"—refers to the least valuable playing card in a thirty-six-
card deck. *Shestyorka* is a disparaging term for the person who occupies the lowest
rung in the prison hierarchy—an errand boy.

them. They stick to themselves. And this is a dangerous thing to say in Russian prisons. You don't joke around with it. If you're playing cards and another guy calls you a *kozyol,* you've got to immediately strike him or stab him, otherwise your own status will get lowered.

"DURING THE SOVIET TIMES, a guy who found himself in prison lost all sense of significance," Boris says. "He was no longer a human being. The Soviet authorities didn't try to improve a guy incarcerated in prison—their only goal was to degrade him, break his will."

Most of the guys in the zone with me had been convicted of robbing apartments, stealing cars, stabbings, being *khuligans.* How the hell are you supposed to become a better person if you're only socializing with other criminals? You can't socialize with an engineer because you've got nothing to talk about. He's an educated, literate person. What language are you going to talk to him in? About what subject? You're not cut from the same cloth.

I was eighteen when I first went into prison. I was twenty-one when I got out. For three years, you find yourself in the environment where you've got to behave the way the other criminals behave. You've got to think the way other criminals think. Otherwise—well, you simply won't survive.

In order to make it through the days, you couldn't risk having a weak thought—not for a minute. I'll give you an example. For two years of my sentence at Colony Number 2, they had us working construction on a tire factory. The inmates did all the heavy labor, mostly with shovels and picks. And almost right away, we started to find the gold teeth.

Boris and his fellow convicts in Bobruisk did not initially realize what had happened on this site, but the construction of the tire factory turned into a gruesome kind of archeology. During Operation Barbarossa, when the Nazis first invaded the Soviet Union, some twenty thousand Jews had been forced to dig their own graves and were shot to death by units of the Einsatzgruppen at Bobruisk. "Almost as soon as we were ordered to begin construction on this tire plant, while we were working on the perimeter fencing, we started finding human remains. Skulls. Bones. Then around two hundred gold dental crowns. It surprised us at first, but someone learned the true story."

Boris recalls that the gold teeth of Jewish Holocaust victims quickly became a form of currency in Colony Number 2.

The teeth were especially valuable to guys who were about to be released soon—they'd trade the crowns for things they might need on the outside. One guy found something like twenty-two teeth. He was kind of proud of the fact that he had the most gold teeth of anyone. This guy was going to be released soon and he wanted to buy my fur hat—that was one of my prized possessions inside. He paid me in gold crowns for it.

Looking back on it now, while we were digging, a part of me is thinking: The Nazis murdered twenty thousand Jews right here. This is like Babi Yar.* There should be a memorial, a plaque, a monument saying, "On this site, twenty thousand Jews were killed." But no, the Soviets decide to build a fucking tire factory.

On the other hand, by now I was a street guy, a *khuligan,* a criminal trying to survive in the zone, so part of me is glad that someone wants to trade me gold teeth for my fur hat. A bunch of gold teeth rattling in my pocket means I can barter for some extra food.

---

* Babi Yar, a large ravine on the northern edge of the city of Kiev in Ukraine, where between 1941 and 1943 the Einsatzgruppen shot more than one hundred thousand victims, mostly Jews. Babi Yar became the symbol of the first stage of killing during the Holocaust and the subject of a famous 1961 poem by Yevgeny Yevtushenko.

One morning I told a friend of mine who was one of the trusties, "Hey, go dig over there," and he ended up finding a gold tenner.*

We kept searching for gold teeth until the camp administration found out what we were doing. They started to crack down—they ordered that anyone found looking for gold teeth along the perimeter of the site would immediately be sent to solitary confinement as punishment.

We have a Russian saying: "Prison is a good school." True, it is a good school, but not for *normal* people. It's a good school for guys who begin and end their lives as criminals. A very good criminal education. Rehabilitation? What fucking rehabilitation? I never saw a guy who became rehabilitated in a Soviet prison. At least within my circles, I didn't know a *single* guy who, after his release, followed a normal path in life. As I said, the Soviets didn't try to improve a person incarcerated in prison—that was never their goal. After enough time inside, for almost all of us, it became impossible to change. In those places, you couldn't become better.

For Boris, the three years spent incarcerated at Bobruisk opened his eyes to the wide variety of methods to exploit the shadow economy—referred to as *na levo,* slang for "on the left."

"Everyone I knew in the zone was busy planning how to make money 'on the left' once they got out: black market, hustling, stealing, doing anything to make enough to live on and eat. Not—as we used to say—in the 'way that was taught by the great Lenin.'"

Boris's sardonic reference is to the famous slogan of Lenin's: "Study, study, and one more time, study!" which was ubiquitously on display in

---

* A ten-ruble coin from the czarist era, featuring a profile of Nicholas II, made of almost pure gold.

Soviet schools. By the time he was twenty years old, Boris was committed to studying only one thing: how to survive as a *blatnoy*. "I had no intention of being a better person once I got out. Doing time in the zone, I was gathering as much knowledge as possible to continue committing crimes, learning how to stay out of the clutches of detectives and *militsiya* and the KGB for as long as possible. In the zone, that's all you do: study any crime possible to make money."

Boris talked to older, more experienced inmates and learned the intricacies of *fartsovka*, reselling foreign-made consumer goods—especially desirable items from the West—at a profit.

Fartsovka involved getting a pair of Levi's jeans for, say, seventy rubles, and reselling them for two hundred. Jeans, cigarettes, alcohol, electronics—anything from the West that was rare and highly desirable—you could resell them at a big profit if you had the right connections.

I learned about the underground foreign currency operations. I also learned about robbing the Sberkassa. Everyone said that the Gosbank was out of reach: too heavily guarded, way too much risk; trying to rob one would be a suicide mission.* Easiest to rob the small savings banks, because although they didn't have all that much cash, they also didn't have much security.

After enough time in the zone—if you put your mind to it—you become a better criminal, a smarter criminal, a criminal with insight into the various traps and pitfalls. Other inmates give you tips on how

---

* Sberkassa was the only banking institution available to Soviet citizens. Wealthier people avoided them because having a lot of money in an account would draw the attention of authorities. Gosbank, the official State bank, financed the entire Soviet economy; there were branches in many cities and towns that moved billions of rubles around the USSR, since the economy was nearly entirely cash based. The Gosbank had huge vaults and armed security, nearly impenetrable to robbery.

to avoid capture by *militsiya,* how not to leave fingerprints if you're going to rob an apartment, how to ensure that you're not seen by witnesses. From that perspective, prison was indeed a good school. As a young criminal you become much more professional.

The three years spent in the labor camp were formative ones for Boris: he'd come in a callow teenage hooligan and left Bobruisk a powerful, labor-hardened twenty-one-year-old who now viewed crime as his vocation.

He'd spent countless hours in the camp listening and learning, and once back on the street, he was ready to apply all this new criminal theory to practice.

CHAPTER 4

DEAD SOULS

When Boris got out of the prison camp, finding a job was the last thing on his mind. "Every day when I woke up, this was my only focus: 'Who can I rob? Which houses are full of jewels and valuables? And most important, how can I rob without getting caught?' Surviving as a convicted criminal was very difficult during the Soviet times because once you had a prison record it was nearly impossible get a decent job."

The most immediate problem Boris faced was his employment history record; this small green passport-sized booklet was one of the most important internal documents in the USSR. In a "worker's paradise" with officially zero unemployment, every able-bodied citizen was obligated to present the employment record book whenever the authorities asked.

When an inmate came out of a Soviet prison, they gave you a release certificate. Let's say you go to a factory looking for a job—first, you go see the head of the hiring department and he asks for your employment history. Before going to prison, I never worked—I'd been a *khuligan*. What fucking work history can I show him? The only thing I can show him is this prison release certificate. Once he sees that I've just come home from three years in the zone, he's not going to hire me. Or if he does, it'll only be the lowest-paying job. As a convicted criminal, you could just get menial work. Go mop the floors. Clean the toilets. Shovel the snow from the sidewalk.

Another thing in the Soviet Union, as soon as you got home from prison, you had to immediately register with the neighborhood *militsiya* inspector. It was the same in every city and town in the Soviet Union. This local cop makes his regular rounds—maybe he's got five streets in his district, maybe fifty buildings. He's constantly nosing around, asking whether anyone's getting into trouble, you know, fishing for information. And this inspector could visit you at home, any time of the day or night, demanding to see your labor book. If you don't have a job, he can send you back to jail for social parasitism. That was the charge: you were literally a "parasite" on the State. You could get up to two years for doing nothing—simply sitting at home.

Boris also still had to deal with the requirement of mandatory conscription into the Soviet Army—young men were required to serve until age twenty-seven; but with a prison record, Boris could no longer hope for a cushy assignment to a sports company.

In prison, I'd already decided that there was no way I was going to spend three years in the fucking army. When I was inside, I learned about a method to get out of doing your military service from some of the older guys. In the zone there was a psychiatric book, a book about psychological illnesses, and I read up on how to get a diagnosis that would make them consider you exempt from military service. I picked "psychopathy"—this was known as Article 7B.

I read the book, studied the symptoms of psychopathy. Once I was released, when it came time for me to be conscripted, I showed up and started displaying these symptoms in front of the army psychiatrist, all the behaviors to show that I had psychopathy. The psychiatrist said I was unfit for military service and marked "7B" in my military service book. I remember him saying, "We can't allow a person like you to carry a weapon!"

Of course, it's possible that Boris didn't need to exaggerate any "symptoms" during his army medical examination and was simply diagnosed by a psychiatrist as genuinely psychopathic and exempt from military service under Article 7B.

By WHATEVER MEANS, Boris had dodged the three years of military service with the clinical diagnosis of a psychopathic personality but still risked returning to prison as a social parasite if he didn't find employment soon.

Back home at my grandmother's house, our neighborhood inspector was constantly hassling me about finding work: "Boris, what are you doing every day? What are you getting into? If you don't find work soon, we will charge you with parasitism and you're going to go back to the labor camp."

Fortunately, I found out about a technical school where I could enroll, get paid a small stipend, and still be able to do whatever the fuck I wanted. So just to keep the local inspector from hassling me, I enrolled. It was a culinary program. I showed up for classes and learned how to cook some dishes.

I didn't plan to be a chef, of course. I only wanted to be a thief! I had leads on a couple of apartments in Gomel—people in the black market who had a bunch of gold and jewels in their places. In those days, anyone getting rich with money from "the left side" was a perfect target. They could never call the cops to file a report of a robbery. I was getting ready to set up these jobs, working out the plans, when my old *khuligan* friend Volodya showed up at my grandmother's place. He'd also been away doing a stretch in the zone, got out about a year before me. Volodya was putting together work crews, painters, who went out to Siberia.

During the mid-1960s, there was a construction boom in the far east of Russia. A running joke was that the population of cities like Gomel would fall by half during the summer months because all the young men were off working in Siberia.

Volodya says, "Biba, what are you doing here in Gomel?" I tell him, "Technical school—I'm in a culinary program." He rolls his eyes. "Yeah? And what are they paying you monthly?" I say, "Twenty-four rubles."

"Look, wrap up with this fucking cooking school already. Come with me for a season. I need a guy like you, a strong guy, someone who can put some discipline in my crew."

I say, "How much do you figure I'll make for a season?"

"Around seven thousand rubles."

When Volodya told me that, I was speechless. Seven thousand rubles for five months? Compared to my student's stipend? I jumped at the chance. Volodya's invitation was the one thing that steered me away from the burglaries and robberies I was planning. That and the fact that I found out I was going to be a father.

BORIS HAD MET THE YOUNG WOMAN who would become his first wife, Valentina—or Valya—when he was twenty-one, not long after coming out of prison.

Valya was a beautiful young girl from a village in the country. She wasn't Jewish. She used to come to the city to have fun. I liked her immediately and we started dating. We had no plans—at that age, you're not really thinking much about the future. As we went on dating, she got pregnant. When she told me she was pregnant, I asked her to get an abortion. But she didn't want to have an abortion.

I wasn't planning on getting married to her at that time. I was fresh out of the zone, a student at the culinary program, and my attitude towards Valya wasn't exactly serious. She gave birth to our daughter, Alesya. Once she was born, my grandmother started in on me, "Boris, this is not good! Look at yourself! You grew up parentless. You had no father in your life. You understand that it's not good for any child to be fatherless."

"So what should I do about it, Mama?"

"Valentina should live here with us—you and her and the child. We'll all live here under one roof."

It made sense to me. I said, "Valya, come! Move in with the baby." She did; we all lived together in my grandmother's house. My grandmother helped with the child-raising, and I got ready to go work with Volodya. I left the culinary program without taking the final exams for the certificate and got ready to go out to Siberia.

When I got out to Irkutsk, I immediately saw the problem with the housepainters. Volodya was right. The painters were a bunch of rowdies. They loved to go on drinking binges. Some of them were experienced painters. All of them were also serious drunks. When payday rolled around, these guys would get their cash—every payday in the USSR was cash only—then go out, blow most of their money on booze, get in bar fights, and then not return to work for who knows how long? Until all their rubles were spent.

It was a miracle if any of them showed up for work Monday morning. I understood what Volodya needed to me to do. We had contracted jobs to finish. He had a timetable to keep. What Volodya needed was an enforcer to keep an eye on the guys he'd hired to work. And if that meant cracking some heads, well, I did what needed to be done.

The first payday rolls around. I say to myself, "Shit, Volodya wasn't kidding when he said I could do very well for myself." The way it worked was, I'd take a cut of all twenty of the painters' salaries. I didn't spend much of my cash out there, and came back from Siberia that first season with just under seven thousand rubles in my pockets. At this time in the USSR, a decent salary might be one hundred rubles per month. An engineer—a professional with an advanced degree— might make one hundred forty rubles a month. Coming back to Gomel with seven thousand rubles, this was the first time I can remember appreciating the concept of having serious money.

But also, after that first season, I realized there was much more money to be made out in Siberia, if you knew how to play the game.

WORKING AS SECURITY with the housepainters was nothing compared to getting your own contract on a State-sponsored construction or renovation job.

I go out there to Siberia with a plan to have my own crew—and we start hiring people in Yakutia. My first signed contract was with a plant that was involved in space technology. They were manufacturing satellites and other things used in the cosmonaut program.

When we get out there, the shops are in a state of total disrepair. The renovation, the painting, it's very technical work. The contract we signed with the plant's administration stipulated that we would place special glass tiles onto the walls and posts. The tiles had to be placed perfectly then painted. The commissioning committee expected the place to look gleaming and clean when we were finished. The factory had to look like a proper space technology plant, not a run-down dump.

By now, in his early twenties, Boris Nayfeld, with three years of prison under his belt, was well versed in how the Soviet Union worked—not in theory, but in practice. Virtually all aspects of everyday business in the USSR involved institutionalized corruption. The system of using influence or connections to get things done was known as *blat*—likely originating from the Yiddish word *blatt,* meaning a "leaf of paper" or "a list."

Boris cut a deal to pay the plant administrator cash under the table. They set up a bold skimming operation, using nonexistent employees. In the United States, such a racket would be called "no-show" jobs. In the Soviet Union, the name had a more literary pedigree.

Myortvye dushi.

"Dead souls."

The phrase comes from the classic satirical novel of the same name by Nikolai Gogol.

Gogol's protagonist in *Dead Souls,* Pavel Ivanovich Chichikov, is a nobleman traveling around the countryside buying records of dead serfs from provincial aristocrats to enhance his standing in society, claiming to have more serfs under his name than he could afford. The novel was widely taught in Soviet schools because it mocks the old czarist way of governing the country; over the decades, the term *myortvye dushi* entered everyday Russian vernacular.

"DEAD SOULS—yes, it was the best racket for us out in Siberia," Boris says. "In terms of theft of state property, this was the big-time money. And so simple. With our contract at the space technology plant, we had twelve real employees from Yakutia doing the work, but we kept forty workers listed on the books. The other twenty-eight didn't exist. They were all dead souls."

Given the importance of the space program to the USSR in the mid-1960s, huge sums of money were being pumped into these renovations—the overall budget approved by some faceless bureaucrat in Moscow. The ingenuity of this scam lay in the fact that it was such meticulous and complicated work, no one—at least, no casual observer—knew exactly how many men it would take to complete the job. A dozen? Two dozen? Three dozen?

And as the boss of the crew I had the authority to pick up everyone's cash on payday and distribute it to the men. I paid the twelve proper workers between one thousand and fifteen hundred rubles per month. What we would have paid those twenty-eight dead souls—that same thousand to fifteen hundred rubles each—went into my pocket.

The gross that first season was two hundred thousand rubles. But it wasn't all mine. I had a partner in Irkutsk. He had the same *myortvye dushi* scam going, but with an aircraft production plant, making SU-25s and SU-27s jets. So two hundred thousand got divided up between me, my partner, and the payoffs under the table. I ended up keeping ninety thousand rubles.

Counting out those ninety thousand rubles on his small cot in Yakutia, Boris realized he'd made more during his first season from dead souls than most hardworking Soviet citizens could hope to earn in a lifetime.

This was no longer petty *khuligan* mischief; Boris was now engaging in the highest level of larceny in the Soviet Union. Embezzlement on a grand scale. There were huge rewards in stealing from the State; there were also huge risks.

CHAPTER 5
THE *BLATNOY*

B oris Nayfeld's first trips out to Siberia offer a window into the precise moment when, according to several leading experts on Soviet organized crime, "the three-tiered edifice known collectively as the Russian mafia began to take shape."*

This was not the criminal brotherhood of the *vory v zakone,* the code-bound thieves' world of the gulags, but a new form of organized crime made up of corrupted Communist officials, black marketeers, and professional criminals.

At the top of the pyramid sat the 1.6 million-member *nomenklatura*— a de facto ruling class of high-level bureaucrats, apparatchiks who'd developed mutually beneficial personal relationships both with citizens engaged in underground economic activity and with professional criminals like Boris Nayfeld.

This level of corruption was unprecedented for a modern

---

* From "The Threat of Russian Organized Crime," a 2001 study by the U.S. Department of Justice, authored by James O. Finckenauer and Yuri A. Voronin.

industrialized nation the size of the USSR. Tribute flowed upward to members of the *nomenklatura,* who were only too happy to line their own pockets. The giant Soviet state apparatus "not only allowed criminal activity, but encouraged, facilitated, and protected it," because the State apparatus itself benefited most from crime.

"Due to absolute State ownership of all available goods and services, there was no legitimate open economy in the USSR," observes Lydia Rosner, a professor at John Jay College of Criminal Justice and one of the earliest specialists in Russian organized crime.

> All private enterprise began with the theft of State goods. This was because all goods were State-owned, and the only way to acquire scarce consumer items was to either pilfer them from the source of production or to steal them from the point of distribution. . . . Thousands of people got rich at the expense of the central USSR budget. People in charge stayed in charge through a combination of power, employment of private procurers for all sorts of goods and services, and acceptance of a totally corrupt system that rewarded this corruption.*

"BY THE NINETEEN SEVENTIES, the underground workshops were popping up everywhere," Boris recalls.

> There was always a black market in the Soviet Union, of course—that's why my father went to the gulag. Even my grandfather, Yosef, when he was working as a *zakroischik,* he made a bit of money "on the left." He'd stitch some clothing and sell it under the table. He'd get cuts of material from guys who worked at fabric factories. The thing is, my grandfather was by no stretch of the imagination a criminal, yet

---

* Lydia Rosner, "The Sexy Russian Mafia," *Criminal Organizations* 10 (1995).

everybody involved could have gone to prison. During the Soviet times *everyone* hustled and took such risks.

But the black market in clothing really took off in the seventies. These little factories making American-style jeans, turtlenecks, polo shirts—anything fashionable in the West—they shot up everywhere. For the average person, it was difficult to buy decent everyday items in the Soviet Union. Raincoats made from Capron fabric were extremely fashionable back then, and you couldn't buy them in any Soviet stores. There was a huge market, but the only way you could get the raw materials, the various polymers, in the quantity they needed was to steal from the State. You'd have to know someone with connections at a factory. And because demand was so great, the underground workshop owners made big, big money.

And this financial windfall created a major problem for those profiting from the shadow economy. "When they first started up, the underground workshop owners had no protection—they were all independent. Unspoken for. The thieves in law realized the time had come to start taxing them. This big *tref* took place, and the *vory* decided to muscle in on the workshop owners, to make them give up a cut of the black cash."

The underground factory owners didn't need much persuading; the arrangement wasn't sheer extortion. The black marketeers essentially wanted to be left alone—they wanted protection from other criminals shaking them down; they wanted protection from street cops, the KGB, and from special *militsiya* units investigating economic crimes.

Meanwhile, the thieves in law had connections with apparatchiks who could divert materials from State-run factories, helping the black market factories to develop and grow. Among the *vory*, it was agreed

---

* An official gathering of thieves in law to come up with joint decisions. Fenya slang, most likely originally from Yiddish.

that a certain percentage would be contributed toward the *obshchak*. By the mid-1970s, by many estimates, roughly half of the consumer goods produced in the Soviet Union reached buyers through the black market.

ACROSS THE USSR, under the *blat* system, embezzling from the State was taking place on a vast scale. All it took was knowing the right factory managers, paying off officials.

"You could make a fortune in the seventies if you were smart, had some balls and the right connections," Boris says. "We didn't even think of it as 'organized crime' yet. To us, it was survival—making a living under the corrupt Communist system. Some guys did it with the underground factories. I did it with my work crews. I'd go out to Siberia each season, put together a crew, and pocket my cut from dead souls. Once the season was over, I'd come back to my hometown loaded with black cash."

After that first season, Boris invited his cousin Benjamin "Venya" Nayfeld, seven years his junior, to come out to Siberia to work with him.

Cousin Venya grew up right near us, in the same neighborhood. He was a strong guy—a weightlifter. He was a champion in the youth and junior divisions, competing in the heavyweight class. In the U.S., people later wrote a lot of bullshit, that he was on the Soviet Olympic team. Venya was a champion, yes, but like me—at the youth and junior level in Belarus. His weightlifting victories helped him enroll at the Gomel State University. But he never completed the Phys Ed degree because he started coming out to Siberia to help me run the work crews.

By quitting university, he was liable to be conscripted in the army, but I got him the best article for copping out. The 7B. The same one I used. I got a doctor at the psychiatric hospital in Gomel to give Venya the diagnosis of "mild psychopathy, unfit for military service."

AFTER A FEW SEASONS running his own work crews in Siberia, Boris was, by the standards of the Soviet Union, an extremely rich young man. Now in his late twenties, he had achieved his youthful goal of being a *blatnoy* and he didn't make much attempt to hide his wealth.

He went to the city's best restaurants with an assortment of girl-friends, bought flashy shirts and jackets made in underground factories. One winter he spent more than 3,500 rubles on black market furs: a sable hat and sealskin coat with a wolverine collar—roughly two years' salary for an engineer or other professional in the USSR.

He also found a jeweler who could make customized gold pieces for him.

In my city I was the first guy to openly wear a gold Star of David. You couldn't buy them in stores in the Soviet Union. I got a jeweler to make one special for me. I wore it over my turtleneck, *openly,* so everyone could see. "I'm a Jew! You got something to say about it?"

You know how many people I beat the shit out of for saying the word *zhid?* We'd be out at a restaurant and some Russian guy would tell one of my friends, *"Zhidovskaya morda!"* If I heard those words I'd snap. Whenever I heard a guy saying *zhid*—no conversation—I'd go straight over and beat the motherfucker senseless.[*]

BORIS WAS BRIMMING WITH THE BRAVADO of a Jewish *blatnoy,* with swagger and reckless aggression, but he was also discovering the para-dox of getting rich in the corrupt Communist state. You could be an

---

[*] *Evrei* is the neutral word for "Jew" in Russian, while *zhid,* originally from Polish, is the most common antisemitic insult—roughly equivalent to "kike" in English. The phrase *Zhidovskaya morda* is extremely derogatory, roughly equivalent to say-ing, "You've got a kike's muzzle!" or "Kike-face!"

"underground millionaire," but what could you actually *do* with all the black cash hidden under your mattress?

At the end of the day, how much caviar could you eat? How much cognac could you drink?

Decent housing, for example, was a chronic problem throughout the USSR. In urban areas many people lived in crowded communal apartments or houses, and any newly constructed residential building required connections and extremely long waits—often five years or more.

I thought I'd be able to buy a nice apartment, since I had a wife and child. I paid five thousand rubles just to get on the waiting list for a new cooperative apartment building. I knew some guys high up at the Gomel basketball team—they'd been allotted a few spots in the queue for a cooperative that was being built. For a onetime payment of five thousand rubles, they gave me a position of a manager on the team.

The entire scheme was a farcical exercise in *blat.*

I'm listed on their books as a guy who manages and travels with the team. They keep the salary I'm being paid as the team manager. They try to make it look like I'm a former basketball player who became a coach so I can qualify for an apartment, but it's fucking ridiculous. I know *nothing* about basketball. I never liked the sport. I'm five foot seven. And look at the height of these basketball players! All told, I spent seven months in the queue and the team still didn't get me an apartment. They returned my five thousand rubles, but they kept drawing the salary for my manager's job on the team.

The coveted new cooperative apartment might have eluded him, but by 1975 Boris arranged to buy a Zhiguli, a lightweight Soviet-made

Italian Fiat, one of the first cars available to Soviet citizens. Though hardly a flashy automobile by Western standards, in the USSR owning a Zhiguli was considered a status symbol. Only a minuscule percentage of Soviet citizens owned private cars; most families with two working adults would have to save up for five or six years to afford one.

A Zhiguli cost forty-five hundred rubles, but there was no way for me to buy it in a dealership. First, there was a long queue for any new cars—some people waited years. Secondly, I couldn't show that kind of income; I only had black cash. I paid some guys I knew seven thousand rubles to get me the latest Zhiguli and registered the car in the name of my uncle—my cousin Venya's father.

As the saying goes, "Envy kills the Russian people." Once I start driving around in a new Zhiguli, wearing my designer shirts, my furs, my Star of David chain, people are constantly pointing, shouting: "Oh, look at this millionaire over here! Look at how much cash he's making!" It's true, ninety thousand rubles for a season was a fortune, but rumors were circulating that I'd actually made three hundred thousand rubles.

At this time in the Soviet Union, if you were caught in possession of anything over ten thousand rubles, you were looking at the death penalty. The best-case scenario meant fifteen years in prison and confiscation of all property. You'd end up broke and barefoot. The worst case was execution by firing squad. If you were caught in possession of *ninety* thousand rubles—that was a certain death sentence.

In the 1970s Soviet Union, any young man driving a new Zhiguli and wearing a sable hat and expensive jewelry was bound to catch the eyes of the authorities.

The *militsiya* pulled me over so many times, I lost fucking count. Bribery was a daily part of life. Even if you tried to hide it, those cops could *smell* it—they knew who had black cash. If you drove a new Zhiguli, if you had on some nice Western clothes, you could expect to be shaken down. It happened with the local cops—the regular patrolmen. But one time I even got pulled over by the chief of a special criminal investigation unit of the *militsiya* in Gomel. He says, "Give me your documents." I said, "Why are you stopping me? You're not a traffic patrolman, you're the *chief*."

This chief asks for my license and keeps it. "I need you to come pick this up at the station," he says. "Meet me there at two o'clock." He makes me park my car on the street. I've got no license, no way to drive home. At two, I show up with my friend Volodya.

The chief looks surprised. "Why do I see two men in my office empty-handed?" he says. He didn't have to say another word. I give Volodya twenty-five rubles, tell him to go to the store to buy four bottles of cognac and some chocolate. When he comes back, an hour or two later, he places the booze and chocolate on the table, between the chief and me. No other words are spoken. "Here's your license, Boris Mikhailovich. You're free to go."

Eventually, the *militsiya* in Gomel started making not-so-subtle threats. One officer in an anti-corruption unit who knew Boris well began to drop an ominous phrase into their conversations.

Vyschaya myera nakazaniya.

"The supreme measure of punishment."

Under the Soviet Union's penal code, this meant execution by firing squad. "When a high-ranking officer in the Soviet Union starts mentioning the 'supreme measure'—I don't care how tough you think you are—you're scared shitless."

MEANWHILE, between the trips to Siberia and shakedowns from corrupt authorities in Gomel, Boris found out that Valentina was expecting their second child. "You know, time flies by so fast. Our daughter Alesya was already five, and Valya told me she was pregnant again. I was feeling the pressure of the cops—constantly thinking about how to avoid the firing squad. 'Valya! Why have another child?' I asked her to consider an abortion. She refused. 'No, Boris! I'm going to have the baby.'

She told me about the pregnancy right before I left for a season in Siberia. And while I was away, she gave birth to a boy. I got back and our son was already in his crib. We named him Valentin. My grandmother started in on me again. She said, "Boris, you have two children now. These children are supposed to have your last name. They have a father—they must carry your name. You must get married."

"What's a signature?" I thought. We went down and registered the marriage. There was no wedding ceremony, no reception, nothing. To me it was just a piece of paper, a marriage in name only, so my kids could be called "Nayfeld."

At that time, I did a lot of partying, going out to restaurants, had various girlfriends. Valya stayed at home raising our two children. She was a good mother. And me? To be honest, I wasn't faithful— I cheated on her all the time. I wasn't anyone's idea of a normal husband. I was rarely home the way a normal father would be. Half the year I'd be in Siberia, and whenever I was in Gomel, I'd go out constantly.

Valya knew all that, I didn't hide it. I mean, I never pretended to be anything other than I am. I never pretended to be a good guy. I suppose being married to me—however many girlfriends I had, however late I stayed out—the arrangement suited Valya because I always provided financially for her and the kids.

THE LUCRATIVE SEASONAL TRIPS to Siberia continued, as did the shake-downs from the cops in Gomel, and Boris says he "sensed the pincers closing in."

> Every morning when I'd wake up, I'd wonder if this was the day I was going to be arrested. The thought of the "supreme measure" was always in my head. I'd go outside, scrape the frost from the windshield of my Zhiguli, and visualize myself standing in front of a military firing squad.
>
> I weighed all my options, thought it through, talked it over with my family. We all decided it would be best if we left the Soviet Union, emigrated to America. And we agreed it was best if the application was completed in my grandmother's name—as head of the family—because we had the documentation to prove that she was one hundred percent Jewish. In the seventies the Soviets were allowing some Jews—the lucky ones—to emigrate to the West. We all planned to leave together: my brother, me, our wives and children. Also, my cousin Venya and his family.
>
> If I hadn't picked up and emigrated when I did—I'm sure it was only a matter of time before I wound up in front of the firing squad.

BEGINNING IN 1970, for the first time, the USSR began to increase its emigration quotas for Jews. Officially, this was done under a policy of "family reunification," allowing Jewish citizens of the USSR to emigrate if they had a letter of invitation from a close relative in Israel. Between 1960 and 1970, only 4,000 Jewish people had left the USSR; the number rose to 250,000 in the following decade.

One key piece of pressure came via trade legislation working its way through the United States Congress. In October 1972, Senator Henry "Scoop" Jackson of Washington State and Representative Charles Vanik of Ohio introduced an amendment that linked Soviet-American trade agreements to the issue of human rights. The amendment ultimately forced the Soviet Union to stop charging exorbitant fees—a so-called head tax—on Jews trying to emigrate. Until that time, Soviet authorities had demanded that emigrants pay back the USSR for the education they'd earned.

The Jackson-Vanik Amendment was finalized as a provision of Title IV of the 1974 Trade Act, signed into law by President Gerald Ford on January 3, 1975.

The legislation was considered so important that, until the ultimate collapse of the Soviet Union in December 1991, many Jews like the Nayfeld family were said to have emigrated "under the Jackson-Vanik Amendment."

The first step in the emigration process was to finagle that invitation from a "long-lost relative" in Israel. Often these relatives were fictitious; the Israeli government and Jewish welfare groups prepared and mailed the letters for Soviet Jews who were trying to emigrate.

"My sister-in-law handled all the paperwork," Boris says. "You couldn't believe the amount of documentation the authorities required. There were piles of papers—things like all our original birth certificates, wedding licenses, educational records—and in the days before photocopiers, the forms had to be typed up with carbon copies. Every detail on every fucking page better be perfect, or the application would be rejected over a technicality."

On top of this, the lines were so long at the Gorispolkom, the Nayfelds thought they'd never get the application processed.

"I knew there was no way we were going to get out of the Soviet Union by waiting our turn," Boris says. "I had to bribe one of the women who worked at the Gorispolkom with a jar of caviar and some black market bath oils just to get a place in the queue."

IT TOOK ROUGHLY SIX MONTHS before the Nayfelds got word that they'd been granted their exit visas. In the weeks before the departure, Boris was busily strategizing how to get all the money he'd made "on the left" out of the Soviet Union.

Like most of the Jewish emigrants looking to leave the USSR with their savings or possessions, Boris had precious little time and fewer options.

By this point, I had more than two hundred thousand rubles stashed away. The money I made with my crews in Siberia, plus all our family savings—my grandmother had sold the house. The thing is, the Soviet Customs Service had all these restrictions. They didn't allow you to bring out anything of real value. An old piece of furniture, a radio, maybe a wedding ring. Nothing could be worth more than two hundred and fifty rubles. Also, foreign currency was illegal.

My first thought was to smuggle out diamonds—there was a plant in Gomel where rough diamonds were polished to produce a brilliant cut. Sometimes the workers stole stones and sold them on the black market. I could have converted all my rubles into diamonds. But there was a widely circulated story that gemstones could be marked with an isotope—we weren't sure if it was true or not—but people warned you that diamonds produced in the Soviet Union gave off some trace amount of radiation. Meaning, the Customs Service had the ability to catch you smuggling at the border.

We don't have a lot of time to figure this out—and while I'm thinking about buying diamonds, I get advice from a couple of friends. They say they've some connection—a few guys in Gomel who can get me rare postage stamps.

I say, "*Stamps?* What the fuck do I know about *stamps?*" But they said that these rare stamps will be easy to smuggle out and easy to sell when we got to the United States.

I didn't know the sellers personally—just some guys in the black market in Gomel. Anyway, I agree to do the deal. I bought a bunch of them—one hundred fifty thousand rubles' worth. Most of my money was spent on this one called the Blue Mauritius that had a catalogue value of roughly half a million dollars. Or so I was told. There were only six in the entire world. Obviously, I wanted to know how one of these extremely rare stamps ended up in Belarus. The guys told me that it was smuggled into the Soviet Union via the port of Odessa by some sea captain in the merchant marines.

The blue two-pence "Post Office," issued by the British colony of Mauritius in 1847, featuring Queen Victoria's portrait in profile, is considered one of the world's rarest stamps. Philatelists say there are twelve authenticated Blue Mauritius stamps in existence. Today, the value for a single Blue Mauritius, in used condition, is $1.7 million. "Officially, our paperwork says we're going to Israel, but first we've got to pass through Austria. In addition to the Blue Mauritius, I bought some Austrian stamps, figuring that that once I get to Vienna, I can sell them at a profit and have some spending money when we get to America."*

BUT AS THE SCHEDULED DEPARTURE DATE approached, the family's entire emigration plan nearly collapsed when Boris's grandmother Riva fell gravely ill.

Mama had so many serious health problems—every morning when she woke up, she needed to take ten different pills. About two months prior

---

* Vienna was the transit point for almost all Soviet emigrant Jews.

to our scheduled departure, she got so sick—her heart, her high blood pressure—that we thought she was dying. We called an ambulance. The local doctors said there was nothing they could do. They could only give her an injection to relieve the pain. I'll never forget how they put it. "Look, your grandmother's old, she's going to die soon."

My grandmother was listed as the head of the family in our emigration documents. The rest of us were following her in this process of family reunification. If Mama died, everything would've fallen apart. We all looked after her, nursed her as best we could. The ambulances kept coming back and forth to our house for weeks, always with the same assessment: "There's nothing we can do. She's on her deathbed." We worried we were going to lose her, right up until day we were emigrating.

The night of the departure, Boris remembers meticulously secreting his trove of rare stamps in packages of sealed Russian cigarettes. He gently pried open the cellophane with a sewing needle, hid the stamps next to the cigarette foil, then resealed the cellophane with a dab of egg white. He also decided to risk smuggling out two small diamonds that he'd bought on the black market for two thousand rubles. He hid the two diamonds in the corrugated cardboard box of a government-approved radio, which he hoped would slip by the Soviet Customs officers undetected. "I figured that with these rare stamps—especially the Blue Mauritius, if I could really get half a million bucks—I should be able to get myself on my feet, maybe even start up a business in the West."

THE NAYFELDS LEFT GOMEL by train on October 6, 1979. They were among the 51,333 Jews emigrating from the USSR via Vienna that year—the peak year of Jewish emigration in the decade.

The border crossing at Brest was successful. The customs inspection didn't find a thing. Not the stamps. Not the diamonds. In Warsaw, we spent one awful night at the railway station. We slept on the floor. We all got so ill with dysentery. My grandmother and my young son Valentin were the sickest. We barely managed to get Mama to Austria alive. She was so ill in Vienna that we called an ambulance. We were sure she was going to die right there.

But the doctors in Vienna were amazing. They fixed her up, gave her some new medications. Within a week, she was feeling better than she had in years. It was my first realization of how different things were in the West. In Gomel, they said there's nothing they could do, she was on death's door. The doctors in Austria got her back to good health.

Before we left Austria for Italy, once we were sure my grandmother was going to be okay, my brother, my cousin, and I talked it over. I'd smuggled out about ten Austrian stamps and we found an actual philatelist's shop. The owner examines them and asks us, "How much do you want?" We tell him we'd like to get three thousand dollars. He laughs in my face. "Three thousand dollars? Are you kidding me? I could sell you these same stamps for a hundred dollars."

Okay, so we realize we've been duped. But I tried not to get too angry. I wasn't sure how, but I'd have to figure out some way to get even with the motherfuckers who ripped me off. I tell my brother and cousin, "Yes, we got burned on the Austrian stamps, but we should be able to do better with the Blue Mauritius once we get to New York."

We traveled from Austria to Italy, where we spent about a month and a half waiting. In Rome, we had to go through quarantine and have meetings with immigration agents. Once you got out of the USSR, you could change your destination from Israel to the U.S.—it required waiting about a month and a half for the approval.

Finally, we were granted visas to come to the United States.

Because my cousin Venya's wife had family who lived in Albany, New York, that was the official destination listed on our U.S. immigration documents. I'll never forget the smile in my grandmother's eyes when Gena and I picked up the family visas.

"Mama, we've been approved," I said. "It's all set—we're going to live in America."

AMERICA.

Four magic syllables, full of promise and wonder, symbolizing liberty and justice, conjuring up an almost mythical world.

But what did it *really* mean for the Soviet immigrants?

In truth, no one was certain what to expect about life in the United States. Soviet propaganda depicted the USA as a dangerous place, over-run by criminals, where you were apt to be mugged the minute you left your house, a dysfunctional and corrupt country filled with unemployment and racial unrest.

The Nayfelds were overjoyed, of course, to be escaping the oppression of the USSR, but like generations of Jews before them, their expectations for starting a new life in *de Goldineh Medineh**—as the imagined utopia was called in Yiddish—were a mix of hope, relief, but also an inchoate anxiety, an unarticulated fear of the unknown.

They would arrive as greenhorns, unable to utter a single word of English—unable even to read the alphabet—unsure how they would ultimately support themselves financially.

Though he understood nothing about free enterprise or capitalism, as they departed Rome, Boris Nayfeld claims that he harbored grand notions of starting up a legitimate business in the United States, using

---

* "The Golden Land," a wishful and imaginative description of America, the country where the "streets were paved with gold."

the black cash he'd sunk into rare postage stamps and diamonds to finance an aboveboard enterprise—something, anything, a taxi business or a jewelry shop . . .

Yet, in Soviet terms, Biba was hardly a naïf: now thirty-two years old, a father of two, he was a prison-toughened crook who'd spent a decade taking huge risks by living outside the law, a *blatnoy* who'd enriched himself handsomely through the crime of Theft from the State.

As he prepared to depart Europe for the United States, Boris knew that whatever fate lay ahead, he was never going to be some nebbish—a nobody—standing on the sidelines.

Whether by legit means or not, in America he was going to find himself at the heart of the action.

PART
TWO

PART
TWO

CHAPTER 6

AMERICA

The Nayfeld family landed at JFK Airport on December 6, 1979, and were met at the arrival terminal by a Russian-speaking social worker from the Jewish community in Albany.

"We spent one night at a hotel near Kennedy Airport, waiting to fly to Albany the next morning," Boris recalls.

Right away, I needed to unload the stamps and diamonds I'd smuggled. That first night I made a phone call to a guy named Marik Tarnopolsky. He was originally from Gomel but grew up in Leningrad. Marik had been in the U.S. already a few years. He drove in from Brooklyn to meet me at the hotel.

He was a short guy—as we joke, "one meter tall including the cap." Kind of plump, round face, always spoke in hushed tones like everything was a big secret. But he seemed trustworthy enough. He had a good sense of humor; we reminisced a bit about people we both knew. I gave Marik the stamps and the diamonds, and told him that

I needed money to get started here in America. He said he'd do his best to get a good price for me.

The next day we all flew up to Albany. The Jewish community welcomed us with open arms. They put us all up in nice apartments. We went to a synagogue to pick up some new clothing that had been donated. They gave us cash each month to sustain our living expenses—I got a bit more because I came with my wife, Valentina, and our two small children.

Credit where credit is due: the Jewish community in Albany totally took care of us during this time. None of us had any clue about life in America. We were given beginner-level English courses. They told us they couldn't keep supporting us indefinitely, so once we'd pick up some English, in about three months, they'd find employment for us. We all went to the school set up at the Jewish Community Center. We could use the swimming pool every day. We lifted weights, played sports—it seemed like a beautiful life.

ALMOST ALL SOVIET-JEWISH EMIGRES from the 1970s and 1980s talk about one moment in the United States or Canada that was so revelatory it was almost a religious experience: their first visit to a supermarket. They were surrounded by such an abundance and diversity of foods they'd never seen in their lives:

> Fresh strawberries and grapes and tomatoes—in the middle of winter!
> Thirty types of cheese!
> Forty types of breakfast cereal!
> Fifty brands and flavors of ice cream!

For some of the new immigrants, strolling the aisles of a massive modern American supermarket was an epiphany: the first concrete realization that all the Soviet propaganda they'd heard about life in the West was a lie.

Boris Nayfeld had an entirely different epiphany.

The first thought that comes into my head is: "Wow, I could steal *all* this fucking stuff!" And I *did*. I used to come to the supermarket after English classes at the Jewish Community Center, stash away all kinds of food on the lower rack of the cart, throw my schoolbooks and papers on top, pay for only a few pieces of fruit, then walk home with a hundred bucks' worth of groceries. Nobody noticed a thing, no security chasing after me. I couldn't believe how easy it was to steal in America.

We used to joke: "Free housing, free classes, all this fresh food there for the taking—now *this* is the communism we've been promised!"

BUT AFTER THREE MONTHS, the carefree days in Albany came to an end.

My brother, Gena, and I were told by the social worker that we had to find work, start supporting our families on our own. I'd sat through all the English classes, but I couldn't say more than a few words. I was sent to some doctor's office in downtown Albany to work as a janitor. I tried it for a few days. But I couldn't picture myself cleaning an office with vacuum and a mop, emptying trash cans, scrubbing toilets. For a guy who'd already done some major criminal things and got used to having quite a bit of money back in the Soviet Union, to work as a fucking janitor? No, frankly, I couldn't imagine that.

And it wasn't just the janitor's job. I couldn't see any future in Albany. It was a small city with maybe ten Russian-speaking families. I wanted to go to New York City, to Brooklyn, to Brighton.

Back in the Byelorussian backwater of Gomel, like most Soviet Jews, Boris and his family knew nothing about the burgeoning Russian-speaking community in Brooklyn.

But after a few days in Albany, they heard the stories.

Brighton Beach.

A seafront enclave where blocks upon blocks of storefront signs bore Cyrillic letters, where you could find restaurants serving *real* Russian rye bread, smoked and salted sturgeon and salmon, pelmeni, okroshka, shashlik, and beef stroganoff; where women did their daily shopping wearing babushkas and shirtless men lounged on the boardwalk playing chess and flipping through the pages of *Novoye Russkoye Slovo.*

Most important to Boris, Brighton Beach was a place where you could apparently make it through an entire month without speaking a word of English.

I wanted to move to a place where the Russians were, where there was some action, where there was some serious money to be made.

I figure I'd call Marik Tarnopolsky to see if he can get me an apartment in New York. Marik lived in Coney Island, in the housing projects at Neptune and Thirty-Sixth Street, by Seagate.

"Well, Marik," I said, "what do you hear about my stamps? Did you get a price for them?"

He says, "Boris, I've got bad news. These are all fakes. The stamps are worthless, you've been had."

I said, "Even the Blue Mauritius?" He tells me, "Yes, that blue one, too. It's a counterfeit—worthless."

Boris's eyes betrayed no emotion; he felt the bile rising in his throat.

I said, "Well, what about my diamonds?" He says, "You can get twenty-eight hundred bucks for these two rocks." I ask him if that's a good price in New York City. "Yes," Marik says, "it's a good price. No one will give you a kopek more."

The number seems low, but I need the cash. "Okay, go ahead and sell them." I tell him to use some of the money to get us an apartment in Brooklyn. A few days later Marik picked us up in Albany and we drove—my wife, kids, and me—to New York. We didn't tell the caseworkers in Albany, we just packed up and left. Everyone else stayed behind for the time being.

Once we get to New York, we move into a three-bedroom apartment in the housing projects, on Neptune Avenue. Marik had arranged everything. Valya, me, and our two kids. Our rent was only ninety dollars per month, including utilities, for a three-bedroom apartment. For low-income people to be able to live in such a nice apartment, on the twenty-fourth floor, with a view! We've got the ocean on the right-hand side. Crack open the window and you can smell the salty sea air. It was a beautiful spot, close to Seagate. It was hard to believe that new immigrants in America could afford to live like this.

WHEN BORIS FIRST ARRIVED IN BROOKLYN, in the spring of 1980, he didn't jump headlong into the world of Soviet émigré crime. He spent a few weeks biding his time, looking for legitimate work, though his lack of English-language skills made that, for all practical purposes, an impossibility.

I figure I'll do what a lot of the new immigrants are doing—drive a taxi. But there was no way in hell I was going to pass an exam for a commercial taxi license. I only spoke a few words in English. Couldn't even read the alphabet. I could manage in Brighton Beach, where almost everyone spoke Russian, but outside of Brighton, I was lost. I met a guy who spoke excellent English—coincidentally, his name was also Boris. He'd been a dentist in Leningrad, but never got his dental license in New York. He owned a used furniture store near Luna Park. At first, I didn't even know his last name. I used to call him Boryek Dantist—Boris the Dentist.

I gave Boryek the Dentist a few bucks; he went down and registered as me and took the driver's test. We looked similar enough—same height, same strong build, but he had darker hair—anyway, he could pass for me in a photo. I rented a taxi from this guy nicknamed Sobaka.* I think I paid five hundred fifty bucks for the month.

Other Russian drivers gave me advice. "Just drive into Manhattan and pull up to some nice hotel," they say. "The most expensive fare is to Kennedy Airport. Only take people who want to go to the airport. You won't have to do any talking."

Sounded like a good plan. I drive to the Hilton Hotel and pick up some people who need to go to Kennedy Airport, but on the way there I'm completely unable to read the signs or the exits. On top of that, I've got no fucking clue about the New York City geography—don't know the five boroughs, don't know which way is east or west—I'm completely lost.

I try to drive to the airport simply using those green roads signs with the picture of the aircraft. I miss the Kennedy exit and end up on Long Island. My passengers are about to have heart attacks because they figure they've missed their flight. I say, "Sorry!" one of the few English words I *do* know, and we barely make it to Kennedy in time.

That night, it's very dark, I pick up a passenger—an African American guy who looks like a doctor. He says, "Take me to the Bronx." I'm saying to myself, "Wait, what is a *bronk*? And what are these *bronks* he's talking about?" I've got no idea where to go. I start driving, get lost, and instead of the Bronx I take him out to Long Island. He notices

---

* Russian for "Dog."

when we're halfway there. "Hey, where are you taking me?" In broken English and Russian and hand gestures I try telling him I don't know the roads, and he should direct me. By some miracle, I get way up to the Bronx, he jumps out, shaking his head, gives me twenty bucks, slamming the door: "Hey, who the hell did you pay for a taxi license?"

That was on a Friday. On Saturday, I make an illegal turn and this limousine plows right into the side of my cab. The limo's fine, like brand-new, but my cab's side doors are completely bashed in. I'm standing there while he files an accident report, then I drive back to Sobaka's place. The insurance deductible was over five hundred bucks. Sobaka took it out of my fares.

I drove a taxi ten hours a day for a week and was still flat fucking broke. I made a vow: "This is the end of my working life in America right here!"

CHAPTER 7

LITTLE ODESSA

Between 1970 and 1980, approximately forty thousand Soviet Jews settled in Brooklyn. By the time Boris Nayfeld arrived, there was already a substantial and entrenched criminal element.

Estimates are inexact, but by the early 1980s, the NYPD suspected "about 500 Russian émigrés" of involvement in criminal activity.* The number may, in fact, have been considerably higher. Many experts now believe that the KGB intentionally released thousands of "undesirables," men with prison convictions, giving them an easy path to emigration.

And a large percentage of the new arrivals—even those who were not professional criminals or who hadn't served terms in the Soviet

---

* "Various federal agencies reported that twelve Russian-émigré crime groups, with an estimated membership of between 400–500 persons, were operating in New York City, while the New York Police Department listed about 500 Russian emigres as being suspected of criminal activities," according to the official report of the Tri-State Joint Soviet-Émigré Organized Crime Project.

prison system—saw nothing wrong with taking legal shortcuts. Bilking the system was widely admired, a demonstration of intelligence and adaptability.

"The immigration from the Soviet Union brought to America's shores many people for whom crime was but ordinary behavior," writes criminologist Lydia Rosner. "Émigrés to Brighton Beach brought with them the social and psychological patterns of behavior and expectations learned in their crime-ridden society. They acted out their homeland psychology through behavior that was gratuitous to Brighton Beach. Schooled in bureaucratic circumvention, these urbanites brought sophisticated skills of system-beating with them."

The narrator of *The Zone,* a novel by the brilliant Soviet-Jewish émigré novelist Sergei Dovlatov, comments wryly on the unintended consequences of newfound liberty in the United States:

> Consider what's going on in our émigré community. The Brighton Beach NEP* is working full blast. It is teeming with gangsters. . . . Not long ago, they opened a brothel there. Four young ladies are Russian and one is Filipino. We cheat the IRS, take cheap shots at our competitors, print God knows what in our newspapers. Former film cameramen sell guns. . . . Restaurant owners collect welfare and even receive food stamps. Drivers' licenses can be bought for a hundred dollars, a graduate degree for two hundred and fifty. It is painful to think that all this vileness is born of freedom, for freedom is equally gracious to the bad and the good.

---

* Brighton Beach NEP—refers to the "New Economic Policy," a brief period in the 1920s during which Lenin allowed some private enterprise to operate in the Soviet Union.

BORIS NAYFELD KNEW what it was to be a professional criminal in the Soviet Union, but he wasn't yet schooled in the finer points of Brooklyn's underworld. In the dense, Russian-speaking enclave of Brighton Beach, it didn't take him long to figure out who the major players were.

"When I first got to Brighton, I didn't know a soul," Boris recalls.

But Marik Tarnopolsky showed me around. He introduced me to the Piterskys and Odesskys.* They were the two main criminal factions in Brighton Beach.

Within a few days of arriving, I already know who's who—I recognize the criminal faces. We can see it in each other's eyes. "A thief knows a thief as a wolf knows a wolf"—that's how we say it. I immediately wanted to blend into that world myself, to start making money in a different way—my own way. Not working for anyone. Be my own boss. Certainly, not working as a fucking janitor or a cabdriver.

Right away, I knew I needed to get armed. When Marik Tarnopolsky gave me the money from the diamonds, one of the first things I bought was a .38-caliber. A snub-nosed Smith & Wesson revolver, like the ones American detectives carried in those days. It was easy to buy a gun on the streets of Brooklyn. In New York at this time, you could buy anything. The .38 only cost me three hundred fifty bucks. I bought myself that piece and started packing it everywhere. I liked that gun because it was so easy to conceal, tucked into your waist, would never jam like a semiautomatic, and packed considerable power.

My first impression of Brighton Beach was terrible. After all the rosy images we'd seen of America in Hollywood movies, Brighton looked

---

* People from Leningrad and Odessa. During the Soviet era, it was common slang to refer to Leningrad by its pre-1917 name "St. Petersburg" truncated as "Piter," and to an emigrant from Leningrad as a "Pitersky."

like the worst slum imaginable. Garbage overflowing on the sidewalks. Streetlights broken—everyone walking home in darkness. Boarded-up ground-floor windows. Flames shooting from trash bins.

In spite of it all, some sections had started to come to life. Shops and restaurants were popping up here and there with Russian signs. Brighton was beginning to take on the look of a Russian-Jewish immigrant district. The rents in Brighton were still fairly cheap, so thousands of immigrants from the Soviet Union settled there. It was especially attractive to the former citizens of Odessa, on the Black Sea. They came from the south of Ukraine and felt most comfortable living by the ocean.

By the late 1970s, Boris says, an ethnic war had broken out in the streets around Brighton and on the boardwalk.

A lot of the Russian Jews were afraid of the Blacks, Puerto Ricans, Mexicans. Older Russian people walking home were getting beaten up and mugged. Store owners were getting stuck up. In those early days, there was a group of us—let's just say Russian guys who weren't afraid of a fight. We used to pick up bats and chains and we'd go to the boardwalk where they were hanging out. There were always a bunch of drug addicts and guys looking for trouble.

We'd chase after them, tell them to get out of the area. It was the only way we could knock them out of Brighton. Some of us got knifed. Some of them got knifed. But little by little, we pushed them out of Brighton. We knocked them back to the Coney Island side. There we made a border. We had a dividing line—right there on the boardwalk—marking Brighton Beach as our Russian section.

NEAR THAT VERY DIVIDING LINE, on Surf Avenue in Coney Island, directly across from Luna Park, there were a cluster of used furniture stores; the strip became a daytime hangout for many Soviet émigrés, newcomers looking for deals to furnish their apartments.

By chance, about five months after he arrived in Brooklyn, Boris heard a seemingly innocent bit of gossip that would change the direction of his criminal life in America.

I'm looking for bargains in a used furniture store and one of the owners, this Pitersky guy named Lyovka Storonkin, asks me where I'm from. I tell him, "Gomel." He laughs. "Oh, yeah? Small world. I was just talking about another guy from Gomel. You know Marik Tarnopolsky? My partner from Piter—" I know he's talking about Boryek the Dentist "—he and Marik ripped off some *lokh* who just got here from Gomel."

That's an old fenya word. A *lokh*. It means "a sucker." An idiot who's easily conned. I stay quiet, show no emotion, waiting to hear more about this stupid *lokh*. Lyovka Storonkin tells me that this dumb guy from Gomel smuggled two brilliant-cut diamonds out of the Soviet Union and gave them to Marik to sell. Marik Tarnopolsky and Boryek the Dentist sold them for about four thousand bucks but only gave the *lokh* twenty-eight hundred.

After I hear this, I waste no time—I call Marik right up, tell him I want to talk to him about something. He says he's been driving a cab all night and needs to sleep. But just from the tone in my voice, he knows something's up. Five minutes after we hang up, he calls me right back, sounding worried. He says, "Boris, I've got to confess something. You know those two diamonds you gave me? Well, let me—" I cut him off. "Marik, let's just meet up tomorrow—you can tell me in person."

The next evening, we're sitting in Marik's blue Buick sedan. I'm in the passenger seat, and I calmly pull out my .38 revolver. "Okay, Marik, what did you want to confess?"

He says, "Listen, I made some money off you, Boris. I mean, I spent a lot of time running around trying to sell the diamonds and the stamps, I figured I'd take something for myself. Like, you know, a commission."

"Marik, if you'd told me you wanted a commission, I'd have said no fucking problem. But I asked if you if twenty-eight hundred was a fair price and you said, 'You won't get a kopek more.'" Marik says, "I'm sorry, Boris. I can give you back five hundred bucks—that's all I took from the deal—but the rest is with my partner."

He admitted that his partner was this same Boryek the Dentist, the Pitersky who'd taken the taxi license test for me. I stared at him before I shoved my gun back in my waist. "Marik, look, I think you're a decent guy. You helped me and my family move down from Albany, but you shouldn't've lied to me. Now you've got to take me to the fucking dentist."

Marik drives over to this apartment house on Eighty-Sixth Street. It's around seven thirty in the evening. I say, "Marik, go ring his buzzer and tell him to come down—but don't tell him I'm here with you."

He buzzes the apartment and when this guy, Boryek the Dentist, gets downstairs, through the open window, I tell him, "Get in the back!" I slide into the back seat next to him, pull out my .38, and stick the barrel hard into his forehead.

"Listen, Boryek, don't fuck with me. How much did you really make on my diamonds?"

He says, "Thirty-five hundred."

"You sure? I'll give you a second to think about it."

I can feel his fear, he's breathing hard, his jaw trembling. But my hand is steady. I press the barrel harder into his forehead.

"Yeah," he says. "Thirty-five hundred."

"Last chance," I say. "Tell me how much you *really* got for my stones. If you're lying, I'm pulling this trigger."

Finally, he says, "Okay, okay, we got forty-two hundred."

As soon as he tells me the real price, I pistol-whip him. Smacked him good in the jaw with the gun. Probably knocked a few of his teeth loose. Then I grabbed his collar. "Listen to me, tomorrow you'll have all my money. If you don't have my money, you're going straight to the afterlife."

The next morning, they both show up at my apartment. Marik keeps apologizing and Boryek the Dentist is like a kid getting caught stealing candy. He smiles at me and says, "My father always told me that if you get caught, you've got to pay up."

They gave me all the cash they'd ripped off. Fourteen hundred bucks in tens and twenties. I count out the cash carefully on the kitchen table. This Boryek turned out to be quite a good guy, actually. Later on, he opened up a lamp business and did very well for himself. We're still close friends to this day.

That was Brighton Beach in the eighties. Everyone getting slick. Everyone scamming everyone. If you saw any opportunity to get over on another guy, you took it in a heartbeat.

For me, that night changed everything. New York's a big city, but the Russian community is tiny. The minute something happens, everyone knows about it. The word spread fast: "Don't fuck with that Boris Gomelsky. He's quick to use his *volyna*."*

Now that we're all squared up, I tell Marik Tarnopolsky. "I want you to help me out with something else. I need to find a way to send all these fake stamps back to Russia."

"Okay, I know a guy," Tarnopolsky says. "He was a *vor v zakone* in Piter—but he lost his crown. His name is Evsei. If anyone in New York can help you out, it's him."

At this point, I knew Marik was talking about Evsei Agron—

---

* *Volyna*—fenya slang for a gun. From "violin."

everyone in Brighton knew he was the top Russian gangster. I told Marik, "Okay, I'll forget about you lying to me if you set up a meeting with Evsei."

The meeting, Boris knew, could potentially change everything, put him on the map as a full-fledged player in the world of American organized crime.

CHAPTER 8

THE UNCROWNED KING

When Boris was introduced to the mobster who would become his criminal mentor, Evsei Agron was in bed recuperating from a freshly inflicted gunshot wound. Agron had refused to cooperate with the NYPD detectives investigating the shooting, vowing to take care of the matter himself.

Marik Tarnopolsky brings me to Evsei's home—he lived in an apartment on Ocean Parkway. We take the elevator to the top floor, Evsei's wife, Maya, opens the door and we find Evsei in bed.

Evsei's crew were in a turf war with a rival crew. A *brigada* led by two brothers from Odessa. As Evsei and three of his guys walked out of a building, they got into a shootout with these Odessa guys. Evsei was wounded. Not life-threatening, but he was laid up in bed recovering.

There must have been five or six of his guys in the place. When I walk into the bedroom, I can hear them plotting. They're busy making all sorts of plans for how to hunt down these rival Odesskys and shoot them one by one.

Marik makes the introductions. "Evsei," he says, "this is our friend from Belarus I was telling you about." I shook Evsei's hand. He wasn't a big man, thinning hair, about fifteen years older than me. But he had such presence. I can see *everything* in his eyes. How can I put this? It was impossible *not* to trust Evsei as soon as I saw him. And Evsei had already heard about me—the street rumors have been circulating quickly in Brighton about me being able to handle myself.

He asked if there was anything he could help me with here in America. I told Evsei about my issue with the counterfeit stamps. Evsei didn't take more than a few seconds to think about it. "Yes, I think I can take care of it," he says. "We'll have to find someone who can bring the stamps back into Russia, and it's going to cost you something."

"That's not a problem," I say.

He stares at me, sizing me up. "Boris, what do you want to do?" he says.

"I can do *anything*—as long as I make some money."

"Would you like to be close to me?"

"Sure, as long as it's mutually beneficial."

After I left, I gave Evsei's offer some thought. Honestly, I didn't want to join up with his *brigada* at that time. I thought I could go on my own, maybe put together my own crew. Evsei was a powerful criminal—he was clearly a strong leader—but he had a lot of enemies. And I realized that once I joined up with him, Evsei's enemies would immediately become *my* enemies.

AGRON WAS BORN IN LENINGRAD IN 1932, and before becoming a *vor v zakone,* he'd mastered one of the most high-status specialties in the Russian underworld—that of a professional pickpocket. In hours of

conversation, Boris learned firsthand the circumstances that forced Evsei
to leave the USSR and come to America in 1975.

> Over the years, I got to know Evsei very well. We spent hours and hours
> talking in restaurants and in the *banya*. He was such a well-educated
> guy. Erudite, cultured. He liked to memorize the great Russian poets.
> Pushkin, Lermontov, Mandelstam. His mind was so sharp. I'd watch
> him with a newspaper sometimes: you couldn't believe how fast he'd
> complete a crossword puzzle in Russian. He saw all the words in
> seconds. He taught me so much, just being around him. He opened my
> eyes to the world: how to read people, how to see through people. I was
> a criminal when I met him, but so inexperienced.
>
> As I got to know him better, Evsei told me all about his life in the
> Soviet Union, how he became a thief in law. As a young man he was
> in university and played football* at a high level, but at the same time
> Evsei was part of a pickpocketing crew, hustling to make money every
> day. The crew included several well-known *vory v zakone*. They traveled
> around doing *konka*.

Konka, a fenya term derived from the first horse-drawn tram line in
1860s St. Petersburg, involves a team of three or four pickpockets, target-
ing people going back and forth from work on streetcars and buses, usually on a payday when everyone in the Soviet Union was carrying cash.

> In *konka,* you're riding on the bus or tram, and one guy jostles, screens,
> or maneuvers the victim into position to be robbed—he's called the
> *tyrshchik.* Once the mark has been pickpocketed, the stolen wallet
> is passed onto another crew member called the *propul,* the getaway
> man, who jumps right off the bus or tram. That way, even if the victim

---

* University-level soccer.

realizes their wallet is missing, even if Evsei and his crew are stopped and questioned by the cops, there's no wallet or cash to be found.

Within the crew, Evsei had the most specialized skill. He was what's called a *pisatel.* That means "writer." He could use a variety of cutting tools, sometimes razor blades, sometimes coins with sharpened edges. In fenya that razor blade or sharpened coin is known as a *pis'mo*—a letter, like you'd put in the mail. Cutting pockets, purses, briefcases, is called "writing letters."

Among Russians of my generation, it was considered a true criminal art form, "writing letters," being able to extract the cash with a *pis'mo* without the person even noticing that he's being pickpocketed. In time, Evsei gained fame among all the criminals in the Soviet Union as one of the best writers in Leningrad.

But Agron was eventually arrested for theft and sentenced to a three-year term inside a penal colony.

At the time, whenever you entered the zone, the inmates would ask about your criminal specialty. You've got to state what crime you committed. Well, Evsei says proudly, "I'm a thief." Next, he gets asked to name the guys who he steals with. Since his pickpocketing crew in Leningrad contains some established thieves in law, the *vory* in the zone welcome him into their ranks. Evsei vows he'll never work, he'll only live by stealing. He swears he'll abide by the code of the *vory v zakone*. He declares himself a thief in prison and is granted the crown.

By the way, the process is different these days. Now, in order to be crowned, there has to be a gathering of two or three *vory v zakone:* you have to go in front of them and tell the story of your life. If you've lived the life as you described it, if you've done prison time, if you've given a clean, clear biography, the *vory* will ask you, finally, "State that you're a thief!"

This is a specific feature of joining the *vory v zakone*. They don't say, "You're now crowned a thief in law," or "We welcome you into our brotherhood of thieves." No. *You* must declare it. *You're* given the final word: "I am a thief!" You've stated who and what you are. Only at that point are you recognized as a *vor v zakone*.

In 1960s Leningrad, being a *pisatel* wasn't Evsei Agron's only racket. Upon his release from prison, Agron worked a high-risk con known as *razgon*. In standard Russian, the word means "acceleration," but in fenya it refers to an elaborate scheme involving criminals impersonating *militsiya* officers.

Evsei told me how he and his guys used to do the *razgon* in Leningrad. Evsei's crew had informers who helped identify guys in the black market, guys stealing state property. People who'd never be able to file police complaints if they got robbed. A perfect target would be a guy who worked as a warehouse manager. Let's say he's been stealing from the State, accumulated a lot of black cash, jewels, gold, antiques, artwork. They phone the wife while the husband is at work—pretending to be another employee at the warehouse—and tell her: "Your husband's been arrested! The *militsiya* are on the way to search the apartment. Get the valuables out of the apartment, the cash, diamonds, gold, quickly! The cops are coming! The less they find, the shorter the sentence will be!"

Of course, Evsei's crew has already been staking out the apartment. The wife throws everything she can carry into a bag and as soon as she gets outside, she's met by a couple of Evsei's guys dressed as cops. Authentic-looking *militsiya* uniforms. Authentic-looking paperwork. They say, "What are you carrying? Please step back into the apartment. Here's the search warrant."

Once back inside, they check the bag stuffed with cash and valuables. They complete the required paperwork, signed by witnesses to the search, then confiscate everything as if it was evidence. When the husband comes home, the wife shouts at him. "What happened? I thought you were arrested!"

"What are you talking about? I was never arrested!"

What can the guys do? He can't call the cops and admit to theft of State property—that could land him in front of the firing squad. It was the perfect crime. Evsei's crew made off with some big scores doing the *razgon*.

As skilled as he was in the criminal arts, Evsei Agron had one Achilles heel: a compulsion for gambling. "Evsei used to tell me about his prized collection of vinyl disks—extremely valuable records in the Soviet times. He collected Dimitrievich, Leshchenko, Lemeshev.* But once he got into gambling, he needed to sell this collection to settle the debts. Because losing at cards and not settling your debts immediately is considered one of the most serious violations of the thieves' code. You must pay up or it's a mark of shame. It will cost you your crown."

In fact, this love of gambling landed Evsei Agron in repeated trouble with the *vory v zakone*. Whenever he had free time, Evsei would go to a *katran*—an underground casino. In cities like Leningrad, *katrans* would often be set up in an apartment where the *vory* could secretly

---

* Alyosha Dimitrievich (1913–1986), popular singer of Russian-Gypsy chansons; Pyotr Leshchenko (1898–1954), known as the "King of Russian Tango"; Sergei Lemeshev (1902–1977), one of the most beloved Russian operatic lyric tenors. In the Soviet Union, owning vinyl recordings by such prestigious artists was a sign of both status and sophistication.

run high-stakes card games, drinking vodka and cognac, and gambling throughout the night.

During one long night at the card table, Evsei loses an enormous sum of money and he's unable to settle up. In Russian we use the word *fuflyzhnik*—a deadbeat, a guy who doesn't pay his gambling debts. When it happened the first time, some other thieves in law helped him put that sum together. But they warn him, "Evsei, don't gamble any more. We helped you out so that you wouldn't be a *fuflyzhnik,* but we're not going to help you next time." Of course, Evsei promises that he won't play cards for money again.

A few months later, Evsei ends up in another *katran,* and he only has a small amount of cash on him. Before starting to play he asks for some credit and another thief in law, a friend of his, guarantees he'll cover any losses. Well, of course, Evsei loses big-time. He has thirty days to come up with the cash. But after thirty days, the friend who guaranteed the money changes his mind. Evsei fails to settle the debt.

They call a *tref.* The top *vory* meet with Evsei and reach a decision: "Evsei, you've gambled and haven't paid your debts. You're a *fuflyzhnik.* You can no longer be a thief in law."

Evsei accepted the sentence. Having lost the crown, he decided to emigrate to America. In the United States, he started doing criminal jobs—pickpocketing and so on—and eventually made enough money to send it back to Russia so he could settle the gambling debt.

In America, Evsei found that no one cared about his lost crown. The title of thief in law by itself meant nothing. At the time Evsei arrived there were three other thieves in law in New York. But none of them had Evsei's brainpower. None had his muscle.

Evsei was a strong leader who was able to put together a serious crew. They worked as pickpockets. Stole gold, diamonds, furs. Made money in racketeering. Arbitrating criminal disputes. *Smenka.*[*] Evsei quickly emerged as the strongest gang leader in Brighton Beach. That's a famous story among us. How Evsei lost his crown as a thief in law in the Soviet Union but quickly became a much bigger name in the world of American criminals.

It took Agron a few months to set the wheels in motion, but he followed through on his promise to help Boris return the counterfeit stamps.

Evsei was so well-connected, he just needed to make a few phone calls. Then he explained the plan to me, exactly how we were going to get those fake stamps back to the motherfuckers who sold them to me. Evsei had arranged for a guy to meet me in Berlin. The guy had a diplomatic passport, so he could bring the stamps unchecked in a pouch into the USSR.

I needed to fly over to West Germany. It was my first time in Berlin. I pulled a few small jobs—robbed a few jewelry stores. That was the quickest way I could raise the money I needed. Then I met with Evsei's connection, paid him four thousand deutschmarks to bring the stamps back into the Soviet Union and return them to these bastards in Gomel.

Once the stamps got back to Gomel, I called up one of the guys who ripped me off. "Okay, so you've got the fakes you sold me. Good. Now, you're going to pay me back everything—in U.S. dollars—or

---

[*] *Smenka*—fenya for a quick-switch scam. Employing sleight-of-hand during a sale to substitute a valuable item with a fake, for example a brilliant-cut diamond with cubic zirconium or a real gold coin with a counterfeit one. Master pickpockets like Agron were particularly skilled at *smenka*.

I promise you this: I'll waste each one of you. One at a time. You understand? Return the money or you won't be among the living."

It didn't take the swindlers long to get Boris back his money—transferred to the United States in dollars. Boris arrived at Evsei's apartment with a bottle of Rémy Martin XO cognac to thank him for his assistance. "Of course, I wanted the money back. But it was the principle of the thing. I was still new in Brooklyn, still establishing my name in America, and I needed to make my reputation as someone who couldn't be fucked with."

CHAPTER 9
THE WRECKING CREW

E schewing Agron's offer to come join his crew full-time, Boris initially attempted to make his living as a freelance jewel thief, a stickup man, and an arsonist.

"My earliest jobs in Brighton were with a small crew of Odesskys," Boris says.

These guys were doing nighttime break-ins of stores and food processing plants. Brighton Beach had a bunch of plants making salted herring and sausages, and we'd burglarize the places at two or three in the morning, then they'd sell the stuff to Russian stores, obviously at discounted prices.

Then we moved on to stealing designer clothes. We went out to Long Island, to the big department stores like Macy's, Saks Fifth Avenue, Lord & Taylor. It was always best to work in teams of two. I worked with this same woman every time. We made it look like we were husband and wife. This woman would pick out the expensive items, designer suits. It was very profitable. We could walk out of a department store with up to five thousand dollars' worth of merchandise and sell it quickly on the streets in Brighton.

But in June 1980, Boris and his female partner were arrested for shoplifting on Long Island.

They caught us red-handed, leaving the store with the merchandise. That was the first time I'd been handcuffed in the U.S. I couldn't make bail, so I spent five nights in jail, waiting for my court-appointed lawyer.

My lawyer says, "If you plead guilty, you'll get no time, only one-year probation." That sounded good to me—you never heard of deals like that in the Soviet Union! You got caught stealing red-handed and *no* prison time? Yes, of course, I promised I would never steal again, was sentenced to one year of probation, then I went right back to Brooklyn to continue stealing.

"WE WEREN'T TOO PARTICULAR about the jobs we did—any way to make a buck," Boris recalls. "There was this Russian fish-smoking plant named Baltika. A businessman asked me to put the plant out of commission. They were his competition. I brought some people along, we climbed onto the plant's roof during the night, poured gasoline down a chimney, and lit it on fire. The place didn't burn down, but the fish-smoking production had to stop for about a month. Which was all that was needed to send the message."

Once his year-long probation for shoplifting was finished, in the summer of 1981, Boris cobbled together a small crew and made a trip to Europe for an ambitious robbery spree that quickly devolved into a comedy of errors. "In the early eighties, I found a partner to do burglaries with named Rezo. He was a Georgian Jew from Queens. He'd lived in Israel before coming to America. Rezo and me got together with a pickpocket called Rynok, originally from Leningrad, and this other guy named Grisha Luydoyed who I'd got to know in Brighton."*

Grisha "Luydoyed" Roizes would, by the mid-1990s, become one of the most infamous names in the Russian underworld; he was the first major Russian mob figure who agreed to work as a cooperating witness with the federal government. According to a former friend, Ludwig "Tarzan" Fainberg, Roizes picked up the nickname "Cannibal" by once biting off the tip of the nose of an NYPD sergeant who had called him a "fucking dirty Jew" after he handcuffed him.

Boris dismisses this widely repeated account as ludicrous. "I don't know where they got all the bullshit stories about Luydoyed," Boris says.

Grisha never bit off a cop's nose. He got the nickname Luydoyed because he had no teeth. He wore dentures. If he pulled them out, all he had was his gums. What Grisha told me was this: one time in the Soviet Union, he made a bet that he'd bite a horse on the ear. Two bottles of vodka, that was the wager. Grisha pulled out his false teeth and snapped them on the horse's ear, he won the two bottles, and after that they started calling him "Luydoyed" as a joke.

Anyway, Grisha Luydoyed had relatives in Copenhagen and he suggested we go over there because there were plenty of jewelry stores just sitting there, waiting to be robbed. He said we could also go to Belgium—Antwerp. There would be jobs for us to do there, too. Russian-owned diamond stores. There were four of us, Rynok, Luydoyed, Rezo, and me. We packed our bags and went to Europe.

---

* *Rynok* means "market," as in a farmers' market. *Luydoyed* means "cannibal." Rezo is a common Georgian first name, not a criminal moniker.

At this time, I only had a white passport.[*] I needed visas to go to Belgium and Denmark. Most of our money went into buying plane tickets, and when we got to Belgium we were almost out of cash. But we figured, why the fuck are we waiting to get to Copenhagen? No time like the present. Let's start robbing right here in Antwerp. Luydoyed is the only one of us with connections—he's able to get us a pistol. He also got us a wig we could use as a disguise. These Antwerp connections also put us onto this one jewelry store. "There's no security at all," Luydoyed says. "The only guy working there is a *pederast*."[†]

Well, I figure, it can't be too difficult to hold this place up. I say, "Who's coming with me?" Suddenly, everyone's quiet. No one wants to do the job. All these fucking tough guys are suddenly acting strange—Luydoyed, Rynok, Rezo—afraid to do a simple stickup? "All right, fuck it—I'll do it myself."

Of course, it's always more difficult to rob alone, but I shove the gun in my waistband and adjust the wig in the mirror. The store's located close to the Central Railway station—that's the heart of the Diamond Quarter. I get there early, waiting for the opening at nine A.M.

As soon as this *pederast* opens the jewelry store, I walk in and point the gun in his face. I say, "Merchandise! Give me merchandise!" This guy starts to scream. Once he starts screaming, I smack his face hard with the pistol. He falls to the floor, screaming louder, louder, louder. Really wailing. It's a busy street, so people on their way to the railway station start gathering outside. It's crazy how fast a mob is

---

[*] By "white passport," Boris means a reentry permit, a passport-like book, allowing U.S. lawful permanent residents to travel abroad and return to the United States.

[†] In Russian, *pederast* is a highly derogatory term for a homosexual—roughly equivalent to "faggot."

forming. I realize, Shit, this job is going bad fast—I've got to get the fuck out of here.

I get out outside, into the street, but I don't know anything about Antwerp—I don't know which way to turn. Then I spot an archway ahead of me. Shadows. Gray stone. Medieval-looking. One guy, a regular citizen in a suit and tie, grabs my arm, tries to stop me from escaping, but I point my gun in his face and he jumps out of the way. When I reach this archway, I rip off the wig, hide the gun, then walk out as calmly as I can. But now there's sirens everywhere and more cops than I can believe—it seems like every cop in Belgium is flooding the streets. *What the fuck?* For an attempted jewelry store holdup?

When I get back to our hotel, I start yelling. "You fucking jerkoffs! You all wanted to come to Europe to make money! What? You think money's just going to fall from the sky? We need to do jobs!" Then we see on TV that there's a terrorism threat by the Red Brigades, and literally two minutes after my escape from the jewelry store, the authorities activated the special police forces to flood all of Antwerp. Cops are everywhere. We realize we can't hang around. We scrape together enough money to get to Denmark.

Once we get to Copenhagen, the plan is to do *konka*. Like Evsei's crew did back in Leningrad. Rynok's a skilled pickpocket. He's a *pisatel*—not on the level of Evsei, but that's his criminal specialty. In Copenhagen we're staying with Luydoyed's family—his brother-in-law was also Grisha, but his nickname was Kosti, or "Bones."

The plan is to get on crowded buses, and Rynok will cut people's pants and purses with his razor to get at the wallets. The rest of us are supposed to create the distraction and make the handoff and get away. But every single time we get on a bus, the driver makes a loud announcement over his speakers. None of us can understand Danish, but we notice people steering clear of us, clutching their bags and purses. We can never get close enough to work the *konka*.

Later on, Grisha Kosti explained what happened. It was common in Denmark for bus drivers to warn passengers to stay on the lookout for pickpockets, telling them to secure their valuables. There were many pickpocketing crews active in Copenhagen—from Chile, France, Spain, all over the place. The bus drivers were always blasting out warnings in Danish. It was impossible to work *konka*.

Now we barely have any cash—we don't even have the money to buy the plane tickets back to New York. This robbery spree in Europe is turning into a fucking disaster. One Sunday Grisha Kosti tells us about this seaside resort town—he says there's lots of jewelry shops there. We head down to the resort town. Once there, we split into pairs and start to walk around, casing the jewelry stores.

I worked as a two-man team with Grisha Luydoyed. He takes off his cheap gold chain and asks for an appraisal—says he wants to sell it. The owner leaves for the back room to weigh the chain. That moment, I lean over and grab everything I can reach from the top shelf: chains, bracelets, diamond rings. We pulled that off in a few stores in this resort town. We made some decent scores. It wasn't a fortune, but we made enough. We flew back to America. All of us except Rynok, who went down to Italy—he had plans to keep pickpocketing among the Russians in Rome.

When they got back to New York, Boris kept up a frenetic pace of "wrecking and robbing," as he puts it, seven days a week. He was working primarily as a jewel thief, then branched out into the world of fine art.

There was this antique dealer from Leningrad—he started giving us leads on Russian-owned shops. I'd go around casing them—I had one guy who was an expert at picking locks and dismantling alarm systems.

The best time would be on a Sunday night—all the nearby shops were closed. On Broadway there was one antique shop and a vacant store with a sign reading, "For Lease." On a Sunday, we broke the locks, got into the vacant store, and closed the door behind us. I used an electric saw to cut through the wall adjoining the antique store while being careful not to trigger the alarm system. Back then, there were none of those motion-sensor alarms—none of those infrared light systems. We got in and picked the place. Paintings, statues, anything made of gold and silver, we hauled it all away.

A few weeks later this same antique dealer gave us a job out of state. This was a made-to-order score. He tells us, "There's an apartment in L.A., you need to fly to California and rob this place while the owners are away. There are two very special paintings there. Don't take anything else, only these two specific paintings." Rezo and I get out there, break in, and rob this apartment. On top of the paintings, we also picked up silver and some gold for ourselves.

We carefully pack up these two expensive paintings, bring them back to New York, and give them to the dealer. In a day or two we met to get our agreed-upon fee. He goes, "You guys trying to pull a fast one? You know, hoodwink me?" I say, "What the fuck are you talking about?" He goes, "The two paintings you brought back are fakes. They're counterfeits."

"That's not my problem, *kozyol*. You ordered us to steal them. We broke into the apartment, and they were hanging on the fucking walls. If you ordered the job, you're responsible for it." He goes, "No, no, no—these are fakes. I didn't want you to steal fakes."

What was the point arguing? I knew I could let Evsei resolve it. He settled a lot of disputes in the criminal world. Whenever these sorts of problems happened between legitimate businessmen and criminals, Evsei would come down with his own ruling. Any argument over money, guys would ask Evsei to act as an impartial judge. He called it as he saw it. If Evsei said, "You must pay," people knew they'd better pay. Evsei didn't have to lift a finger because there were enough people around him who were ready to go get the money for him. All he had to do is give the verdict.

I went to see Evsei on this issue with these fake paintings and asked him to make a ruling. He considered the facts, called the guy up, and took our side in the dispute, "You gave my friends the job. My friends completed this job. It is not their problem if the paintings hanging on the walls were fakes. Pay what was agreed." Once Evsei spoke, that was it. Rezo and I got paid twenty thousand each for those two paintings, even though they were fakes. No more discussion. In criminal matters, Evsei's word was final.

BORIS ALWAYS HAD HIS EARS OPEN for potential scores—even if they were halfway around the world.

Late in 1982, I got this tip from a guy in Brooklyn about a really good score. A diamond processing plant in Israel, a factory where they cut the rough stones. The guy tells me it will be an easy job. There's an employee on the inside—one of the diamond cutters is in on the setup. This inside guy knows the whole schedule, when the boss and wife go in and out, how much merchandise is going to be inside the factory on any given day.

I tell him, "Sure, I'll take the job." I ask Rezo to come because he speaks good Hebrew. He lived in Israel for two years before coming to America. He's also got good connections in the Georgian-Jewish community there in case we need a hideout.

We fly to Rome first to reconnect with Rynok. By the time we get there, Rynok's already stolen a bunch of credit cards. We rent a car and start to charge up stuff at expensive boutiques. Gucci, Versace, Armani,

Prada, whatever. We've got to keep it under a thousand bucks per transaction, otherwise the merchants have to phone in for authorization. We make about fifteen grand in one day, enough merchandise to finance our tickets to Israel, hotel rooms, and flights back to New York.

When we land in Tel Aviv, Rezo meets up with the people he knows from the Georgian-Jewish community, they give us a pistol and a machete, and we start staking out the job. We know the owner and his wife show up at the jewelry factory at exactly nine A.M. First thing they do every day is lay out the rough diamonds for their employees to finish—and the diamond cutters all got there by nine thirty.

Rezo and me walk in, pretending to be selling these special disks they use in cutting diamonds. Rezo starts talking in Hebrew, offering him our disks, and the owner says he's not interested. He's really obnoxious about it, shooing us out of the store. I pull out the gun and point it at his head, and Rezo pulls out the machete, we get everybody down on the floor and tie up their hands.

Rezo does all the talking in Hebrew. We grab all the uncut stones laid out on the workbenches, plus we remove any rings and valuables the owner and his wife have on them personally. The owner's pleading with Rezo, "Don't hurt us, I'll open the safe for you." Obviously, I don't know what he's saying—they're all yapping in Hebrew. In the meantime, Rezo starts looking scared, panicky, I don't know what's up—but I can tell he wants to get the fuck out of there.

We get out of there with a decent score, about forty-five thousand dollars' worth of rough stones. We've already got a ticket to fly out of Israel that afternoon. First, we settle up with Rezo's Georgian friends, the guys who gave us the gun and the machete. We paid them in diamonds. Then we fly straight out of Tel Aviv to JFK.

The local police investigated, interrogated everyone at the factory, all the employees. Our inside guy, the diamond cutter, was questioned but he stayed strong—didn't say a word to the cops.

I figured it was a nice, clean score—we got some diamonds, the owner would collect on the insurance, no one got hurt. But as soon as we got back to New York we heard from this inside guy. "The *safe!*" he says. "Why didn't you guys clean it out?"

Turns out the safe was filled with three hundred thousand dollars' worth of uncut diamonds. "The safe! *That* was the score," he says. "He was ready to open it!"

And now I'm fuming. We went through all that hassle, only to blow the whole fucking job? "What happened?" I say to Rezo. "Why didn't you have him open it, *sooka?*"*

Rezo says, "Look, I didn't know if the safe was wired—maybe it had one of those silent alarms that goes straight to the cops."

"A silent alarm? What's the fucking difference? We were already *inside*. We could have cleaned the fucking thing out easily in thirty seconds—we had plenty of time to get away."

It burned me so bad, leaving three hundred thousand bucks' worth of diamonds in that safe, I tell Rezo, "That's it, we're done. I'm not going to work with you again. You need to look for another partner."

The next day, I set up a meeting with Evsei at his apartment and I tell him what happened on this diamond job in Israel. Evsei says, "Listen, Boris, you're a serious guy. You know how to make money. You know how to handle yourself. Enough with this traveling all over the place. Come with me. Stay close to me. Like I've been telling you, I could use you in my crew."

SITTING IN AGRON'S LIVING ROOM, glancing at the shelves lined with hundreds of Russian-language books, Boris mulled Evsei's offer in

---

* *Sooka*—"bitch."

silence. He realized his own freelance criminal ventures weren't paying off—he still had so much to learn.

Wasn't he only delaying the inevitable?

Right then and there, I stopped trying to do my own thing, stopped trying to run my own crew, and came to work with Evsei full-time.

Evsei tells me, "Boris, bring a couple more good guys—we're going to need strong people with us." I already had a friend named Ilya Zeltzer—we called him Zelya. We hadn't done any jobs together, but we'd hang out, socializing and drinking at restaurants. He was from Kishinev, had a sharp wit, loved to have a good time. I knew he was a solid guy. I called him straightaway: "Zelya. You're going to work with us!" Also, my cousin Venya. His size alone intimidated a lot of people. I brought Zelya and Venya onboard and we helped add muscle to Evsei's crew.

For Boris, it was a calculated risk: While Agron's enemies would instantly become *his* enemies, this was an opportunity to step up in the underworld ranks.

The chance to become Evsei Agron's right-hand man, to learn the day-to-day workings of the rackets from a powerful boss, made it a risk well worth taking.

CHAPTER 10

THE *BRATVA*

The Russian-Jewish mob in Brighton Beach headed by Evsei Agron was often referred to in both the press and official FBI documents as the *Organizatsiya*. But that label is a misnomer. There was little organization, no hierarchical structure like in Cosa Nostra families. In Brighton Beach, there were always many competing factions, and each group tended to be amorphous, operating with fluidity, a collective of independent criminals coming together opportunistically to work for a shared purpose.

Boris explains that a crew like Evsei Agron's was less a structured criminal organization than a *bratva*—a "brotherhood."

"The *Italyakhas* have their military-style ranks: boss, underboss, captain, soldier.* Russians don't have any of that. We're all like brothers. We have a leader, of course—Evsei was our *starshiy*. The rest of us are equals. When we do a crime, we all eat the same. If Ilya Zeltzer and I

---

* When discussing members of Cosa Nostra, Boris generally opts for a unique piece of Russian slang; rather than the standard word for an "Italian"—*Italyanets*—he'll often refer to an *Italyakha,* or "big Italian," indicating a certain level of respect.

do a jewelry job, let's say we bring fifty grand, or a hundred grand, we put it on the table. All our proceeds go into the *obshchak*—the common fund. With a Russian crew, everything's shared equally."

Evsei Agron is listed in several law enforcement documents, including the exhaustive "Tri-State Joint Soviet-Émigré Organized Crime Project," as the "self-styled" and "original Godfather" of the Russian Mafia in the United States. Contemporaneous news accounts sometimes referred to him as "the Little Don" of Brighton Beach.

"We used to laugh when we heard things like that," Boris says.

Russians never used those words. "Godfather," we only learned about that from the movies. For us—I mean *real* Russian criminals—we'll use the word *starshiy*—leader. Or in fenya, you'll talk about a *pakhan*—that means chief. But that's used more when you're in the zone.

Russian organized crime operates totally different from the *Italyakhas*. The best way I can describe it to you is using another fenya word. *Korennoy*. That comes from the word *koren*. Root. You know, like the roots of a tree. That's a special kind of criminal partnership. If someone asks me who I'm working with on a job, I'll say, "Evsei is my *korennoy*." It means that we're so close, so connected, all our criminal proceeds are joined at the roots. In real-life terms, it means, if I go do a robbery job and Evsei's not personally involved—he knows nothing at all about it—doesn't matter; since he's my *korennoy* I need to share the proceeds equally with him.

THERE WERE A SEEMINGLY ENDLESS VARIETY of frauds and swindles being worked within the Soviet émigré underworld, almost always preying on fellow immigrants who, due to their experiences in the USSR, would rarely report anything to the police. A particularly distinctive Russian con job in the early '80s was known as *schneyer*.

Schneyer is yet another fenya term—originally from Yiddish—for a scam involving valuables, usually diamonds and gold. One version of *schneyer* that was popular in the early '80s was minting counterfeit coins that looked like they were from the czarist times. Almost everyone who'd lived in the Soviet Union—especially jewelers—knew that the ten-ruble coin featuring the portrait of Nicholas II was made of 90 percent pure gold.

"To work this *schneyer* properly, you need some authentic ten-ruble coins—preferably four or five," Boris says. "We had our people who could manufacture fakes—they were almost identical-looking to the ten-ruble coins. At the time, you could get one hundred twenty dollars for a ten-ruble coin on Forty-Seventh Street in the Diamond District."

Working *schneyer* requires a great deal of theatricality, right down to the costuming and props. "We dressed up as sailors—Russian merchant marines. We were wearing the actual uniforms of the merchant fleet. In my pocket, I even had some Soviet naval medals with me—not to sell them, just to add authenticity to my story."

The guys we scammed were in the meat business. "We've just come on a ship from Russia," I tell them. "We've got some coins we need to unload quickly." Now, we've got five real ten-ruble coins and a thousand counterfeit ones in various bags. We go to a jeweler with them, because obviously they want to check the weight, to make sure the gold is real. We do the *smenka*—the quick switch—whenever they want a certain coin checked, we make sure the jeweler is examining an authentic ten-ruble coin, not one of the fakes.

If the real ten-ruble coins were worth one hundred twenty bucks apiece, we only asked for sixty. We only targeted Jews from the Soviet Union who had black cash, guys always trying to get ahold of sweet things they could resell at a profit.

We pulled it off more than once—making fifty and sixty grand each time. If you were good at *schneyer*—if you had a pickpocket's sleight-of-hand—you not only managed to sell the counterfeits, you kept your real ten-ruble coins, palming them and slipping them into your pocket after they'd been checked by the jeweler.

IT WASN'T LONG BEFORE the Soviet émigré criminals realized that, as easily as they could defraud other Jewish immigrants, they could set their sights on scamming multinational insurance companies. Exploiting any chinks in institutional armor came naturally to crooks who'd turned the act of stealing from the Soviet state into a criminal art form.

One day I come up with an idea for an insurance scam, talk it over with Evsei and the guys, then walk into one of the antique dealers who used to play ball with us. I make him a proposition. "Here's my idea. Why don't you get some expensive items on consignment to take to an antique show? Load it all into a van. Me and my guys will rob you on the way to the show. We'll pull guns on you, you just play along, act like you're really being robbed. You collect from the insurance company. We give you back the merchandise, and you can sell it on the side. We split the score down the middle. Fifty percent to you, fifty percent to us."

He says, "Hey, that's not a bad plan. I'll think about it."

About three months after he said, "I'll think about it," I'm reading the Russian newspaper and I see a story about this same fucking antique dealer. It says he took a lot of valuable artwork, antiques, and other merchandise to an auction on consignment. On the way back he stayed for the night at a motel. While he was sleeping, over a hundred seventy thousand bucks' worth of merchandise got stolen along with his personal car. That was a nice touch, I thought. Getting his personal car ripped off.

I immediately showed the article to Evsei and the guys in our crew. "Evsei, this was our fucking idea. This was our job. This *kozyol* went ahead and did it without us! What, he thinks he can stiff us?" Evsei agreed—he said we should see the guy and get our fifty percent.

I went with Kadik—Arkady Shteinberg. We staked out the antique dealer, caught up with him one fine day as he was walking to work.

Kadik's driving and I'm smiling when I say, "Hey, why don't you get into the car? I think we need to talk." We sit him in the car and drive to a quiet street. I pull out my *volyna* and stick it to his head.

"You snake! What, you decided to stiff us? Think we don't read the newspapers? Look, either you pay us half of what you got from the insurance, or I'll whack you right here."

With my .38 pressed to his temple, the guy quickly saw our point of view. He agreed to cough up half from that insurance score.

THE STEADIEST INCOME STREAM for Russian mobsters in New York came not from swindles or robberies but by providing *krysha*—literally a "roof." This was an updated Russian version of the ethnic protection rackets that had plagued immigrant communities in American cities since the days of the Sicilian Black Hand extortionists.

You need to pay people like us to protect you from people like us.

Soviet émigré restaurateurs, jewelers, furriers, and furniture store owners would often give a cut of the monthly gross—as much as 20 or 30 percent—to ensure protection from other organized crime groups.

"During the early nineteen eighties, Evsei got paid by many businessmen for *krysha*, all over Brighton Beach, Sheepshead Bay, Coney Island, the Diamond District in Manhattan, anywhere there were Russian Jews, we'd get *krysha*. Before the gasoline business, *krysha* was the most lucrative of our rackets.

"We didn't start with the rough stuff," Boris claims. "We always made a friendly visit, gave them the option to pay *krysha* willingly. If they didn't want to pay, okay, then they'd need some convincing. It might start with a message. Some broken windows, a Molotov cocktail, a pistol whipping. And then, depending on the circumstance, it could escalate. More often than not, they agreed to pay."

Few of the new immigrants, conditioned as they were by years of terror from the Soviet authorities, trusted the police in the United States. Complaints to law enforcement about demands for *krysha* were almost unheard-of.

Before I joined up with him, Evsei had this guy named Vilya Puzyretsky working with him, collecting money from a few places, restaurants like the National. But this Vilya was a big-time drug addict. He made his name in the underworld because he knifed someone while settling a dispute—that gave his criminal reputation a bit of a lift, but as a person, he was a fucking nobody. A huge addict constantly shooting up heroin. Whenever I spoke with Evsei about him, I'd ask, "How can you be dealing with this *narkoman*?"

Evsei told me, "You know, Boris, I started out with Vilya, I can't just cast him aside."

But more and more, Evsei began to rely on Boris and his hulking cousin Venya to collect money and threaten those unwilling to come under his *krysha*.

Evsei could see perfectly well that Vilya was a drug addict. Yet he kept him around out of loyalty. Then we started to see that Vilya was lying, skimming, cheating us. By definition, a drug addict cannot be an honest person. He can't be trusted in business. He can't be an honorable criminal. Because he always needs money for his habit.

This *narkomanyuga!** We were together on a couple of jobs with

* *Narkoman* is "a drug addict." *Narkomanyuga!* means roughly, "big-time junkie!"

him. We cleaned out a few stores at nighttime. Everything needs to go into the *obshchak*. But Vilya would grab some of the merchandise on the side and start selling it around Brighton, skimming from us. Like I said, he always needed to support his habit.

I once did a burglary job with Vilya—just me and him. We made off with a good score of pearls. We drove up to Canada to sell them. We had a buyer up there in Montreal. I couldn't believe it: he needed to stop for his heroin fix on the way to Canada. I saw him, shooting that junk into his arm!

When we got back to Brooklyn, I said to Evsei, "I don't want anything to do with this *narkoman* again." At that point, yes, Evsei decided to distance himself from Vilya. That was Puzyretsky. Pure *kozyol*. Eventually, someone took him out—he was shot and killed in the National. Well, as they say, a dog's death for a dog.[*]

MOST ENGLISH-LANGUAGE ACCOUNTS of BRIGHTON Beach in the '80s describe Evsei Agron as a terrifying presence, a predatory, sadistic boss—more feared than respected.

One particularly lurid detail, reported in a 1989 *New York Times* front-page story and widely repeated in numerous books, is that Agron would carry an electric cattle prod like a walking stick, using the farm implement to shock anyone who refused to pay his extortionate demands for protection.[†]

---

[*] Emil "Vilya" Puzyretsky was murdered inside the National on May 11, 1991. A gunman shot him twice at close range with a silencer-equipped handgun and several more times after he fell to the floor. None of the numerous eyewitnesses would identify the shooter, and the homicide remains unsolved.

[†] "Soviet Emigre Mob Outgrows Brooklyn, and Fear Spreads," by Ralph Blumenthal with Celestine Bohlen, *New York Times,* June 4, 1989.

"All those stories about Evsei with a cattle prod are pure nonsense," Boris says.

> At one time, before I joined up with him, Evsei carried a stun gun. You know, a Taser, like the cops use. A lot of people started carrying those things back then for self-defense.
>
> But like I told you, Evsei was a skilled pickpocket—a *pisatel*—he wasn't a goon. By the time I was with him, Evsei almost always had a pistol, either a .25-caliber or a .32. I trusted my .38 revolver— not those little guns—but he liked them because they're so easy to conceal. Evsei could take care of himself. He'd been in more than a few shootouts.
>
> When it came to disputes over the *krysha,* threatening people to pay up, it was me, Cousin Venya, and Zelya who handled the physical stuff. And believe me, if someone needed convincing, you wouldn't see us walking around Brooklyn like farmers with cattle prods.

FOR THE TIME BEING, Boris had found his criminal niche.

A role that came naturally to him.

The muscle.

He enjoyed being Evsei Agron's enforcer.

Soon, the chilling flash of those pale blue eyes struck fear into nearly everyone in Brooklyn's Russian-speaking community. Very few debtors or recalcitrant business owners refused to pay up after a visit from Boris and his massive cousin Venya.

Moreover, as Boris drove the boss around the streets of South Brooklyn—Brighton Beach, Coney Island, Sheepshead Bay, Gravesend—he realized, at last, that he'd found his new home.

CHAPTER 11

EL CARIBE

Evsei Agron and his crew liked to conduct business in the many restaurants of Brighton Beach or in the relative privacy of the Russian baths. But by early 1983, a country club and catering hall called El Caribe, located in the Mill Basin section of Brooklyn, would become their de facto headquarters.

"This is how we got started with El Caribe," Boris says.

Evsei had a relative named Sergei who was a builder. He comes to Evsei with this idea to build a fitness center—a swimming pool, health club, weight room. Sergei has all the plans laid out. But he doesn't have investors. He asks us to be partners and invest with him— finance the construction. Evsei turns to me and my cousin Venya with an invitation to go in on this project. Once we start looking into it, the plans, the blueprints, the numbers, I tell him: "Evsei, I'm not a businessman. I don't know anything about running a legit business. My cousin and I will contribute our due share, but I'm not going to be hands-on with it. I leave the decisions up to you." Evsei gave Sergei the go-ahead, and we all fronted him the money.

That's when Sergei finds this guy Dr. Morton Levine, who has a big catering hall in Mill Basin. We sign a contract with this Levine— he owns the building and the property—we've got the rights to use an office upstairs at the catering hall and run the downstairs swimming pools and fitness club. I think it cost us about two hundred and sixty thousand to build the fitness club and swimming pool.

Naturally, the *Italyakhas* were also around the place all the time. We knew the various crimes and rackets they were mixed up in. We could all see what was happening to this Levine. It was well-known that he was working with the *Italyakhas*. He ended up in their jaws. They turned him into their hound.

According to an affidavit sworn by an FBI special agent, Dr. Morton Levine openly aided the illegal activities of the Lucchese crime family; Lucchese underboss Anthony "Gaspipe" Casso said he regarded Levine as "someone who would do anything for him." Many other members of the Five Families frequented the catering hall, including Gambino boss John Gotti, who hosted a large Christmas party there in 1988.

"Gotti was a great guy," Levine told the *Washington Post* in 2019. "So was 'Gaspipe.'" In the same interview Levine admitted to being the go-to doctor for many Italian mobsters in Brooklyn. "I was 'il dottore de tutti de capos,'" Levine said. "I was in a neighborhood with a lot of Italian families. You treat the mother, the father. They recommend you."*

Levine's connections to Italian and Russian organized crime figures came under great scrutiny during the presidency of Donald Trump,

---

* "Michael Cohen's Secret Agenda," by Paul Schwartzman, *Washington Post*, February 9, 2019.

when it was revealed that Levine's nieces and nephews were also part owners of El Caribe. One nephew, Michael Cohen, Trump's personal attorney, supposedly sold his share in El Caribe before Trump's presidential run in 2016.[*]

"ONE NEW YEAR'S EVE the top *Italyakhas* gathered at El Caribe," Boris recalls.

Soldiers, captains, underbosses, bosses. They all partied it up. I was invited, Evsei, my cousin Venya, Kadik, Igor, everybody in our crew. It didn't happen often, but that one New Year's we partied together. To be honest, I didn't like it much because the Americans—the Italian Americans—do New Year's very differently from us Russians.

At first, the health club was just an investment opportunity. We didn't plan it this way, but El Caribe turned out to be a perfect office for us because we could meet with Russians and Italian criminals—and do so without drawing much attention. Nothing looked suspicious. We'd talk criminal business while we were pumping iron. The fitness club was one of the best places to talk without the risk of being bugged or filmed by the government. El Caribe had a big outdoor pool with cabanas, and when the weather was warm, we liked to sit out back and play cards. We felt secure there. Our introductions to all the Italian criminals took place precisely at El Caribe.

At this time, the government couldn't even imagine that the Italian Mafia and Russian criminals would be gathering, working out deals, making decisions together.

---

[*] None of Dr. Levine's nieces and nephews were ever implicated in the organized crime activities that Boris alleges took place at El Caribe.

None of us—Evsei, myself, Venya—did much in the way of managing the actual fitness center. Honestly, we all just came over to work out. Except Evsei. He didn't go in for sports. Well, you know, we say, "among the pickpockets, pickpocketing *is* their sport." The rest of us, we lifted weights with the Italians and talked business. Sometimes Russians came in there with proposals for criminal jobs. Mostly asking for our help extracting money.

By the mid-1980s, Boris says, almost all questions having to do with Russian organized crime in Brighton Beach were decided at El Caribe. "There were many adjudications at El Caribe—it was a good place to make decisions on criminal disputes. But over time, it became well-known that we were the owners—Evsei, me, and Venya. You'd hear people saying it in Brighton, 'Over at El Caribe, there's Russian criminals alongside Mafia, the *bratva* rubbing shoulders with *Italyakhas*.'"

Federal agents also picked up on these street rumors and soon had El Caribe under constant surveillance. "After we owned the place for about a year, we knew that the FBI was keeping a close watch on Evsei. He was *always* being followed. We'd often see the federal cars that tailed us, trying to be slick, swapping one sedan for another. We could see the government watching us whenever we came or left El Caribe. We had to be vigilant. If I was driving Evsei home, I'd often circle the block two or three times to make sure no fed was on my tail."

By 1983, BORIS AND HIS cousin Venya were known as Brighton Beach's most formidable enforcers. Boris's instantaneous use of violence, the lightning flashes of his temper, became infamous within Russian criminal circles, while the bearded Venya—standing five nine and two hundred eighty pounds—was known for his prodigious strength.

Many accounts of the Brighton Beach underworld in the 1980s erro-
neously describe the cousins as the terrifying "Nayfeld Brothers."[*]

On August 21, 1983, Venya Nayfeld was involved in a fight at the
Sadko restaurant that resulted in the death of an eighteen-year-old
named Zurab Minakhi. The killing has become one of the darkest
stories in Brighton's underworld lore—supposedly illustrative of the
brazenness and savagery of the Russian mob—though the facts have
long been shrouded in rumor and sensationalism.

"This is what actually happened that night," Boris recalls.

We were at Sadko. Venya, Evsei, Zelya, myself, and some others. We
already ate somewhere else, and we just came late to listen to the
music. Sadko always had top entertainers. That night Alik Milos was
playing and Lyubka Uspenskaya was singing. We'd normally arrive at
Sadko after one in the morning, to drink coffee and listen to the music.

About an hour after we sit down, there's a bunch of these young
Georgian Jews out partying, making lots of noise. One of them was
playing the big shot—as we say, pretending to be a *blatnoy*.

He comes over to our table. Really drunk, loud, he starts sizing us
up. He says, "So-and-so is a thief in law," and "So-in-so is *not* a thief
in law!" Venya tells him, "Listen, leave us alone! It's not your place
to be talking about who's a thief in law. Get away from here!"

The kid looks insulted, angry, but he walks away.

I'm planning to stay at Sadko maybe another hour. Venya says he's
going to leave. To be honest, I can't remember whether he left alone
or with some girl. I stayed a while longer with Evsei and the others, so
I wasn't outside when it all happened. What I'm telling you is based

---

[*] This confusion likely stems from the fact that the Russian term for "a male first
cousin," *dvoyurodnii brat,* contains the word for "brother" (*brat*). Boris's actual
brother, Gena, was never involved in criminal activity, organized or otherwise.

on Venya's account and what the other witnesses said. As Venya was leaving, this same Georgian Jew who was bothering us along with two or three of his buddies start yelling at my cousin: "You! Come over here! You wanted to tell me something?"

Venya says, "Look, I'm on my way home—what do you want?"

The Georgian guy pulls out a knife and comes at Venya. Now, Venya is a big, strong guy, and he intercepts the knife, grabs the guy's wrist, and redirects the blade. During the struggle, Venya stabs the kid straight in the heart. There were many witnesses, and they all said the same thing: the Georgian kid was the instigator. He came at Venya with a knife.

Anyway, the kid's lying there bleeding to death, Venya realizes the cops are going to investigate this as a murder. So he's kind of panicked and doesn't go home, but goes to crash at a buddy's apartment.

The next day, Evsei and I meet with Venya. My cousin's not sure what he should do. Evsei says, "You acted in self-defense. I have a good lawyer. He'll take the case and you'll be found not guilty." This lawyer was about eighty years old, but Evsei was very tight with him. He was kind of a famous defense attorney. Evsei and Venya went to his office in downtown Brooklyn. I didn't go with them. Venya described what happened outside Sadko and the lawyer agreed to take the case.

There was all sorts of garbage written later about the incident, like Venya lifted the guy up off the ground with one hand and stabbed him with the other.* There were many, many witnesses who testified as to what *really* happened. They told the police in great detail. The young

---

* Robert Friedman in *Red Mafiya* writes that "the black-bearded Benjamin [Nayfeld], a former member of the Soviet Olympic weightlifting team, was a bear of a man with a twenty-two-inch neck. He once killed a Jewish youth in a Brighton Beach parking lot in front of dozens of witnesses by picking him up like a ragdoll with one hand and plunging a knife into his heart with the other."

Georgian pulled a knife, came at my cousin, there was a struggle, Venya overpowered him. The kid, almost accidentally, was stabbed with his own knife.

Here's what I *did* see: earlier in the night, this same young kid, very drunk, harassed others in Sadko. Besides the argument with Venya, he was belligerent towards other guys. Witnesses gave statements that this young Georgian picked fights with at least three different people in Sadko.

Evsei's eighty-year-old lawyer friend represented Venya. Venya turned himself in, and in the end, it was judged that he was acting in self-defense. My cousin was never charged with murder.

About three or four months later, we find out that this dead kid's dad—a wealthy Georgian Jew in Queens—is looking to get vengeance. We get wind of the fact he's planning to put a contract on Venya. When I hear about it, I arrange a meeting with this father. I come out to Queens, alone, and we sit down outside on a bench.

I tell him, "Listen, we heard you've been trying to hire someone to get rid of my cousin Venya. You're looking to take revenge?"

The father stares at me. "What are you trying to say?"

I tell him, "If anything happens to my cousin, you need to understand one thing: we'll make your entire *family* pay. Why start a feud? What happened, happened. It's over. What's more, I saw how your son was acting in Sadko. Your son behaved improperly."

The father sat there for a while and then said, "You know what? I submit your cousin to God. I am not doing anything. Let God decide what happens to him."

By mid-1983, our crew was well-known, not just in New York but out of state, too. Evsei formed alliances with some of the other Russian groups across the U.S., and we'd do jobs jointly from time to time.

We'd get calls for work—especially money-extraction jobs—in cities where there wasn't an established Russian criminal organization.

One time, Evsei, Zelya, and me flew out to L.A. We got called in to settle this dispute. One partner had stiffed another partner and we were given the job of collecting what was owed. Once we got to L.A., we were met by some of Evsei's friends from Leningrad. They took care of us; we moved into a hotel and started to do our research, working out a plan for how we were going to track the guy down and get him to pay the money he owed.

One night, we've got a bit of downtime, and Zelya and me went out restaurant hopping. Misha Shufutinsky* had moved from Brighton to L.A. by this the time. He and a partner opened up this restaurant called Kapitan. Zelya and me went out with two young chicks. Some Russian girls we met in L.A. We go to Misha's, then another place called the Black Sea. As soon as we come in, there's a group of about twenty young Russians there. About ten guys with ten chicks. At first glance I can see these guys are looking for trouble.

When we come in, one of the guys recognizes the girl I'm with. He shouts, "You! Come over here!"

I don't know what's going on—maybe she used to date him or something. She's about to go over to his table, but I stop her. "Listen, why don't you sit here? You came with us. Sit down with us, have a drink. Later, you can go over and say hello."

The guys are all in their twenties. I look over. They're staring hard at us, and I hear one of them say in Russian: "Oh, what's gonna happen now? There's gonna be a fucking *sea* of blood." I'd been drinking a lot, but I heard that part clearly. I get up from the table and I tell Zelya, "Let's go over there and teach these punks a lesson."

---

* Mikhail Zakharovich Shufutinsky—one of the most popular Soviet-Jewish émigré singers. More on Shufutinsky on page 138.

I didn't have a gun on me, but I picked up this knife from the table, you know, a steak knife with a serrated blade. I head straight for their table. Zelya's right beside me. In the meantime, the owner's wife—she knows me from Brighton—she sees me approaching with this knife, coming up to the chief punk, the leader with the big mouth.

I grab him by the hair—he had very long hair—and yank his head towards me and go to slice his throat with the knife. The owner's wife sticks her hand in the way and I accidentally cut her. The knife falls to the floor, she's bleeding everywhere, it's just fucking mayhem.

We start to beat up these young punks. There's only two of us but we take on the bunch of them. Many of the young guys are too scared to join the fight. Just Zelya and me are throwing punches right and left. We kicked the living shit out of them. The owner and his wife are pleading with us to stop. "Biba! Leave, please! The cops will be here any minute!" So Zelya and me pick up our girls and leave.

The kid whose throat I'd nearly cut turned out to be the son of a guy Evsei had known back in Leningrad. The next day the father calls Evsei. "Please, Evsei, call off your dogs! Tell your men that my boy meant no offense. He had no idea who he was dealing with. He was drunk!"

The thing is, I was drunk, too. And the next day, once I was sober, I realized how lucky I was. This wasn't like Venya and the Georgian kid at Sadko, where my cousin could plead self-defense.

Zelya kept saying, "Biba, what if you'd *killed* the kid?"

He was right. First of all, I didn't realize that the state of California had the death penalty for murder. And second, at that time I didn't have the kind of money you need to go into hiding. To go on the run for a serious crime like murder, you need to forget your family and friends, you need to forget *everything* in your life. You think that's easy? It takes a lot of cash to do that—to keep changing documents, moving every few weeks, and so on.

I talked it over with Zelya. I said, "Better not to get drunk again when we're doing business—especially out of town."

Ilya Zeltzer amazed me that night. He was fearless. That was one thing about Zelya—when I was with him, I didn't need any other backup. Having him there was like having three or four guys. Later I saw, sadly, that he was willing to give his life for me.

BORIS ALWAYS VIEWED "money-extracting" assignments like that one out in Los Angeles as the most complicated, and potentially danger-fraught, aspect of mob life.

With money extraction, of course, the payoff's good—our cut was always fifty percent—but the risk's also high. The people we're collecting for almost always have dirty money. They can't go to the cops, they can't go to the courts, so they come to us. When you're collecting money on behalf of someone else, the repercussions are different than a typical criminal job. The level of risk to you personally is different.

When you're doing a job on your own, when you go to rob stores, apartments, factories—that's one thing. It's your decision. The consequences are straightforward. If you get away with it, you get away with it. If you're caught, okay, you go to fucking jail.

Sometimes we'd get money-extraction jobs for two or three million dollars. When you're talking about that kind of cash, *anything*'s possible. Let's say one partner screws the other out of a few million, then he totally disappears. Now you get called in to collect this debt— well, you better think long and hard about the consequences.

First of all, the guy's just ripped off a few million bucks, which means he has the resources to take you out. For a hundred grand, he can pay someone to kill you before you get to him. And he's got the resources to stay underground for some time. If he's a well-connected criminal, a guy with some experience, most likely he'll try to arrange a kind of negotiation, paying off part of the debt, but not all of it.

Then there are also many people who flat-out refuse to return what's owed, who won't go for any kind of negotiation to settle the issue. Okay, now, you've accepted the job of collecting, if you fail to carry out the job, you lose face in the eyes of the customers. Not only the customers. The rumor will spread around the entire criminal world: "So-and-so was given the job to collect and he failed."

Overnight, your reputation is shot. If you don't recover the money—how can I explain it?—you get this feeling of a little worm constantly gnawing on the insides of your stomach. That's why it's always necessary to think hard about the money-extraction job before saying yes. You need to investigate the person's background, their history, who they might be connected to. You make a character sketch, obtain as much precise data as you can before agreeing to get the money. If you don't, well, you might be walking across a minefield.

Of course, sometimes you realize the guy is never going to pay what's owed. He's never going to negotiate. You've got to settle the issue by other methods. Guys who refuse to pay might get blinded with acid or have their bones broken. Some guys are crippled for life. In these cases, it's better not to go around issuing warnings. You simply do what you need to do.

That's the only way to preserve your criminal reputation. You've accepted the job: if you can't extract the money, you need to make sure there are some serious consequences. But you've also incurred serious consequences for yourself. You're risking a long-term enemy, someone who'll bear a grudge against you for years. For the rest of his life, this guy can be a risk to take revenge.

We finished that job in L.A. We collected the money we'd been sent to there get. If I remember correctly, it was two hundred grand. Almost as soon as we got back to Brooklyn, we get another call from L.A. There was this guy Tolik Pitersky. He'd stiffed one of his partners out in California—something medically related—for eighty thousand bucks and ran off to New York.

Me and my crew start looking for this Tolik. Eventually we get this address, not far from Kings Highway. We stake him out on a one-way street, waiting for him to come out and get into his car, and we'll intercept him. He comes out. Doesn't see us. As he pulls away, about to pass our car, he suddenly spots us, throws his car in reverse and gets away by driving backwards, like sixty miles an hour, against the flow of traffic. We all had guns on us and didn't want to go flying around Brooklyn, in reverse, attracting attention. We figured, fine, we'll catch up with Tolik another day.

Brooklyn's a big place but, like I said, Russian circles are tiny, and we knew he couldn't duck us for long. One day I'm sitting in the office at El Caribe. The office was downstairs, next to our pool and fitness center. I get a call from the girl working upstairs: "Boris, these two Italians are here with someone. They want to talk to you." I asked her to let them downstairs.

One of the *Italyakhas* was named Anthony—a young, athletic guy, dark hair, dark eyes. I knew him already because we used to work out together in our fitness center. The second *Italyakha* didn't do any talking. And the third guy with them was this fucking Pitersky deadbeat Tolik.

Anthony says, "Boris, we need to talk to you." I give Tolik a stare. In Russian I say, "You *kozyol*! Wait outside! I want to talk to these *Italyakhas* without you listening to the conversation. Get out of the fucking room!" Tolik leaves. I ask Anthony, "Okay, what's up?"

Anthony says, "Our boss sent us to straighten out this problem." I knew their boss was Gaspipe Casso, one of the heavyweight Lucchese gangsters in Brooklyn. I say, "What kind of problem could we have? I've never done business with you or your boss."

Anthony goes, "My boss invested a lot of money in this guy Anatoly. He's doing some business for us." I tell him, "Okay, your boss invested with Anatoly. That's fine. But the thing is, this snake is stiffing people. He takes money, he runs off, he doesn't pay his debts. We've got a job to do, too. He's got to pay what he owes."

"Boris, this guy says you're driving around looking to whack him. I'm telling you—you can't whack him yet. He's got a job to finish for us."

I say, "I'm not trying to *kill* him. Why would I kill him? He owes money. Anthony, how's he going to pay me if he's *dead*?"

"Boris," he says. "I'm asking you for a favor. Don't touch him until he's finished the job for us." I tell him, "No problem. We're not going to touch him until you're done with him—then we can settle up what he owes." We shake hands and they leave El Caribe.

A few months pass. Tolik starts to hang out in Russian restaurants—Odessa, Sadko, Metropol, the National—talking about how he's with Gaspipe and his crew. He's running his mouth: "The *Italyakhas* made a deal with Biba not to touch me! I can party it up!"

I get wind of all this, but I'm still waiting for these guys from Gaspipe's crew to give me the go-ahead so I can settle our business.

Then one day I see a story in the Russian newspaper. It says there was a car discovered at a parking lot at Manhattan Beach. Inside the car, they found the body of this very same Tolik. The body had five bullets in it, and the insurance shot to the head.

We later found out what Gaspipe's crew had been using Tolik for. They opened a company in Tolik's name. They bought cars, electronics, all kinds of equipment, took out bank loans—Tolik was just the front. They used his name to run up a line of credit, stealing millions. Well, they got what they needed from Tolik. "The Moor has done his duty; the Moor can go."*

In my opinion, they were one of the most bloodthirsty of the *Italyakha* families—the Lucchese family. And especially Gaspipe's crew in Bensonhurst. For people like me who grew up in the Soviet Union, the only thing we knew about the Mafia was what we'd seen in movies like *The Godfather*. We didn't really know how they operated on the street.

Boris's perceptions of the Italian American mob might indeed have been filtered entirely though the romantic lens of Hollywood. Meanwhile, he and the rapidly growing community of Soviet émigrés were busy manufacturing their own cinematic—and often deadly—nighttime playland on the seaside of Brooklyn.

---

* In Russian, this common expression is often attributed to Shakespeare's *Othello*, but actually comes from *Fiesco's Conspiracy at Genoa* by Friedrich Schiller. The phrase means that you have no need for someone once they've finished doing what you've asked them to do.

CHAPTER 12

BROOKLYN NOCTURNE

Studying photos of Brighton Beach's nightlife in the early to mid-'80s—the raucous scenes inside the famous Russian supper clubs—it's easy to see Little Odessa as a community steeped in nostalgia. But it's an ersatz nostalgia: a longing for a world that never existed. On the shores of South Brooklyn, the immigrants created an entirely novel cultural scene.

"Brighton Beach is, in fact, a collection of old Soviet fantasies," one perceptive *Washington Post* columnist wrote. "It is how the beleaguered communist worker imagined that America would look."

The crowded restaurants and nightclubs clustered along Brighton Beach Avenue offered a fever dream of Western opulence filtered through a Slavic sensibility. An esthetic borrowed, in part, from Odessa's Belle Époque architecture: medallioned ceilings, crystal chandeliers, gilded ornaments, red velvet curtains, compass points inlaid in polished parquet dance floors. Throw in a dash of American glitz: some restaurants offered up Las Vegas–style floor shows; others Sinatra-like crooners belting out Russian chansons. The tables were crowded with towering, tiered trays of caviar, lobster, smoked fish. Waiters in bow ties juggled plates of chicken Kiev and beef stroganoff. The bottles of Stolichnaya, of course, never stopped flowing.

And gangsters were ubiquitous in Brighton Beach nightlife. Organized crime figures like Evsei Agron and Boris Nayfeld had silent (or in many cases not-so-silent) partnerships in the restaurants and nightclubs. According to Boris, they also served as early patrons for many of the era's leading singers and performers.

"By the time I met him, Evsei had married Maya Rozova," Boris recalls.

Maya was a singer who'd emigrated from Russia and began her career in New York, performing with her first husband, Alex Shabashov. In my opinion, among the immigrants nobody performed the Russian romance* better than Maya. She had a rich voice, did beautiful renditions, accompanying herself on the piano.

Evsei fell in love with her, and it so happened that she fell in love with him. By the time they married, there were only a few Russian restaurants, Fiddler on the Roof, Sadko, Metropol, Odessa, Paradise, the National. We always had good relationships with the owners; Maya and Alex Shabashov started their careers at the National.

The best times we ever had in Brighton were when Evsei and I started to hang out during the evenings together as friends—before the second attempt on his life. By 1983, the majority of the Russians I knew in New York were criminals. It didn't take much for them to get angry and pull out their guns. Even the youngsters—the kids who weren't serious criminals—they'd get drunk at a restaurant and fights

---

* By "Russian romance," Boris is referring to the traditional lyrical sentimental song, often with a Romani influence, that was developed and popularized in imperial Russia.

would break out. Someone needed to manage the situation, keep order, otherwise the violence would start hurting the business. That's where Evsei would come in. For a cut of the monthly take, we provided the *krysha* to many of the restaurants, so they'd remain free of violence. When I joined up with Evsei full-time, as I mentioned, he and Vilya were already providing the *krysha* at the National.

People don't remember the good things Evsei did, only the bad. Yes, he was a criminal. Yes, he made his money strictly by criminal means. But he also used his money and his power to help a lot of people. For example, many musicians who arrived from the Soviet Union in Brighton without money or connections, Evsei helped them get work.

I remember when Misha Shufutinsky arrived in New York, around 1981. Today, he's a big star, one of the leading bards in Russia. Misha's a fine singer and musician. He writes his own arrangements. He's got a great standing among the singers. But back then, when he first got to New York from the Soviet Union, Misha couldn't even get a job at the smallest restaurant in Brighton Beach. Nobody would take him. Nobody had heard of him, and all the restaurants said they already had enough musicians. Maya knew he was talented and asked Evsei to help get Misha get a job.

We got him a regular singing gig at Fiddler on the Roof. That was the start of everything for Misha. I always got on well with him. Even today, as big as he's become, Misha Shufutinsky is just a normal guy—a member of the intelligentsia—whenever I've seen him, he's always grateful for the support we gave him finding employment when he was first starting out.[*]

---

[*] Mikhail Zakharovich Shufutinsky, born in Moscow in 1948, the preeminent singer of Russian chanson music. He began his career in Brighton Beach in 1981 and became hugely popular in Russia after the collapse of the Soviet Union. Many of his chansons deal with the *blatnoy* subculture and émigré life in New York. He was awarded the title of Meritorious Artist of Russia in 2013.

And it wasn't only the musicians. There were so many immigrants looking to start up businesses who simply needed financing. Evsei would give them money to get their business off the ground. You could say Evsei acted as a banker for new immigrants who had no credit or standing with the American banks. Sure, he didn't lend money for free; people had to pay back with interest. But who lends money free? Does any bank lend a start-up business money without charging interest?

There was this one jeweler called Simochka. Evsei gave him fifty thousand bucks to start up his own jewelry factory. The guy was a wizard with his fingers. His jewelry was truly artwork. We became great friends and would all go to the *banya* together once a week.

In all criminal matters, Evsei was one of the fairest people. Yes, there were occasions where he'd let things slide, I mean who doesn't make mistakes? Everyone makes mistakes. But as a criminal, Evsei was one of the best. He had an *excellent* criminal name.

Even though he was pushing fifty, Evsei was out with me in Brighton almost every night. The reason we did so much restaurant hopping was because of Maya. Maya would be singing at a spot and Evsei would go there to pick her up when she finished at two or three in the morning. Many nights, Evsei and I would go out and start at one spot, then continue drinking and partying, because he needed to pick her up when she was finished performing. The National, Sadko, Odessa, Fiddler on the Roof. We'd make stops at all of them.

Naturally, since we were out every night, I was always meeting women, even though I had a wife and two kids at home. I mean, I made no secret of it. Everyone knew that I wasn't a good husband. It was no different than back in Gomel. In New York I cheated on Valentina constantly. We lived together under the same roof, but when I'd get home it was often six or seven in the morning and I'd ask her to fix me a hot bowl of borsht for breakfast as she was getting ready to go off to work.

Looking back on it all now, Valentina was a good mother, a good wife. She had ambition. She not only learned English, she enrolled in a college to study nursing. She became a registered nurse. When I remembered her as the young country girl I'd met in Gomel, it amazed me: I never would've expected that Valya could work so hard to get an education in the United States—studying biology, chemistry, mathematics—all in English, mind you. Had I been a *normal* husband, who knows? She may have studied even further. But I wasn't a normal husband, I was constantly out all night and cheating on her.

While out partying at the Metropol, the largest Russian restaurant in Brooklyn, Boris met an attractive blond eighteen-year-old Jewish girl from Ukraine named Angela Kiperman, who would later become his second wife. "I was at Metropol and I saw my friend Alik Aronov partying. I can't remember what the occasion was—a birthday or something. In any event, I saw Angela sitting at their table. She smiled at me, I invited her for a dance. The band was playing chansons and we danced for quite a while that night."

Boris was already known in Brighton's restaurants and clubs for his ballroom dancing skill. During his wild *khuligan* days in Belarus, his older brother, Gena, had taken dancing lessons, and Boris—ever a quick learner—picked up the steps by studying his brother.

"As we danced, Angela told me a bit about herself—that she was from Kharkiv," Boris recalls. "She was only eighteen—I was already thirty-four or thirty-five. I can't remember how we connected next, but we met up and went to a restaurant. That was our first date. Over the months, we started a relationship, going out to restaurants, dancing. She was living in Queens with her parents, working at a Manhattan salon, doing manicures and pedicures. I didn't think anything serious was going to come of it—never imagined we'd one day get married and have a child. But as we say, 'The deeper into the forest you go, the more firewood you find.'"*

This was the brief period in the early eighties when Evsei and me were going out and having fun in Brighton. Everywhere we went, cognac, caviar, young beautiful women wanting to meet us. It was the peak of pleasure—let's put it that way.

But it was also at that time that I realized that I'd crossed over a line. I'd become a *complete* criminal. My life, my mentality, and all my actions were wired to be of a criminal nature. Twenty-four hours a day, seven days a week.

Evsei's enemies were always looking to make moves against him. And our nights out started to get more and more dangerous. There was this one night when Evsei was taking Maya to work. As Maya went into the restaurant, some guys made a move on Evsei—we never found out who they were.

Evsei pulls out his .25 and shoots one of them in the stomach, jumps in his car, and speeds away immediately. Evsei calls me up, tells me to come right over to his place. When I get there, he says he shot a guy in the gut and asks me to dispose of the weapon. I take his .25 and toss it into the ocean. The shooting wasn't reported anywhere. We didn't know if the guy was badly wounded or if he died. Either way, we got away with it.

BUT BEING THE BOSS of the Russian mob in America meant Evsei Agron always had a target on his back. By 1984, a war over the protection rackets in the Diamond District and Brighton Beach had been brewing with

---

* A famous Russian proverb meaning "As things go on, they get more complicated."

a crew led by a Russian-born, ex–Israeli Defense Forces veteran named Boris Goldberg. Goldberg, who wore Coke-bottle glasses, was known as "Borya Ochkarik."* He led a cowboy crew, based out of a warehouse in Chelsea, involved in armed robberies, extortion, and drug trafficking.

This Borya Ochkarik had longstanding beefs with Evsei. In fact, Evsei had been having problems with Borya Ochkarik long before I came to work for him. They were beefing over *krysha*. And Borya Ochkarik decided to assassinate Evsei in order to take control of all the rackets on Forty-Seventh Street.

Within his crew, Borya Ochkarik had a professional killer named Charlie Rivera—a skinny Latino guy. Actually, I heard he was half Latino and half Sicilian, but who knows?

Charlie went everywhere with a Russian-Jewish kid named Evan. One day, there was an internal dispute within the gang—some kind of shootout in Manhattan. One of their own crew got wounded. We're sitting in the offices at El Caribe and the guy who got wounded, Ilyusha Lysy,[†] suddenly comes to see us. Our whole crew is sitting there, and he says, "Evsei, I've come to warn you about something."

We can see he's been wounded. We heard about the shootout. "Warn me about what?" Evsei says. Ilyusha Lysy says, "Evsei, there's going to be an attempt on your life." We listened to his story. I said, "Okay, an assassination attempt. Who's planning it?" He tells us it's Borya Ochkarik. Now I want all the details: "Where? When? How are they going to try to take out Evsei?" He says Borya and his crew rented an apartment across the street from Evsei's building and a sniper with a rifle is going to take Evsei out.

---

* *Ochkarik*—a Russian pejorative for someone who wears glasses; roughly equivalent to "Four Eyes."

† *Lysy* is roughly equivalent to "Baldie."

As soon as Ilyusha Lysy left the downstairs fitness center at El Caribe, Evsei Agron narrowed his gaze in suspicion, glancing between Boris and Venya.

"Why would this guy suddenly come to warn me about being killed?"

"Maybe to get in good with us," Boris said.

"No," Evsei said. "I think he's just trying to draw us into their beef— have us settle it. He wants to use us to kill Ochkarik and all his dogs."

"Do we make a move against them?"

"Not yet," Evsei said. "For now, we wait."

The second attempt on Agron's life occurred on the evening of January 24, 1984.

"It was a cold night, snow mixed with rain, and I was off doing a job," Boris recalls.

We had to settle up a dispute about *krysha* with a jeweler on Forty-Seventh Street who refused to pay up. Evsei told me a message needed to be sent. I drove out to Long Island with Zelya. We lit a Molotov cocktail, tossed it into this guy's front window, then we drove back to Brooklyn.

Around eleven that night, I get a phone call about Evsei getting shot. I race to the hospital in my Lincoln. Evsei was laid up in the ER, badly wounded. It was amazing he was still alive. The shooter had snuck up on him from behind, in the parking garage, shot him in the head with a .25—but somehow, the bullet didn't kill him. The slug was still in his head and couldn't be safely removed. Evsei was conscious, but his eye was damaged. In the end, half his face was paralyzed.

I said, "Evsei, did you see who shot you?"

Evsei tells me, "No, I didn't see the face. The only thing I saw was the feet—a pair of small boots."

We realize now we've made a bad mistake. We should have paid more attention to the tip-off from Ilyusha Lysy. I should never have left Evsei's side. Now we start to zero in on Borya Ochkarik. We decide that we're going to kill the entire crew. One by one. We start to stake them out by their homes. We follow them everywhere, looking for a clear chance to open fire. We tail Charlie and Evan first. Charlie Rivera was the only real threat posed to us in that entire crew. Get rid of Charlie and everything else would be easy. Every day, we're following Charlie and Evan's car, trying to figure out the best time to whack them.

But we never got a clear chance. A few days later, our friend Simochka the jeweler calls me up: "Boris," he says, "Charlie and Evan want to meet with you."

"Meet with me about what?"

Simochka says, "I don't know—they just want to talk."

"Okay, fine, set it up," I say. We get to Simochka's jewelry factory in Brighton. I'm with Zelya, both of us carrying our pieces. Charlie comes in with Evan. Evan does the talking—he speaks Russian but with an accent, because he was little when his parents took him out of Russia. His Russian name was Ivan, but he wanted to sound more American, so he changed it to Evan. He was translating for Charlie. Charlie goes, "Boris, I know you've been following us, but we didn't shoot Evsei. We didn't try to kill him."

"Oh, you didn't?"

"No, Boris, I give you my word of honor." He swore he was telling the truth in front of Simochka and everyone. I said, "All right, Charlie, if it wasn't you, fine, we're going to keep looking for whoever did it."

We weren't just going to take Charlie's word for it, obviously. But in the meantime, we got a tip that a contract on Evsei had been taken by another one of our rivals, Slavik Ovoschnik.*

Slavik Ovoschnik had just been locked up on an extortion charge and, even in his wounded state, Evsei says, "If it was Slava Ovoschnik, I'll fucking shoot him down *personally* the minute he gets out." The truth was, we couldn't really be sure—there were so many people trying to take out Evsei in those days.

After the shooting, everything changed for Evsei and all of us. All the fun times in Brighton got left in the past. We had to watch our backs constantly. Evsei stopped driving his own car—I'd take him everywhere in my Lincoln. I'd pack my .38 and take him to the apartment, wait until he got safely inside.

Our enemies knew that they could find Evsei, me, and our entire crew at El Caribe. And we also knew this wasn't going to be the last attempt on Evsei. Sooner or later, someone was going to try again. We were on alert every time we exited El Caribe. Before heading home, we'd always drive a lap around the country club first to see if anyone was following us. I always had my gun in my waistband.

In fact, not long after that second shooting, we decided to sell our interests in El Caribe to Marat Balagula. After Evsei got shot in the face, we weren't keeping up with paying the expenses and the fucking taxes owed. Like I said, I'm no businessman—I'm strictly a criminal. Marat came to us with a proposition. "I'll buy you guys out of El Caribe. My company needs tax write-offs and I'll be able to show the club's operating expenses on my returns." Evsei and I sat down, talked it over, and sold the club to Marat for, I think, two hundred eighty thousand.

---

* Vyacheslav Lyubarsky, a Brighton Beach jewel thief, swindler, and racketeer, generally known by the nickname Slava "Ovoschnik"—meaning "Slava the Vegetable Seller."

Agron, his face now distorted into a perpetual grimace, never wielded the same power within the Brighton Beach underworld after the 1984 shooting.

THE ATTEMPTED MURDER remained unsolved until September 1991, when Boris Goldberg—or Borya Ochkarik—was arrested and charged in a sweeping RICO case in the Eastern District of New York. According to federal prosecutors, the "Goldberg Crime Group" was indeed behind the shooting of Evsei Agron in January 1984.

In 1992, Goldberg pled guilty to charges including cocaine trafficking, extortion, armed robbery, and the attempted murder of Agron.

Boris Nayfeld would hear a firsthand confession from the shooter in federal jail. In 1994, facing RICO charges himself, Boris was held in the Metropolitan Correctional Center (MCC) in Lower Manhattan.

While I was in MCC, one of the guards takes a Polaroid of me, brings it around to every cell, asking whether anyone has a beef with me or vice versa. Because if there was situation where I wanted to kill someone, or someone wanted to kill me, they'd have to find me a different floor in MCC. All of a sudden, this Russian crook, a Pitersky who robbed banks with the *Italyakhas,* approaches me. "Boris," he says, "Charlie and Evan are here on this floor. They're asking whether you've got a beef with them or not." Charlie and Evan both got long sentences for killing a security guard during a jewelry store robbery—something like forty years.

I said, "What kind of beef? Well, we once thought maybe they shot Evsei . . . but that was a long, long time ago. I've got no beef with them now."

They release me into the population, and I hear that Charlie Rivera wants to see me. I go and find him. He's sitting there with Evan.

Charlie says, "Boris, remember that day when I swore that I wasn't the one who shot Evsei?"

"Yes, of course, I remember."

He says, "Well, it *was* me. I did shoot him." He tells me that Borya Ochkarik put out the contract. Charlie did the shooting. Evan drove the getaway car. Charlie looks up at me and says, "Is this gonna be a problem between us?"

I stared at both of them for a long time. "Look, Charlie, let's leave it alone," I said finally. "It's water under the bridge."

We're talking about something that happened ten years back.

Yes, he lied to my face. But it was so far in the past it seems like another lifetime. Charlie and Evan have already got their sentences—they've got forty years to do, and I'm in the middle of my own RICO case. I mean, we're all stuck in fucking jail. Who knows what's going to happen to any of us? Who knows what tomorrow holds? There's only one thing I know for sure. This is not the time or place to be settling old scores.

FOLLOWING THE FAILED ATTEMPT on Agron's life, by early 1984, Boris's criminal mentor receded from the day-to-day activities of his crew.

"Evsei still provided some useful advice, but he began to distance himself from the business," Boris recalls. "He started to rely more and more on me to take care of all our operations. Tears were always dripping from one of his eyes. Half his face looked frozen, like a guy who'd had a stroke. After the shooting he was basically a disabled person. He was no longer the same Evsei."

And as Agron's power waned, another guileful Soviet émigré made his ascendance in the Brighton Beach underworld, one who would have an enormous influence on Boris Nayfeld's ever-expanding criminal portfolio.

CHAPTER 13

THE LONG CON

Among all the hustlers, swindlers, and gunmen in the Soviet émigré underworld, it was an unimposing-looking immigrant from the south of Ukraine named Marat Balagula who would emerge as the racketeering mastermind of Brighton Beach.

Though Balagula's family was originally from Odessa, he was born in 1943 in Orenburg, a small city in southwest Russia, near Kazakhstan, when his mother fled during the Nazi invasion of the USSR. After the war, the family returned to Odessa; Marat studied economics in university, then worked on board a Soviet cruise ship, the *Ivan Franko,* as a bartender. He emigrated to the United States with his family in 1977, settling first in Washington Heights, finding work as a textile cutter. He quickly gravitated toward the underworld of Brighton Beach, and emerged as one of the brightest criminal minds among the Soviet émigrés.

Balagula was often described as a brilliant and charming opportunist. In photographs from the 1980s, paunchy and balding, in a sports jacket with tie slightly askew, he looks more like a weary furniture salesman than a mobster. Yet it was perhaps Balagula who best embodied the distinctive characteristics of Russian organized criminals in the United States: "urban in origin, well educated, and industrially and technologically skilled."

Like many of the émigrés, Balagula enjoyed embellishing his past in the USSR. American journalists credulously repeated a story that Balagula was so well-connected in the Soviet Union that a young Mikhail Gorbachev, a regional Communist Party boss at the time, showed up at Balagula's thirtieth birthday party to pay his respects. A photo of the two together was said to have been one of Balagula's prized possessions. No such photo exists, since Gorbachev and Balagula never met.[*]

There were many ludicrous legends of Balagula's "Midas-like wealth," including claims that he masterminded "a fleet of supertankers that plied the high seas," once tried to purchase an island off the coast of South Africa, and installed gilded doors, costing ten thousand dollars apiece, in his Long Island home.

Boris Nayfeld recalls Balagula's far more quotidian—and plausible-sounding—beginnings in Brooklyn's underworld. Before they stole tens of millions of dollars together in the fuel rackets, Boris began working as muscle for Balagula—doing freelance arson jobs.

I met Marat when I first got to Brooklyn. In the early days, he had a crew of about five guys. He had this auto repair shop in Coney Island. He used to hire me to torch cars. They'd give me the description of a certain car to set on fire and I'd get three hundred bucks for torching it. I had no idea of the techniques they used to write these cars off with insurance companies—that didn't interest me. I just did my work, lighting up cars.

---

[*] In 2019, when I interviewed Marat's daughter, Aksana Balagula Straschnow, in Brooklyn, she described the story as laughable and assured me that her late father had never known the famed Soviet leader.

When I met him, Marat was a businessman—first he owned Sadko, the first Russian restaurant in Brighton Beach, then he opened Odessa—so we'd see him around a lot when we went out at night.

Marat didn't have the personality of a criminal. By nature, he was a jumpy, nervous guy. As we say, "he was afraid of the squeaking wheels on a cart." But he was cunning. A very cunning guy. As his criminal business started to expand, he needed guys like me for muscle, to handle the rougher stuff. I did some freelancing for them besides arson, mostly extracting money out of deadbeats who stiffed them.

By the time I became Evsei's right-hand man in 1983, Marat was also starting to become closer friends with me. He'd invite me to his restaurants—honestly, he had a lot more money than me by then. He was doing very well, financially.

Boris found himself playing an uncharacteristically diplomatic role in the interpersonal dynamic of the Brighton *bratva*—serving as a kind of buffer between Agron and Balagula.

There was always some friction there. Evsei wasn't fond of Marat. And Marat wasn't fond of Evsei. But in my eyes, there was a huge difference between them. Marat had a head for numbers; he was a smart businessman, but he was no gangster. Evsei was a big-time criminal both in Russia and in the U.S. He was a gangster *and* a businessman. Marat never argued with Evsei, never fought with Evsei on any issue, he always tried to oblige Evsei in every way. Yet there was always that hostility. A grudge—never spoken about—that obviously went back some time.

Though Evsei Agron was indisputably the most powerful Russian mobster in Brighton Beach, by the early 1980s Marat Balagula had emerged as a force in his own right—a savvy entrepreneur and a financier of businesses, both legitimate and criminal. Balagula always had an eye for spotting talent, and he exhibited a degree of foresight, a patience with long-term investments that was often lacking in the typically mercurial and impulsive gangsters of Little Odessa. This was certainly the case when a terminally ill hustler arrived on the scene in Brighton with a plan to run an elaborate con in the Diamond District.

"This guy Aron Kishka shows up in Brooklyn one day," Boris recalls.

He was a specialist in working *schneyer*. He'd been in Germany before he came to work with us in New York—I'd met him a couple of times over in Europe. He showed us a variation on *schneyer* we'd never seen. Most criminals doing a *schneyer* job were looking to make fifty or a hundred thousand. That's the most I ever made doing *schneyer* with the ten-ruble coins, you know, when we dressed up as Russian merchant marines. To me, it was a quick scam you'd pull in a day—usually best done out of town.

Aron Kishka told us we needed to work the *schneyer* as a long con. If we played it out right, we could steal over a million bucks. Instead of conning some *lokh* in a single day, his *schneyer* required months and months of planning and patience.

As soon as Marat hears about this, he likes the idea. He invites Aron Kishka to work with him. Aron has his eyes set on the Diamond District in Manhattan, but he doesn't have the start-up money to work his *schneyer*. Marat fronts him a hundred thousand dollars to get started.

Step one is renting out an office near Forty-Seventh Street. Aron says that the office needs to be on an upper floor and have an entrance and a back room with its own exit. It's crucial that this back exit not be visible from the front of the office. Step two is to build a reputation—start buying up stones. Aron's targets were always Hasidic Jews in the diamond trade. In major diamond centers like the one in midtown

Manhattan there are always people looking to sell their cut stones—especially if you're offering good prices.

Aron was knowledgeable enough about gems not to seem like an amateur, and he could negotiate in Yiddish, which made the Hasidic Jews entering his second-floor office feel at ease.

He needed to get a reputation as a buyer in the Diamond District, so in the first month or so, he didn't care if he operated at a loss. He purchased a bunch of stones and sold them quickly—the point wasn't making a profit, it was to create a cash flow and steady traffic of customers. Over the weeks he began luring in more and more Hasidic Jews, making sure they became comfortable sitting in that office and doing business.

Boris was impressed by the sophistication of the swindle. Aron Kishka wasn't really trading diamonds; his true commodity was his reputation. This was paramount in the close-knit community of Manhattan's Diamond District, where it isn't uncommon for million-dollar deals to be done strictly on a handshake.

Another thing you have to understand about Aron Kishka—this was a guy with nothing to lose. He had colon cancer. Even before we met him in New York, he had surgery. The guy knew he was dying. He wore one of those bags on his body, you know—he couldn't go to the bathroom normally. The fact that he had terminal cancer worked to his advantage. People felt sympathy for him. Everyone knew he probably didn't have more than a year to live.*

Anyway, he kept building up his business for a few solid months,

---

* *Kishka*, in Ashkenazi Jewish cuisine, refers to a once-popular dish of grains, minced meat, and chicken fat stuffed inside the lining of beef intestines. In Yiddish, and many East Slavic languages, the word *kishka* means "guts," hence, the derivation of the nickname of this terminally ill swindler Aron.

luring in more and more sellers. When he had a good reputation in the
Diamond District, when the sellers felt comfortable in his office, he set
a date to do the *schneyer*. He put out word one day that he was buying
a lot of cut diamonds. His regular clients, these Hasidic Jews who knew
him, came by with their stones. Aron studied the diamonds, quoted
good prices—in one day, he managed to pull in over a million dollars'
worth of stones. He made sure everyone could see him locking the
jewels in the safe in the back room. He told them he was going to the
bank to cash a check necessary to make such a big purchase.

By this time, the sellers all trusted him. They'd done enough
business with Aron that no one batted an eye when he left. These
Hasidic Jews sat waiting in what they thought was an empty office,
with their jewels secured in the safe. But what the sellers didn't realize
is that there was a back exit, and Aron had a partner, a guy named
Yakov—nicknamed Yasha—who no one had ever seen. And while they
were in the front room waiting, Yasha emptied the diamonds out of
the safe. It was a trick safe, with a hidden opening in the back. In any
event, Yasha was so quick and quiet, no one noticed. Then he slipped
out the back exit. The Hasidic Jews sat there in the office waiting and
waiting. By the time they figured out something was suspicious, Aron
Kishka and Yasha were halfway to Brighton Beach with over a million
bucks' worth of diamonds.

Aron Kishka starts selling off the stones in Brighton. He unloads
them at cut-rate prices—what's the difference? It's all profit to him
anyway. And these are *top*-quality stones, so everyone wants some.

He gave Marat the lion's share of the diamonds since he'd put
up the hundred thousand to finance the *schneyer*. I bought some
diamonds for myself, and so did Evsei and the rest of our crew.

And Aron Kishka? It was his last job in New York. His cancer
progressed fast. He got locked up by the feds in MCC—not for this
schneyer job, for something else—and was facing deportation from the

U.S. But before he could be deported, he died. Aron was only on the scene in Brighton for a short while, but we all remembered what he'd taught us . . .

Much later, we decided to pull it off a second time over in Antwerp—the biggest diamond market in the world.

But first, Boris and the other Brighton Beach gangsters would dive headlong into a grander shell game, employing an everyday commodity with an even higher payoff than the rarest of gemstones.

Gasoline.

CHAPTER 14

GASOLINE

It was Marat Balagula who introduced us to gasoline," Boris recalls. "He wasn't the first to figure out how to steal the gasoline tax, but Marat perfected the scheme. More than anyone else, Marat figured out how to explode the profits. I have to give Marat credit. I made my first serious money—my first million dollars—with Marat."

Criminals had been bootlegging gasoline in the United States, albeit on a small scale, long before the arrival of Soviet émigré criminals. Prior to the 1980s, New York State required individual gas stations to collect and pay fuel taxes. The original gasoline bootleggers worked on the retail level; many were Greek and Turkish immigrants who sold gasoline, failed to pay the required taxes, then went out of business before the tax collectors could catch up with them.

In 1982, New York State changed its legislation, shifting the tax responsibility from individual stations to the wholesale suppliers. Lawmakers thought it would be easier to collect taxes once a year from a few wholesalers than from thousands of gas stations. Soviet émigré gangsters immediately saw the opportunity to exploit a glaring weakness in the system: a provision in the new law allowed wholesale distribution companies to trade or resell gasoline among themselves, with only the last company—the one selling the gasoline to the stations—responsible for collecting the taxes due.

In so-called daisy chain schemes, licensed fuel companies, owned and controlled by mobsters, would purchase wholesale gasoline, then move it through a series of bogus sales using dummy wholesale companies. The gasoline never physically moved; the dummy companies simply filed invoices along with fraudulent tax exemption forms. After a labyrinthine series of transactions, one of the dummy corporations in the chain was designated the "burn company," the one ostensibly responsible for paying the taxes.

Instead of paying the government, the burn company simply vanished. At the end of the year, tax collectors were left sorting out a complex paper trail that led to a dead end. An empty office, no officers or employees. None of the previous distributors in the daisy chain could be charged with wrongdoing since they had valid invoices for the sales and had filed valid tax-exemption forms.

For ingenious criminals like Marat Balagula and Boris Nayfeld who'd grown up in the Soviet Union's culture of institutionalized corruption, gasoline-tax fraud was just as an extension of the crime of stealing from the State. Siphoning off billions of dollars owed to the government seemed a safe racket: a faceless, victimless crime. Consumers at the pump had few complaints; the filling stations owned by, or connected to, Russian and Italian organized crime groups could sell gasoline at a cheaper price per gallon, since they weren't paying any of the tax anyway.*

---

* In 1986, the estimated national average of federal, state, and sales taxes for gasoline was about forty cents a gallon.

"You didn't even have to be a good businessman to steal a huge amount of money in gasoline," Boris says. "My cousin Venya and me set up a fuel company. We made it look incredibly complicated to the feds but, in fact, the concept was simple. We were middlemen between the gasoline suppliers and the stations. We didn't move gasoline, we only moved pieces of paper. Today, the system is computerized—you couldn't get away with what we got away with. But back in the eighties and nineties, all we needed to do was generate a whole lot of invoices for sales and file tax-exemption forms."

Russian mobsters added another clever twist to the scheme. "We started hiring people from other countries—guys who were here with green cards," Boris says. "Mostly Poles, Hungarians, Rumanians—people from Eastern Europe who were in the United States legally but wanted to go back to live in Europe. We offered them a hundred grand to create dummy companies in their names. Their documents were used to register companies and to steal the taxes. We'd have them get their official gasoline distribution licenses, file all the necessary forms, then we'd give them a big chunk of cash to simply disappear. 'Here's a hundred grand,' we'd say, 'just fucking leave America forever.'"

By the mid-1980s, Marat Balagula had emerged as the dominant player in the massive gasoline-tax scam. Balagula controlled a half dozen terminals on the waterfront, a fleet of delivery trucks, and had an ownership stake in dozens of gasoline stations.

"How did Marat gain control of the whole market? He didn't have to buy up companies himself," Boris says. "Whenever any Russian would open a gasoline distribution company, Marat would negotiate a certain percentage for us. It could be ten, fifteen, or twenty percent in that company, depending on each deal. We'd supply the wholesale gasoline, and we'd have a small partnership stake in their company. With the number of companies involved, when you added it all up, it was some fucking serious money."

Indeed, by the mid-1980s, stealing fuel tax had become the biggest new revenue stream for organized crime in several generations; only the trade in illegal narcotics came close in terms of the income being generated for the mob.

IN ALL HIS GASOLINE BUSINESSES, Balagula was in partnership with Anthony "Gaspipe" Casso of the Lucchese crime family. One federal investigator described the division of labor in the gasoline scam succinctly:

"The Russians supplied the brains, and the Mafia supplied the hit men."

But Boris calls that an oversimplification.

Here's how it worked: Gaspipe gave Marat protection from other Italians; I gave Marat protection from other Russians. Within the Russian crime world, Marat was under my *krysha*. If any Russians tried to fuck with Marat's businesses, I dealt with them.

Honestly, ever since that situation when they whacked Tolik, I didn't trust the *Italyakhas*. I knew that Gaspipe was a treacherous fucking guy. But then gasoline took off. And in gasoline, Marat was already doing lots of work with the *Italyakhas*. From that point, we couldn't avoid it, we *had* to do business with them: the money we were making together was just too good.

It would have been difficult to leave the Italians out of the gasoline business for the simple reason that they had arrived generations earlier than us Russians. They were established. They had a one-hundred-year head start on us here in America.

The *Italyakhas* already had their own people in the police department, in the city administration, and they owned many gas stations. They had their fuel terminals on the waterfront. They had the unions that controlled the waterfront. Yes, the Russians could have tried to run the gasoline-tax racket on our own, but we would have crossed paths with the *Italyakhas* sooner or later. It was the smart move to make the gasoline business a joint venture, a partnership with the *Italyakhas*.

Marat always took me along to his negotiations--especially with Italians. With me there, he felt more confident. And I always packed my .38 to these meetings in case the negotiations got difficult.

THE SCALE OF THE EMBEZZLEMENT was unimaginable to American law enforcement authorities. In 1996 testimony before the United States Senate's subcommittee investigating Russian organized crime in the United States, Edward Federico Jr., the director of national operations division, Criminal Investigations, of the Internal Revenue Service, testified about the difficulty of trying to combat Russian mobsters in their "motor-fuel-excise-tax-evasion schemes."

"We have identified some significant characteristics of the Russian organized criminal in this newly established criminal enterprise," Federico said. "They display a remarkable aptitude for sophisticated white collar crime. They are ruthless, employing threats, intimidation, and violence to further their aims. They are very adaptable. They are not monopolistic. They are very fluid. These characteristics are particularly true of those individuals involved in motor-fuel-excise-tax schemes investigated by the IRS. What started out as a novel fraud scheme contrived on Long Island quickly evolved into a billion-dollar-a-year compliance problem for us and the nation."*

---

* Full testimony can be found in *Russian Organized Crime in the United States: Hearing Before the Permanent Subcommittee on Investigations of the Committee on Governmental Affairs, U.S. Senate, One Hundred Fourth Congress, Second Session, May 15, 1996* (Washington, D.C.: U.S. Government Printing Office, 1996).

Federico noted that approximately $20 billion in motor-fuel excise taxes was collected annually by federal and state governments and that roughly 5 percent—or $1 billion—was stolen each year by "Russian organized crime groups and their Cosa Nostra partners."

Three of the five Cosa Nostra families in New York—Colombo, Genovese, and Lucchese—had their own Russian partners and formed what they called a gasoline cartel. When Gambino boss John Gotti heard about the scope of the tax scam, he was overheard on a FBI bug saying, "I gotta do it right now! Right now I gotta do it!" A decision was made to allow the Gambino family, and its own Russian associates, into the cartel. Only the Bonanno family was shut out of the gasoline-tax racket.

The most high-profile Cosa Nostra mobster to profit from the gasoline-tax scheme was Michael Franzese, then a twentysomething member of the Colombo family. Gasoline had made him one of the Mafia's biggest earners; he rapidly attained the rank of caporegime and the press dubbed him "the Yuppie Don" for his jet-set lifestyle and flashy ventures into the film industry. After his conviction for tax evasion and gas bootlegging, Franzese testified before the U.S. Senate's hearings on Russian organized crime.

"In early 1980, while I was a Colombo family soldier, Lawrence Iorizzo, a major independent gasoline wholesaler based in Long Island, New York, came to me for protection. Iorizzo and Russian organized crime figures working independently of one another each figured out how to orchestrate one of the most lucrative government rip-offs of all time—stealing gas-tax money," Franzese said, adding, "the Russians pioneered and perfected these schemes."

I SPOKE TO FRANZESE at length recently about his role in the gas-tax racket and his partnership with two Soviet émigrés, David Bogatin and

Lev Persits, and the Rumanian-born Michael Markowitz: "They were gentlemen with me, and I was a gentleman with them," he said. "We were together for at least five years, and they were the best partners I ever had. We made a lot of money together. They were very progressive, they worked hard, they brought a lot to the table.

"Marat [Balagula] was also a very smart guy," Franzese added. "I sat down with Marat a couple of times—he bought gas from us, and I think we bought some from him. There was always stuff going on in the street, who's trying to horn in, who's trying to get a piece of the business. Everyone wanted a piece of the gas business. There was so much money involved."*

Franzese testified before the U.S. Senate subcommittee that for roughly four and a half years he was running his gasoline scams in New York, Pennsylvania, Connecticut, and Florida, and he stole hundreds of millions of tax dollars. "Our profits ran anywhere from two to thirty cents per gallon, and at one point we were moving four hundred to five hundred million gallons per month."

During our conversation, Franzese elaborated on how the gasoline scheme had exploded for him out on Long Island after he offered protection to the 450-pound Iorizzo and went into partnership with Markowitz, Bogatin, and Persits.

When I first went to my boss [Carmine "Junior" Persico] with this deal, I said, "Junior, listen, I'm gonna show you more money than you ever saw in your life. I'm telling you, I got something special here. This is gold. But if we start putting it out there, they're gonna blow it like everything else. This has to be a controlled circumstance. I'm gonna put accountants on the payroll, we're gonna keep this very tight, but you gotta protect me. You can't let anyone else get involved. If we sit

* From an interview I conducted with Michael Franzese on January 14, 2022.

down, you gotta take my side—you can't be playing politics with this."
Junior's exact words were "show me." And I showed him.

At its peak, Franzese's operation was arguably the largest within the
sprawling gas-tax racket.

"I was pulling down eight-to-ten million a week—some weeks it
might be five, other weeks fifteen, but it averaged out to eight-to-ten
million in cash that the Russians were bringing me weekly," Franzese
tells me. "I'm giving two million a week to the boss of our family. Two
million in cash weekly, that buys a lot of loyalty."

And beyond the hundreds of millions in untaxed income, Franzese
found he liked socializing with his Russian-speaking partners.

Once a week, every Wednesday or Thursday, I'd go to Brighton Beach and
meet with them. They had a club there that was unbelievable. There was a
long table like I'd never seen before, and we'd congregate, women all over
the place, and trays of lobster. Lobster. Lobster. They *love* their lobster, I'll
tell you that. And their famous drinks. We partied a lot together. We went
to Florida together—because I had my own jet plane at that point—and
they'd come down to Miami with me to party. They were great guys. It
really was a beautiful marriage—Russians and Italians working together.

At our peak, I controlled over three hundred gas stations, and
we had eight Panamanian [distribution] companies. I was pulling
down eight-to-ten million cash a week. But remember, I was just *one*
operation—there were other families with their own operations, and
just think about how much they might have been bringing in. The feds
estimated it a billion dollars a year in lost taxes, but believe me, it was
much, much more than that.

The oft-made comparison between the profits from gasoline bootlegging and narcotics trafficking is inexact, Franzese assured me. "I will

say this emphatically: there wasn't that kind of cash flow and revenue since the days of Prohibition. For Cosa Nostra, there was Prohibition and then there was gas."

"YES, ALL OUR CRIMES prior to gasoline could be considered pocket change," Boris recalls.

> We went from pulling jobs of a few hundred thousand to stealing millions and millions—and getting away with it for ages. It took *years* before the FBI and the IRS figured out how we were doing it. Of course, whatever money I made with Marat, I divvied up with the *bratva*. Evsei, Zelya, Kadik, Igor, everyone. All of us shared equally in the profits.
>
> Many, many Russian criminals got rich from gasoline. And Marat controlled the entire market. He set the prices at so many stations all over the region. Like most of us, Marat loved to gamble—I don't know a Russian criminal who doesn't love to play cards.
>
> When the big cash started to flow from gasoline, we started going down to the Atlantic City casinos to party. We'd get the best suites— and the casinos always comped us with the best of everything. Cognac, steak, lobster. Everything on the house. Sometimes Marat would be at the tables in Atlantic City and lose a hundred thousand in a night. Or more. It was nothing to him. The next day, he'd raise the price of gasoline by a cent or two and immediately make all the money he'd lost.

It became a running Russian joke throughout the émigré community: you could always tell how Marat did at the gambling tables in Atlantic City by the price of gasoline at the pump the next day.

CHAPTER 15

MURDER ON OCEAN PARKWAY

On May 4, 1985, a bright sunny morning in Brooklyn, Boris Nayfeld got into his burgundy Lincoln Town Car and drove to Ocean Parkway to pick up Evsei Agron for their weekly trip across the East River into Manhattan; every Saturday, they liked to spend the morning at the historic Russian and Turkish Baths on East Tenth Street, relaxing and talking business with friends in the nearly two-hundred-degree *banya*. "The night before, we'd been out at a restaurant and when I dropped him off at his place I said, 'Okay, Evsei, see you tomorrow as usual.'"

But there was nothing usual about this bright May morning in Brooklyn.

We always liked to be at the *banya* in time for the first steam, so I'd pick up Evsei early. We had a little group that usually went together. Sometimes I picked up our friend Simochka the jeweler, sometimes Simochka used to drive himself. Other guys met us there, like Lyonya

Usaty*—one of Evsei's oldest friends from the Soviet Union—he also like to be at the first steam on Saturdays.

Obviously, there were no cell phones back then, and before I left my place, I called and said, "Evsei, once I get there, I'll just ring the buzzer. Come straight downstairs." It was such a beautiful Saturday morning—nice and warm—and when I got to his building on Ocean Parkway, by Church Avenue, it was around half past seven. And since it was the weekend, it was impossible to find a parking spot. I could have left the car at a fire hydrant. But in that area, normally the police came by and left a ticket quickly.

I got out, buzzed the intercom for his apartment, then got back into the car. I sat with my engine running, right by the hydrant in front of the main entrance. Five minutes pass. Ten minutes. Fifteen. I just keep sitting there, waiting. I'm thinking, this isn't typical for Evsei, he's usually right on time.

After about twenty minutes, Boris walked over to the intercom panel and pressed the buzzer again. This time Maya answered.

"Who this?"

"Maya, it's Boris. Where's Evsei?"

"Boris, he left a long time ago."

"How long?"

"At least twenty minutes," Maya said.

I get back in my Lincoln, shaking my head. Maya said he left, but I never saw him exit through the front doors. I figured that maybe Simochka had decided to drive after all, and he'd picked him up a few

---

* *Lyonya* is short for Leonid. *Usaty* is Russian for "moustache." "Lenny Whiskers" is the closest English equivalent. Lyonya Usaty now goes by the name Leonard Lev; a former restauranteur who'd been partners with Marat Balagula, Lev is primarily known as a concert promoter and film producer. See more on page 302.

minutes before me. I drove straight over the bridge into Manhattan. I figured I'd see Evsei and Simochka at the *banya*.

But when I got to the *banya,* there's hardly anyone there—for first steam, the place is usually quiet, maybe a couple of people. Boris Tuberman, one of the *banya* owners, was standing at the front desk. I said, "Borya, has Evsei been by?"

"No," he says. "Haven't seen him."

I go into the changing room and I start to undress. But I didn't even get into the steam before a phone call comes in at the front desk. It's Lyonya Usaty: "Boris, Evsei was killed just now!" I hang up the phone, throw my clothes back on, and drive back to Brooklyn as fast as I can. The whole drive back from Manhattan into Brooklyn is a blur.

I double-park the car and rush upstairs. Evsei is lying just short of the elevator, and the cops are there. The cops ask for my name, where I'm coming from. I tell them, "I was at the *banya.* I got a call saying Evsei's been killed, so I came straight over." They took down my information and said, "You need to leave because we're gathering neighbors' statements. We'll be in touch with you."

I was in shock as I drove away. I started thinking it all through. How did anyone walk out past me? I'd been right outside the main entrance and I saw no one suspicious. What I didn't consider at the time was the building's fire escape. Whoever did the shooting must have used it to exit and slipped around the back. The building didn't have surveillance cameras, so there was no way of being sure.

Everyone knew that I was the one driving Evsei. Everyone knew our routine—that we liked to go to the *banya* on Saturday morning. The police called me in and interrogated me at the precinct house. They told me I was a suspect. They said that I was under suspicion of having organized Evsei's murder, supposedly to take his place, running the rackets. I told these cops, "Are you crazy? I could never have planned anything against Evsei. He was my best friend!"

They never arrested me, and I volunteered to take a lie detector test. They placed all the polygraph wires on me, then they asked me questions and I answered them. Since I had nothing to do with it, I passed the lie detector test.

The details of the killing only came out later. When I pressed the buzzer the first time, Evsei walked out of the apartment. He didn't say anything in the intercom, didn't reply to me—just walked out of the apartment towards the elevator. He passed by the door to the stairway exit, and the shooter must have been standing behind that exit door. When he saw Evsei walk past that small window, he came out and opened fire. He used a small caliber with a silencer. That's why Maya didn't hear any gunshots. When Evsei dropped down, the killer walked over to him, made the execution shot to the head, and then he must have got away down the fire escape.

On Sunday, the day after Evsei was killed, I met with Marat at the Metropol. Igor Grafman's place. Marat was with his girlfriend, Natalia—the three of us were sitting together, and I was really feeling upset. I was drinking to take away some of the tension. Marat says, "Why do you feel so bad for him getting killed? Don't feel sorry." Then he says—I'll never forget these words: "He should have been killed a long time ago."

We hadn't even buried Evsei yet. He'd barely been dead twenty-four hours. I glared at him. "Marat! Why are you saying these things? You never talked like this about Evsei when he was alive. You always tried to appease him. Why start on this now?" Marat shrugged and stared back at me. "Listen, Marat, to me, Evsei was a dear friend. I understand that he didn't always speak nicely of you and you didn't always speak nicely of him. But you never dared say anything like this to him—not to his face—not while he was alive."

Marat says, "Boris, I gave you the opportunities to make money. I brought *you* into gasoline. Who you shared money with, whether or not you gave Evsei a chance to make money, it was of no interest to me."

That's the kind of conversation we had on that Sunday after Evsei's death. These words got stuck in my mind. I'd long been aware of Marat's attitude towards Evsei. He always was deferential to his face. But deep down Marat held a big grudge against Evsei for something.[*]

For years there has been much speculation that Marat Balagula and Boris Nayfeld together planned the assassination of Evsei Agron. Some accounts of the aftermath of Evsei's murder depict Boris strolling into the office at El Caribe where Marat was holding court, like some treacherous Praetorian guard after the assassination of an emperor.

At Metropole, the day after the murder, Marat seemed very pleased that Evsei was gone. He spoke in such a disparaging tone. "Oh, come on, Boris!" he said, "Evsei was not as good as you think."

It was later written in a newspaper article that I was suspected in the murder. Also, in [Robert] Friedman's book, he slips in that I was under a cloud of suspicion, that I was behind the killing of Evsei in order to take everything over. These are absolute lies. Blatant untruths.[†]

People who say such things don't understand the relationship I had with Evsei. To me Evsei was a *real* man. One of the smartest I've ever known. When we first met, I didn't know seventy percent of what Evsei had locked up in his brain. I was a criminal when I met him, but I was just a street guy. Evsei opened my eyes to the world of the thieves

---

[*] Marat's mistress, Natalia, was never charged with any crime related to the activities Boris is recounting here.

[†] Boris is referring to a passage in Robert Friedman's *Red Mafiya: How the Russian Mob Has Invaded America* (New York: Little, Brown and Company, 2000), which implicates both Boris and Marat in Evsei's unsolved murder.

in law. He explained their essence to me. Evsei had big ideas, he understood business, was so sophisticated in how he dealt with people.

Whatever rumors circulated, whatever lies were written, pointing fingers at me for the murder—I know the truth. Looking back all these years later, yes, I can say Evsei was my best friend. But he was more than a friend—in terms of our criminal life, he was like my father.

In the days after the murder, Boris and the rest of Evsei's crew began to run through the possible suspects.

At first, we thought it must have been continuation of the problems with Borya Ochkarik. But we had no proof it was Charlie and Evan or anyone from Borya's crew. We buried Evsei at Washington Cemetery—on McDonald Avenue and the Bay Parkway. Of course, there were a lot of people at the wake at Zhenka's café. At the wake, I sat replaying the tape in my mind and started to suspect Vadik Reznikov.

About a month earlier, I parked my Lincoln and I'm walking to Evsei's, almost at the building. I see Vadik. He's crossing Ocean Parkway. There's this kind of a bridge there, and he's walking in my direction. I was surprised to see Vadik—it wasn't like we were in Brighton Beach. Not many Russians lived around Evsei.

I said, "Vadik! What are you doing here? Where are you coming from?"

He goes, "I was just at a friend's place nearby here, heading home."

It seemed a bit strange at the time, but it didn't raise any alarm bells. Then I remembered a second time when I saw Vadik near Evsei's building. Now I realized that Vadik was probably casing the place, trying to figure out all the possible entrances and exits ahead of time. Figuring out what route he'd make his getaway.

Brighton Beach in the mid-1980s was filled with ruthless killers, and one of the most brazen was Vladimir Reznikov—nicknamed "Vadik Reznik"—a Kiev-born gunman who'd done prison time in the USSR and made a name for himself in Brighton Beach by committing a public murder and then beating the case.

I first got to know Vadik in 1982, after he killed Rachmiel Dementev. Dementev was a criminal who worked as a pickpocket, pulled scams, *smenka* jobs. He was quite a bit older than me. When Vadik landed in America from Ukraine, like everyone else in our circle, he had no intentions of getting honest employment. Many in Brighton knew him from his days in the Soviet Union as a criminal, so Rachmiel took him along on jobs.

After they'd made some money together, Rachmiel and Vadik had a falling-out. I don't know exactly what happened, I'm just repeating what Evsei and others told me. There was a big argument between Vadik and Rachmiel, and Rachmiel said he wouldn't work with Vadik anymore. It was New Year's Day at the National restaurant. Rachmiel was there with his relatives. Vadik showed up, sat down with Rachmiel, and they started to get into it with each other. That's when Rachmiel said, "You *musoryenok*!"*

In our world, calling someone a *musor*—in public—that's serious business. It means you've been working with the fucking cops. It's like saying *kozyol*. For Russian criminals, you don't throw that label *musor* on someone casually.

Rachmiel calls Vadik a *musoryenok* and Vadik says, "Fine, wait here, I'll be right back." Vadik goes outside to his car, brings back his *volyna*.

---

* *Musor*, the Russian word for "garbage," is fenya slang for the police. *Musoryenok* is the diminutive form, equivalent to "Little piggy!"

He came straight over and shot Rachmiel dead on the spot. He killed him right there in the restaurant in front of everyone and then went on the lam. He stayed in hiding for a long while. The police knew who did the shooting and were only looking for the motive. Vadik managed to convince some witnesses to change their stories, made it look like he was acting in self-defense. Only then did he turn himself in.

"BY THE TIME I GOT TO KNOW VADIK, he was already starting to lose his mind," Boris says. "He used to say that when he was in his jail cell, the guards were sending invisible rays into his brain. They were shooting in some kind of rays to torture him. Even back then, he was starting to go crazy. He was also heavily into cocaine. He did not shoot up junk, but everyone knew he snorted a lot of cocaine."

After the murder of Dementev, Vladimir Reznikov became partners with one of the strangest figures in the Soviet émigré circles, an author-cum-swindler named Yuri Brokhin. Born in Dnepropetrovsk, Ukraine, in 1934, Brokhin worked as a screenwriter and film director in the Soviet Union, emigrated to the United States in 1972, and published two books, *Hustling on Gorky Street: Sex and Crime in Russia Today* and *Big Red Machine: The Rise and Fall of Soviet Olympic Champions*. For the first, he'd immersed himself in the Moscow underworld for three years, learning the tricks of the trade from various street criminals.

Evsei knew this writer Brokhin really well. By the time he was in New York, he was more of a criminal than a writer. Vadik hooked up with Brokhin and they did *schneyer*. Brokhin had this one really large diamond with a brilliant cut. He had a perfect copy made from zirconium. They worked the *smenka*. They'd show the real stone and get a jeweler to quote a price. If the rock was appraised, for say fifty thousand, they'd only ask for twenty-five thousand. After the appraisal, they had the skill, the sleight-of-hand, to switch the real stone for a fake right under the jeweler's nose.

Brokhin lived in an apartment in Manhattan with his wife. One day he came home and found she'd drowned in the bathtub. It was officially ruled a suicide. But there was another version to the story, the version that Evsei told—everyone in Brighton had heard it. Brokhin and Vadik Reznik had helped her drown. While she was in the bathtub, they grabbed her by her feet, violently yanked her, holding her under until she died. Brokhin got a large life insurance settlement for her. Like Vadik, Brokhin was also using cocaine in a big way. And once he received the insurance settlement, he either shorted or stiffed Vadik on his agreed-upon share.

On December 5, 1982, the forty-eight-year-old Brokhin was found murdered in his own bed, according to police accounts, shot with a .25-caliber in the head. Since there were no signs of forced entry, the police theorized that Brokhin had likely known the killer—and $15,000 in cash was found in the apartment. No arrests were ever made.

Several times Evsei told me that Vadik was the killer. He was never arrested for it, but a lot of people had their suspicions. Once a criminal like Vadik commits murder for the first time, he gets obsessed. You could say he gets a taste for blood. By 1985, everyone in Brighton knew that Vadik had come unhinged. He got away with the first murder, killing Dementev in the National. He got away with the second murder, killing Brokhin in his apartment. Now we realized he'd killed Evsei. Vadik figured, like all of us figured, that in America, unless you get caught red-handed, it's very difficult for the *musors* to prove that you've murdered someone.

I remembered all this about Vadik only after Evsei was gone—I thought about the two times I'd seen Vadik in Evsei's neighborhood and I figured that he was most likely the killer. But I had no proof. It wasn't one hundred percent clear to me until early in 1986, when he made a move against me and the rest of my crew in our offices in Sheepshead Bay. Only then did I put things together. I realized that it must have been Vadik who'd murdered Evsei. His motive was to take control of our share of the gasoline business.

THE FULL STORY behind the murder of Evsei Agron will likely never be known.

No arrests were ever made; nearly four decades later, the homicide remains unsolved.

Boris maintains that the killing of Evsei left a void in his life—one that he filled with days and nights of nonstop action, moving forward constantly, steadily, like a great white shark.

Agron's death marked the end of an era and brought about a sea change in the Soviet émigré underworld.

For ten years, since the mid-1970s, the rackets of Brighton Beach had belonged to Evsei's *brigada*.

And even in his diminished state—face half frozen, one eye forever weeping—Agron still provided a figurehead of leadership.

Yes, he was a boss of the old school, yet Agron had adapted quickly to life in America, combining the savviness of a businessman and a ruthlessness of a prison-hardened *vor*.

Boris Nayfeld, by his own admission, lacked Evsei's understanding of legitimate business.

Marat Balagula, for all his cunning, had none of the traits of a bona fide gangster.

But working in tandem, Boris and Marat—this new two-headed Hydra—would prove to be a formidable force in organized crime.

Balagula was constantly generating or financing brazen schemes and ideas, his vision far more ambitious and international in scope than Agron's.

And Boris Nayfeld had a clear brief: "My business was to make sure no one fucked with Marat's business."

Boris Nayfeld on the famed Brighton Beach boardwalk in
the summer of 2021.

Boris's biological mother, Ekaterina Nayfeld, who abandoned him at age three, while Boris's father, Mikhail, was serving a sentence for black market activity in a gulag in far eastern Russia.

Yosef and Riva Nayfeld, Boris's grandparents who raised him in Gomel, Belarus. Throughout his life, he always referred to his grandmother as "Mama," and he considered Riva and Yosef to be his "true" parents.

Boris (*in front*) being hugged by his older brother, Gennady (or "Gena"), in their school uniforms in front of a fountain in Gomel.

The small house in Gomel in which Boris was raised—lacking any modern conveniences, even indoor plumbing—and which served as the communal family home until the Nayfeld family emigrated to the United States in late 1979.

Boris (*far left*) in an undated photo at a nursery. Since infancy, Boris has been known as "Biba"—a nickname given to him due to his round cheeks, bright blue eyes, and cherubic appearance. When he was two years old, his grandparents often said, "he resembled a toy doll."

Boris and his older brother, Gena, in a fragile photo, sent by Ekaterina to Mikhail at the gulag. Dated February 28, 1949, when Gena was just over two years old and Boris was fifteen months. On the back, Ekaterina wrote the following note in purple ink (translated from the original Russian):

To our loving father from your two sons Gennady Mikhail[ovich] and Boris Mikhai[lovich]. Remember us, dear father, and don't forget that somewhere you have kids and come back as soon as you can, otherwise it's very painful that our childhood will pass without [our] father. The time that we will spend with you, dear father, will be precious to us.

Waiting, Nayfeld

Boris (*center*) with two now-deceased *khuligan* friends in Gomel in the late 1960s. To Boris's left is his close friend Tolik Plotkin, leader of a group of *banditen*—or bandits. Plotkin was sentenced to juvenile prison, and after his release, he died under mysterious circumstances. The Soviet police said it was suicide, but many suspected Plotkin was murdered.

Boris (*center foreground*) in a work zone of a Soviet prison camp—he was sentenced to three years of hard labor in Penal Colony Number 2 at Bobruisk, located 157 kilometers to the west of Gomel. Boris was incarcerated for the crime of *khuliganstvo*—hooliganism—from age eighteen to twenty-one. The time spent in prison, among older and more experienced *blatnye,* was formative to his becoming a lifelong "professional" criminal.

Boris holding his niece in front of the family home in Gomel, circa 1972.

Boris (*front row, center*) with a large group of his criminal friends at Gomel's city hall for the wedding of one of his *khuligan* friends. Note that Boris is proudly and openly wearing his Magen David ("Star of David") pendant, a bold act given the official antisemitism of the Soviet era. With money he'd made on the black market, he had a jeweler design the Star of David specifically for him, since Jewish religious pendants were not sold in the USSR.

Nayfeld in Belarus, circa 1978, when he was a young *blatnoy* (or "professional criminal"). He's wearing more than 3,500 rubles' worth of black market furs: a sable hat and a sealskin coat with a wolverine collar would have been two years' salary for an engineer or other well-paid citizen of the USSR.

Boris with his criminal mentor, Evsei Agron, the original boss of Brighton's underworld. The Leningrad-born Agron had been a *vor v zakone*—or "thief in law"—in the USSR, and by the late 1970s, he was undisputed as the most powerful gangster among the Soviet émigré community in the United States.

Evsei with his second wife, Maya Rozova—noted singer of Russian chansons—at a popular Brighton Beach supper club.

The front entrance of the El Caribe country club, a well-known meeting place for organized crime, both for members of the Italian American Mafia and the Russian *bratva*. Evsei and Boris financed the building of a fitness center at El Caribe, which became their de facto office and the locus of Soviet émigré criminal activity in the United States. Boris says, for years "the government couldn't even imagine that the Italian Mafia and Russian criminals would be gathering, working out deals, making decisions together."

Manhattan's famed Diamond District, on West Forty-Seventh Street. In the tight-knit, largely Yiddish-speaking diamond districts of New York and Antwerp, it's not uncommon for gem merchants—like the three Orthodox Jewish men shown here—to do multi-million-dollar deals strictly on a handshake. Boris was behind several massive swindles—in both New York and Antwerp—in which millions of dollars' worth of diamonds were stolen.

Boris (*seated at center*) with his arm around a girlfriend in a Moscow restaurant in the early 1990s. Around the table toasting Boris are three of the most prominent *vory v zakone* of the 1990s—Timokha, Givi Rezany, and Rafik Svo—who were all later murdered in separate incidents by fellow gangsters.

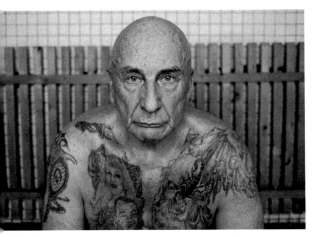

Boris in 2018, posing for an Associated Press photographer in the *banya*—Russian bathhouse—in Sheepshead Bay, Brooklyn. He shows off his numerous prison-inked tattoos, which for Russian criminals can be read like a storybook—as Boris says, "a criminal's autobiography."

Boris, fresh out of federal prison in Colorado after serving a five-year sentence for racketeering and money laundering, returns to Brighton Beach in a Lincoln Town Car in a moment captured by a *New York Times* photographer in 2018.

Boris, photographed by the author, cutting up a traditional Russian fruit pastry during a dinner at his palatial Staten Island home in the summer of 2019. Boris is a surprisingly good cook. After his first stint in prison in the USSR, he briefly attended culinary school. He never completed the diploma, as he quickly started to make a name for himself in the underworld, working criminal rackets in Siberia while facing the death penalty for the crime of "Theft from the State."

CHAPTER 16

THE BIG *SCHNEYER*

Evsei hadn't been dead for more than a month when Boris and Marat got a proposition for a major diamond score oversees. "This guy called Igor Babai, came by the office at El Caribe with his partner, Edik. Igor says, 'Hey, remember Aron Kishka? Let's work the same *schneyer*. But this time in Antwerp.' They explained their plan, we talked it over—Marat thought it was a solid idea. He still had his share of the diamonds from the Aron Kishka job, about half a million dollars' worth, and he invested with them to get the job going."

For centuries, Antwerp has been the world capital of diamonds. Approximately 84 percent of the world's rough diamonds are cut and sold in the city's famed Diamond Quarter. Nearly $50 billion in diamonds is traded each year in Antwerp.

Many diamond merchants have historically been Jewish refugees fleeing antisemitism: medieval expulsions, czarist pogroms, Nazi persecution, Soviet oppression. From the Middle Ages onward, European Jews were forbidden to buy land or engage in agriculture and concentrated instead on banking and such specialized professions as the cutting, polishing, and trading of gems. Diamonds and other gemstones are perfect investments for a beleaguered minority: small items bearing a high value, portable, easy to conceal in times of sudden danger.

But these same attributes also make diamonds ideal contraband. They can cross borders undetected. For mobsters constantly looking for ways to launder money, diamonds offer a perfect vehicle. Millions in illicit cash can quickly be converted into high-value assets that are easy to conceal and move undetected across international borders.

"I flew to Belgium with Igor and Edik," Boris recalls.

We went looking for a suitable office in the Antwerp Diamond Quarter. We needed to find one with the same layout that Aron Kishka used on Forty-Seventh Street—a comfortable front room for conducting business and a back room with a second exit which no one could see from the front.

It took us a few days, but we fixed the place up: sofas, chairs, desks, phones. We hired a girl to work there as a secretary. She happened to be a rabbi's daughter. Igor and Edik came up with that twist. They realized that if you have a local rabbi's daughter in the front office as a secretary, then these Hasidic diamond sellers will immediately feel more relaxed.

We each had our roles in the *schneyer*. Edik was supposed to be the expert in gems. He had the jeweler's loupe and could talk like an actual gemologist. Igor worked in the front of the store. He did the negotiating and buying. I was there to represent Marat Balagula's interests. I was his eyes and ears. Basically. I handled the security—keeping an eye on the diamonds and the cash.

Before we could start trading, we took Marat's diamonds to Switzerland to use as collateral. Marat had a rich friend living in Zurich named Sasha Gramatsky. Sasha agreed to front us the money in exchange for the diamonds. He put the stones in a safety deposit box at a bank in Zurich and gave us two hundred thousand dollars cash to run our business in Antwerp.

We felt it would be safer to live in Brussels and commute five days a week to Antwerp. We lived in this rented flat in Brussels that had three separate rooms. I lived in one with my girlfriend, Angela—she flew over from New York to be with me for a few months. Igor and his wife lived in the other, Edik and his girlfriend in the third.

We rented a car in my name. A silver Toyota. For months it became like a regular job, commuting to work from Brussels to Antwerp first thing in the morning. Every day we were buying stones. We followed Aron Kishka's game plan. Igor and Edik had to seem knowledgeable but not haggle over the price too much. Didn't matter if we lost money on each deal. The important thing was building a reputation for buying at fair prices and developing a steady flow of clients.

We needed a lot of cash for this job, but even though we had a small safe, I didn't want to risk leaving it. I used to take all our cash with us in a briefcase when we locked up and drove back to our flat in Brussels. One night, when we were starting up, we went to a Chinese restaurant not far from our apartment in Brussels. I had close to two hundred thousand cash in a briefcase. I put the case under the table, we ate and left. When we got back to our flat, I suddenly realized I didn't have the briefcase with me. We all ran like crazy back to the restaurant. These Belgians, the restaurant staff, were such honest people. Amazingly honest. The case was sitting there waiting for me. "Here, sir, you left this," they said. Imagine if that briefcase had gone missing? We would have started that job two hundred grand in the hole.

At one point, I had to fly back to New York to handle a few things with the gasoline business with Marat. And as I was leaving, I told Igor and Edik to return the Toyota, and get a different car with their own documents. "All right, we'll return it," Edik says. But when I flew back to Belgium, I found out they kept the Toyota in my name and even extended the rental another month. "Well, what's the fucking difference?" I said, "They didn't return it, but it should all be all right." I didn't realize that a couple of years later, this same rental car was going to bite me in the ass.

We spent several months working this *schneyer,* driving back and forth between our apartment in Belgium and buying diamonds in Antwerp.

Then we set the date. We put the word out we were looking to do a lot of buying. We booked as many sellers as possible. I was in that back room, making sure no one ever saw my face. Igor and the rabbi's daughter were in the reception area, and Edik would come from the back to the front since he was constantly doing appraisals of the merchandise.

Boris could hear the Yiddish chatter of the Hasidim up front, and from time to time the secretary would offer the sellers coffee or water. "The rabbi's daughter had no idea about the scheme, of course—she thought we were real diamond merchants. Totally on the up-and-up. I don't even think she knew there was a back exit to the place."

Once they had a sizable collection of diamonds in the back room, the whole con was over in a flash. Months of work and planning had gone into the setup. It all ended in seconds.

I nod at Edik, slip all the stones into my pocket, and walk out the exit. I got into my rented Toyota and vanished. In the meantime, Igor and Edik stayed in plain view of the sellers. Everyone was calm, kibbitzing, acting carefree.

After fifteen minutes passed, Igor left the sellers in the reception, stepped into the back to check on things, then he and Edik put on their coats and disappeared out the back way. I met them at our rendezvous spot a few blocks away, and we drove from Antwerp back to Brussels. It turned out that the diamonds in my pocket were worth one and a half million dollars. Our office? We just abandoned it. We'd leased it in a fake name, paid cash for the rent, so no one could trace us.

We found out later how it all played out. We were on the road back to Brussels by the time the Hasidic sellers realized that something funny was going on. The rabbi's daughter went into the second room and was shocked to find that there was no one there. They called the police, and Antwerp detectives started an investigation. But there was nothing linking us to the office—at least that's what we assumed. We vanished. Became ghosts.

If I remember correctly, we flew out of Brussels that same day. The one and a half million in diamonds got split up. Igor and Edik took their share of the stones. I got my cut. Of course, when I got back to New York, I brought Marat his share of the diamonds, as well as the ones we left in the safety deposit box with Sasha Gramatsky in Switzerland.

It was a great score, but it was the last diamond _schneyer_ that Marat ever financed. We probably would have tried it again—in another city—but by mid-1985 our gasoline businesses were booming. And on top of that, Marat, Zelya, Venya, and me were all about get caught up in this fucking credit card fiasco back in Brooklyn.

By the winter of 1985, new opportunities to swindle and steal were coming in daily. The gasoline-tax racket provided a huge stream of illegal income, but Boris Nayfeld, Marat Balagula, and their associates continued to juggle smaller scores in New York and across the United States and Europe.

In fact, it was the most routine of financial scams—credit card fraud—that nearly brought down the entire crew. It defies logic and common sense, but the basic operating principle of the Brighton Beach mob in those days seems to have been to grab every piece of low-hanging fruit. No cost-benefit analysis ever went into their decisions.

"When you're a full-time criminal," Boris says, "you don't stop and think, 'Hey, should I take a chance racking up a few hundred thousand in this credit card scam while we're steadily bringing in millions with gasoline?' No, your brain doesn't work that way. You're always thinking of new ways to get over. A job is a job. If there's a score there for taking, you take it."

In February 1985—three months before the murder of Evsei Agron—a small-time Brooklyn crook named Robert Fasano approached Marat Balagula looking for help. Fasano had contacts at Merrill Lynch from whom he got the names and account numbers of more than two dozen customers whose Visa cards could be used against the value of their investment portfolios.

In today's age of multi-million-dollar cybertheft and credit cards embedded with sophisticated microchips, the crudeness of the crime seems almost ludicrous. But in the mid-1980s, this was a cutting-edge hustle; it was known as a "white plastic" scam. Ordinary rectangles of plastic were embossed with the legitimate cardholder's name, number, and the expiration date of the card. Since the merchant needed to be a willing participant in the theft, there was no effort to make the fake credit cards look authentic.

"The whole mess with these credit cards started because Marat had made a connection to an *Italyakha* named Fasano," Boris said.

He introduced Fasano to me and my cousin Venya and Zelya. Fasano needed a way to charge up all kinds of goods on the cards.

Of course, we were only comfortable dealing with other Russians. If we found a store where we could charge ten thousand dollars of merchandise, then we'd offer the store owner twenty percent. In other words, he keeps the merchandise and makes two thousand bucks for a few minutes of his time. All he needs to do is run the charges through, give us eight thousand in cash which we split fifty-fifty with Fasano. We did it with furniture, furs, and diamonds—we didn't touch the merchandise. The owner simply gets authorization for the credit card sales, keeps the stuff, takes twenty percent, and gives the rest to us.

According to prosecutors, on February 20, 1985, the first store the crew hit was Venezia Furniture on Kings Highway in Brooklyn. The owners, two Soviet émigrés, called up Visa to get authorization for a $12,000 furniture purchase. The sale was approved, and the entire transaction was over in minutes. Next, Boris, Venya, and Zelya drove to Philadelphia and visited Misha of Siberia Furs. They charged a $7,500 lynx coat to one of the cards. Then off to Askari Jewelers. Their stolen credit-card shopping spree lasted a few weeks, and they managed to rack up more than $300,000 in bogus purchases of furniture, furs, and jewelry.

But the scheme fell apart when Fasano was arrested, agreed to cooperate with special agents of the United States Secret Service—the federal agency with investigative jurisdiction over credit-card-related felonies—and gather evidence against his accomplices.

What happened was this lowlife, instead of going to jail, he decides to set us up. He calls and says we need to have another meeting, that he's got some new cards and we need to discuss the terms. The meeting was just me, Venya, and Zelya—Marat wasn't there. We didn't realize that Fasano had been nabbed by the feds and—in order to lessen his sentence—he agreed to wear a wire.

We met at a restaurant in Brooklyn. I can't remember the name of the place. I'm sitting down with Venya and Zelya and across from us sits Fasano. There was another guy there that we didn't know—he turned out to be an undercover fed. They were secretly recording everything we said.

They start discussing how the next round of credit card charges is going to be arranged. At the time, I didn't speak good enough English to follow any of it. They were talking very fast. My cousin Venya spoke English really well, Zelya spoke well enough to follow. I keep asking them what the hell they're talking about. Venya says, "It's all right, just wait, we'll explain everything afterwards."

When they all got busted, I kept waiting to get picked up—but nobody accused me of anything. Not one fucking charge. The feds locked up Venya and Zelya as well as Marat, of course—because they'd made lots of other recordings of Marat on the phone.

The case made headlines as one of the first major credit card prosecutions involving Russian organized crime in the United States.

My cousin Venya got good legal advice. His lawyer saw the evidence and told Venya straight up, "You better plead guilty." It meant up to three years in prison and a large fine. Zelya was also in the middle of plea bargaining. But Marat was so confident he could beat the case that he hired Barry Slotnik, a big-time defense lawyer, to try to beat the case.

Marat spent something like seven hundred fifty thousand in legal fees, trying to fight this fucking case. But at this time Marat was loaded—the money was rolling in from gasoline, so he didn't give a damn how much he paid the lawyers. That's the way Marat was, always thinking he could outsmart everybody. He was the only one who thought he could beat the feds at trial.

Boris was never arrested in the case. He was somewhat astonished, given his active involvement in the entire sordid scheme. But he managed to remain free for only one reason: his rudimentary level of English. "Since I couldn't understand what was going on during the conversations, my voice wasn't on any of the recordings used by the prosecution.

The feds knew I was involved, they knew I was at the meetings, that I was in all the stores charging merchandise. Of course, they wanted to arrest me. But they didn't have my voice on tape. For once I was happy my English was so fucking bad—I hadn't been paying attention in those classes they gave us in Albany when we first came over from the Soviet Union. Not understanding what the fuck was going on was the *only* thing that kept me out of prison."

YET NOT UNDERSTANDING what was going on during conversations— English or otherwise—hadn't prevented Boris Nayfeld from profiting handsomely in the gasoline rackets.

By February 1986, Boris, his cousin Venya, and the rest of his crew spent most of their days at the Platenum Energy Company, a dummy corporation with offices on the ground floor of a building on the corner of Avenue U and Batchelder Street in the Sheepshead Bay section of Brooklyn.

A three-story multifamily redbrick town house built in 1960, 2101 Batchelder Street is located on a quiet block lined with trees; it was a most unlikely location for the headquarters of a thriving wholesale gasoline company with the word "Platinum" misspelled in its papers of incorporation.

And yet, by 1986, for Boris Nayfeld and his crew, the Platenum Energy offices had become a hotbed of criminal activity, primarily fuel-tax evasion—but the office also served as their de facto social club, a hangout where they would accept collection jobs, agree to provide *krysha,* and even consummate the occasional gun deal.

CHAPTER 17

AMBUSH ON AVENUE U

In late December 1985, in those same Platenum Energy offices, Boris Nayfeld had sold the Uzi 9 mm submachine gun that would, a few weeks later, be used in a brazen daylight attempt to murder him.

"I got ahold of this Uzi that only fired single shots," Boris recalls.

I didn't have a way to convert it from semi to fully automatic, so it was pretty much useless to me. Around Christmastime, this guy named Misha Vax comes around and asks me to sell it to him. Everyone in our crew carried either a .38 or .45, so there was no need for a machine gun. I decided to sell Misha Vax the Uzi for fifteen hundred bucks.

When I sold Vax the Uzi, of course, I didn't know that they were plotting against us. But they quickly converted the Uzi to fully automatic. They also got their hands on a second machine gun from somewhere. They figured with two machine guns they could easily cut us all down.

I'll give those motherfuckers credit—they were clever in how they set us up. The Friday before the attack, they sent this guy Feliks—Feliks

Chernigovsky—to our Platenum office. Feliks walked with a bad limp. One of his legs was prosthetic.

This Feliks was a fucking nobody in the criminal world. A *prikhlebatel* incapable of generating anything himself. At the time, I didn't know he was connected to Misha Vax or anyone else. Friday evening, he drops by our office, saying, "Boryek, how are things?"

I tell him, "All right, thank God."

He says, "Let's play clabber."†

"Fine," I say. "Clabber it is. Just for the hell of it, or for keeps?"

"I tell you what," Feliks says, "if you win, I'll take you and all your friends out for lunch—any restaurant you choose. If I win, then you take me and my friends out."

I nod and start shuffling the deck. The gasoline business was going very well. We were sitting on *a lot* of cash. We start to play a few hands of clabber and I won. Looking back, I'm sure this fucking lame Feliks threw the game—I mean, he intentionally lost, because that was his whole role in the plot. It was part of the setup. He needed to make sure me and the whole crew would later on be in the same spot, at the same time. After he lost, he asked when I wanted to go out to eat. I tell him, "Let's do it on Monday, around half past noon."

Our company was officially run by a guy named Roma Katzelson, he went by the nickname Zhivoglot.‡ He was from Bobruisk. A good guy. He knew how to sell gasoline. He was our frontman: Marat provided us

---

* *Prikhlebatel*—someone who eats soup or porridge from another person's bowl. A sponger, moocher, hanger-on.

† Clabber is a trick-taking card game of apparent Dutch origin—where it was called "Klaberjass." It uses only the highest twenty-four cards in the deck—ace to nine—and has long been popular within the Russian-Jewish community.

‡ *Zhivoglot*—can mean a glutton, parasite, a ruthless bloodsucker—literally, "one who swallows its prey alive."

with the wholesale gasoline and advised us on pricing, Roma Zhivoglot ran the day-to-day, filing the necessary tax-exemption forms, and negotiating sales with other distributors.

We had a young lady working as an accountant, and luckily she didn't come to work that Monday for whatever reason—or God knows what would have happened to her.

Monday morning, the office was quiet. It was just me, Zelya, and my cousin Venya. This guy called Fimka dropped by around 11:30 with his son, who was about six years old. Fimka was a good guy, close friends with Zelya. Zelya was playing cards with Venya, sitting at a table that was placed directly in front of the door. They'd been hanging out there for about fifteen minutes when I said, "Fimka, why don't you take your kid and go home?"

It's not like I had a premonition that something bad was about to happen, I just wanted them out of the office. "We're going to lock up soon and go out to eat," I said. Fimka stayed another five minutes and left with his son.

JUST AFTER 11:45 A.M., Misha Vax returned to the office and told Boris that he needed to discuss some pressing business.

"Borya, I've got a request for you," Vax said. "We got stiffed by Kapusta."*

"Okay, you got stiffed by Kapusta." Boris shrugged. "What do you want from me?"

"Kapusta owes us a hundred thirty thousand."

"And?"

"And can you help us collect?"

---

* *Kapusta*—Russian for "cabbage"—was the nickname of Sasha Skolnick, well known in Brighton Beach criminal circles as a professional gambler.

"Sure, but this ain't the Red Cross, Misha. If we collect, you know we take half."

"Not a problem," Vax said. "You'll get your half, Borya!"

"For the next fifteen minutes, Misha Vax is hanging around the office, talking about this collecting job—but we don't know that he's part of the whole setup," Boris recalls.

Shortly after noon, lame Feliks comes by and asks how soon until we go out to eat. He limps around the office, towards the far corner, then down the corridor where our accountant's office is located. He walks around, sees there's nobody else in the offices and, on the way back, he says, "All right, Boryek, I'm going to wait for you outside."

Looking back now, I realize it was this *kozyol's* job: to case the joint in advance of the attack, to make sure we're all in place. And as he exits—we don't notice this, of course—Feliks doesn't shut the front door completely. We had a secure door, with a buzzer system to let people in. We kept lots of cash in the office and we were always careful. We could see who was coming though the window and if it was someone we didn't know, we'd never open the door.

At 12:15, the door suddenly bursts open and this guy in a dark blue trench coat is inside. He's trying to disguise his face by wearing a dark blue hat with lowered brim and sunglasses.

Zelya's the one sitting closest to the door, in the middle of his card game with my cousin Venya. Zelya turns around, startled, jumps to his feet. At this moment the gunman pulls the Uzi from inside his trench coat. The *same* Uzi I sold Misha Vax. I recognized it instantly.

Zelya yells, "We're being robbed!" and throws himself forward at this guy. The gunman starts firing, a quick burst of automatic fire.

Eight rounds hit Zelya. He's killed instantly. But his quick thinking saved us. He gave up his life to save our lives. As he was being shot to death, Zelya kept charging towards the gunman, and the weight of his body pushed the guy back through the office door. At that same moment, a second gunman—we never found out who—starts shooting through the window, glass is shattering everywhere. It's complete fucking mayhem.

I realize now there are two assassins creating a crossfire with machine guns to make sure they kill me and everyone close to me. Misha Vax is bleeding, badly wounded, shot in the chest. Vax didn't hit the floor when the shooting started—which was most likely their plan—but instead he ran straight towards the shooting. In all the confusion, Vax escapes through the front door.

When Zelya pushed the shooter out of the office, he hit him with enough force to knock off the guy's hat and glasses. He's getting ready to come through the door a second time to finish the job, but now I can see his face really well. Without the cap and glasses, there's no doubt.

It's Vadik Reznikov.

Time freezes.

Everything is clear to me—now it all makes sense.

Vadik murdered Evsei and now he's trying to kill the rest of us. If any of us are going to survive, that fucking door needs to be slammed shut. If Vadik manages to get back inside with the Uzi, he's going to mow down all of us.

My cousin is down on the floor next to the table. I see he's got his gun but he's not shooting. I jump up, manage to shut the door, turning sideways, making myself a narrow target, standing just on one side but stretching my hands out to slam the door. While I'm pushing it closed, another burst from the Uzi rips through the door, and I get hit between my thumb and index finger. The bullet rips clean through my hand.

My main thought is to grab a gun and start shooting back—but I don't have my piece on me. I run into a back room where I've got some weapons stashed in the ceiling, remove a panel, grab this .25 pistol, rack it and jump outside onto the porch, ready to start blasting. Zelya is laying there dead. I see that one of the bullets knocked out his eye.

In the heat of the moment I didn't even feel that I was shot. But there's blood streaming from my hand and dripping everywhere. Once I'm out on the porch I can hear police sirens in the distance, getting louder, getting closer. In the meantime, I see Vadik Reznik jumping into his Nissan, along with Misha Vax, and they escape.

When I get back into the office, my cousin is still on the floor with his pistol. I say, "Venya, why the fuck didn't you shoot?"

"How can I shoot when I'm out on bail?" he says.

"*Bail?* What the *fuck* are you talking about? What's more important—your bail or our *lives?*"

He was free on a quarter-million dollars bail, awaiting sentencing for the credit card case with Marat and Zelya. I'm furious he didn't return fire, but Zelya is lying there dead, one eye blown out of his head. The *musors* are getting closer and I don't have time to argue with Venya.

I'm so pumped up, I forgot I was bleeding. I look down at the pistol in my hand. It was completely saturated in my blood. With all the adrenaline pumping, I'm not feeling any pain. I needed to get rid of my *volyna* fast. I quickly washed the gun off in the sink, sirens getting closer and closer. Everything was covered in blood. I cleaned the pistol grip and trigger as best I could, trying to get rid of any fingerprints. Then I placed the gun back into its hiding spot in the ceiling. Venya also stashed away his piece.

The sirens are right in front of the office, on Avenue U, the *musors* arrive, start trying to figure out who shot who. Later they told us there was a total of thirty-eight rounds fired inside the office. It was a miracle

all of us weren't fucking corpses. They took me straight to Coney Island
Hospital because I was bleeding pretty heavily from the wound and
needed treatment.

All the guys in our crew came to see me, gathering around my
hospital bed. Kadik, Igor, Venya—our whole crew. They asked, "Boryek,
did you see who did the shooting?"

I told them yes. I'd seen Vadik Reznik's face clearly. Vadik killed Zelya
with the Uzi. I told everyone that when Zelya knocked off the hat and
glasses, I stared directly into Vadik's eyes. I said to my cousin: "Venya,
I'm going to recuperate here for a little while longer. A few more days.
Once I'm discharged, you take the steering wheel and I will fuck these
guys up, one by one. I'm going to shoot the holy fuck out of them. We're
going to catch Vadik first and I'm going to whack that motherfucker."

Boris had the gunshot wound in his right hand stitched up and
spent three days in Coney Island Hospital; by the time he was discharged, his cousin Venya was in police custody, having voluntarily sur-
rendered to begin serving his sentence for credit card fraud. Misha Vax
was hospitalized with a serious gunshot wound to the lung and then
charged as an accomplice in the murder of Elia Zeltzer.

Misha Vax got arrested. He'd been seen by eyewitnesses getting into the
car along with Vadik, fleeing the scene. He didn't do any shooting, but
the police were trying to piece it all together and put together a murder
case against him.

The *musors* keep asking me, "Did you see Michael Vax alongside
the other assailants?" I tell them, "No, I didn't even see anything. I
don't know who shot us." The cops say, "Boris, we believe you *do* know
the shooters, you just don't want to talk. But you're going to have to tell
us who you saw."

I keep repeating my story. Didn't see a face. Don't know who might have done it. Don't know shit. And I start putting on this whole act like I'm too shaken up to deal with all their questions. "You know something? I'm in such a state at the moment, I'm wounded here, I don't want to talk further about this subject."

When I got out of the hospital, since my cousin Venya was already in jail, I approached a close friend of the late Zelya—I'm not going to name him because he's still alive. I asked him, "Hey, will you come along with me? I need a good wheelman." He said, yes, he would. He gets behind the wheel of my Lincoln, while I'm packing my .38. I've got on a hat and a mask and we start driving around Brighton Beach, Coney Island, Sheepshead Bay, going to the *banyas* and the restaurants, looking for any sign of Vadik.

But this fucking snake was not easy to pin down. Vadik was nowhere to be seen. He knew that, sooner or later, someone would finger him and tell the *musors:* "It was Reznik."

I wasn't going to tell the *musors* a fucking thing. I wanted to settle scores with Vadik Reznik, with Misha Vax, with lame fucking Feliks, and everyone else who was part of the attack. Meanwhile, Misha Vax was still in jail, sending out messages to Vadik to hurry up and bail him out, otherwise he might start talking.

The cops are watching me, pressuring me to testify, and I figure I better get the hell out of town for a while. Sasha Gramatsky, the rich friend of Marat's who fronted us the cash for the diamond *schneyer* in Antwerp, says: "Boris, you've been wounded—why don't you go down to Miami to recuperate? I'll take care of everything."

I fly down to Miami. Sasha Gramatsky set up a luxury suite for me, got me a beautiful girl. Well, I had a good time with her. She had a curious life story. She told me she was a schoolteacher during the week but moonlighted as an escort.

Sitting there in Florida, it began to make sense to me now, the more I thought about it. The first step for Vadik was killing Evsei. The next step was getting us all in our office in Sheepshead Bay and whack us out—because as long as I was still alive, I was providing a *krysha* to Marat Balagula.

With me and my crew out of the way, they could make a move on Marat. The thing is, they didn't want Marat *dead*. Marat was the golden goose. Everyone knew he was the brains in the gasoline business. They wanted him alive, just under their thumb. They needed to take us all out so that they could control all the millions in cash Marat generated.

I get back from Miami and the police are still pressing me to testify against Vadik Reznik and Misha Vax. When I told the crew in the hospital that I'd seen Vadik's face clearly in the doorway, I'd been speaking in Russian, of course. But someone must have heard me and informed the cops that I'd seen the shooter's face.

No matter how many times I tell the *musors*, "I don't know who shot us," they keep saying, "Yes, you do!" And now they're threatening me with a court order.

IN RETROSPECT, Boris says he felt like his entire world was caving in around him.

Evsei murdered.

Now Zelya.

His entire crew frightened, scattered, in utter disarray.

And the incessant pressure from these fucking homicide detectives to testify.

That's when Marat Balagula figured it would be best to get me out of the country for a while. He goes, "You know what, Boris? Why don't you go to Africa?"

I stare at Marat. *"Africa?"*

"Yes, Africa," Marat says. "Let some time pass. Soon enough, all this commotion will end. If there are no witnesses, if you don't testify, the *musors* won't have a case."

I mull it over: it sounds like a good plan. I'll disappear, we'll let some time pass, and then we can take care of Vadik and the rest of them. Marat was out on bail for the credit card case, but he'd managed to keep traveling around the world, making money everywhere he could. One of the major investments he had was some diamond mine in Africa.

So next thing I know, still recovering from the gunshot wound to my hand, I'm on a flight to Sierra Leone—a country I'd barely heard of, let alone planned to live in for seven months.

CHAPTER 18

A BEND IN THE RIVER

When Boris Nayfeld arrived in Sierra Leone he found that Freetown, the coastal capital, had become a haven for Soviet émigré criminals of all stripes: diamond smugglers, arms dealers, money launderers, drug traffickers. The Pied Piper of the West African adventure was a Lithuanian-Jewish espionage agent named Shabtai Kalmanovich.

"It was Kalmanovich who convinced Marat to invest in Africa," Boris recalls.

He managed to get Marat to go in on this diamond mine in Sierra Leone. Shabtai Kalmanovich lured a lot of Russians to do business in Sierra Leone. At this time General [Joseph] Momoh had just become president—he and his wife were close to Shabtai Kalmanovich.

I'd met Kalmanovich sometime earlier in Germany. He was close to Fima Laskin. Kalmanovich was more twisted than a pig's dick, as they say. Kalmanovich worked for two intelligence services at the same time. He was a double agent for the KGB and the Israelis. None of us suspected he was a spy, of course. But you knew as soon as you met him that something was off—Kalmanovich was as slippery as they come.

A small man with long wavy hair and a copper tan, Kalmanovich was born in Soviet Lithuania in 1947, and moved to Israel with his family in 1971. By many accounts, Kalmanovich agreed to work as a KGB sleeper agent in exchange for an emigration permit. He became an adviser to Israeli prime minister Golda Meir, and the Shin Bet security services recruited him to spy on the Soviets. He arrived in Sierra Leone in the mid-1980s as a businessman—his ventures included running the country's only bus company—but he reputedly also helped finance the rise to power of Joseph Momoh in November 1985.

Sierra Leone is home to one of the richest motherlodes of diamonds on earth; by the mid-1980s, under President Momoh's regime—due, in part, to the presence of Kalmanovich—it was also considered one of the world's most corrupt nations. At Kalmanovich's invitation, Russian mobsters like Marat Balagula pounced at the opportunity to wash tens of millions of dollars they were stealing in gasoline tax in the United States, through a variety of business ventures, including mineral exploration.

"President Momoh granted Marat Balagula the rights to mine diamonds from this river inland," Boris says. "Kalmanovich had a percentage of the mine also. By the time I got to Sierra Leone, Marat and his company had already invested over two million dollars in the mining prospect. Marat wanted me there as his eyes and ears—to make sure the diamond mine started producing."

Much of the mineral wealth of Sierra Leone is in the interior Kono District, and can only be extracted by alluvial mining of the riverbeds.

The engineers dammed off one of the bends in the river and started to fill it with dirt to create a pocket from which the water could be pumped out. After this area was drained, the plan was to start looking for the diamonds in the riverbed with shovels and pans.

I was living in a village without any electricity or running water. Completely out in the bush. I stayed in this villa that had been specially built for an assembly of African leaders some time ago. Once the assembly was over, the villas were empty and rented out. It was like a hostel. I had a local guy who cooked all the meals and took care of the place. We had diesel generators to run lights and appliances.

I spent most of my time at the bend in the river where Marat had the mineral lease. Every day, I'd make my way through the bush to the river. They were supposed to be getting prepared to start producing diamonds. Basically, I was overseeing the workers. I carried a shotgun on my shoulder and a .38 in my waist. Once they started panning for diamonds, it would be easy to steal the rough stones, so I had to keep my eyes open all the time.

But the whole mining operation was a disaster. A real fucking mess. For one thing, no one understood the climate in Sierra Leone. The best I could understand it, there are only two seasons in that part of Africa: it's hot in the summer and it rains in the winter. When I got there in February 1986, it was the rainy season. Every night, as soon as the sun set, there were these downpours. Such rains! To me, it seemed like waterfalls coming from the black sky. During the daylight, the workers kept digging and digging, pumping out the water from the dammed-off area, then at night these incredible rains would undo all the work of the previous day.

The village didn't have electricity—everything ran on diesel generators. Outside, it would be total darkness, and throughout the rain, I could hear people dancing and drinking all night long. There was also no working shower, and one day I decide to wash myself in the river. I lathered myself with soap and dove in, then came out to dry in the sun. The next day my entire body was covered with huge pustules. I'd never seen anything like it. It was like in the ten plagues. I drove in to see a doctor in Freetown—a Belgian guy. He looked at the pustules covering me from head to toe and asked, "What did you do to yourself?"

I tell him, "I bathed in the river." He stares at me like I'm a madman. "You can't do that!" he says. "But they all do it," I say, "all the locals wash themselves in the river."

"No, no, no," he says. "This is *their* country. They're used to the water. If you try to do it, you'll get very sick." He gave me some medication and ointment, told me that every morning I needed to pour some water into a wash basin, add some antiseptic, and then I could wash.

Boris remembers sitting in darkness during a fierce tropical rainstorm, listening to the people in the distance dancing and singing along to a radio. His mind was thousands of miles away, fixated on revenge. He was biding his time until he could fly back to New York and settle scores with Vadik Reznikov.

I'm stuck in that village, covered in fucking pustules, rain pelting down all night, and I keep seeing Vadik's face—remembering how he killed Zelya and how he killed Evsei, how he tried to kill me and my cousin. I'm just waiting for a call telling me I can fly back and waste this worthless piece of shit.

After I'd been there a few weeks, I flew over Angela. Marat also brought his girlfriend, Natalia. Marat never stayed for long, just a week or so for vacation. He had a bunch of business going on in South Africa. Fima Laskin also flew in from Berlin a lot. They never came deep into the bush with me, to the river where the diamond-mining lease was. They all stayed in the best hotels in Freetown. At the time, many people came to Sierra Leone on vacation—especially Belgians. There were beautiful beaches, the hotels were so cheap, just thirty or forty dollars per night.

But the cheap hotels also attracted a lot of European tourists. Men of deviant orientation. It took me a while to figure out what was going on. I'd see all these strange-looking Belgians, Germans, Frenchmen—it turned out, they came to Sierra Leone because prostitution was open, and there was a huge amount of trafficking in children. European men came looking for African kids as young as ten or eleven. Imagine, a tourist destination for child molesters! But that was the thing about Sierra Leone in the mideighties. Everything you can possibly imagine was going on there.

Marat's friend Sasha Gramatsky would fly in sometimes to vacation. Gramatsky at this time had sheepskin-coat-making plants in Poland. He lived in Berlin but also had an American residency permit. He was wealthy, but not nearly as rich as he would later be, after the Soviet Union fell.

One morning, we're in Freetown, in one of the best hotels. Down by the pool at eleven A.M. Sasha Gramatsky has a plane to catch that night at seven P.M. I'm just sitting by the pool, relaxing, and Sasha asks me if I want to play cards. Gramatsky really liked to gamble. He was the kind of cardplayer we call *zamazlivy*—a guy who hates to lose even a small amount and just keeps chasing it, digging a deeper and deeper hole.

Some people can walk away once they lose, but not Gramatsky. He was compulsive with cards. We start playing clabber. We're wagering cognac. Instead of dollars, we're betting bottles of Cordon Bleu. Within a few hours, I've won about two hundred bottles of cognac, I look at my watch, and he needs to get ready to go to the airport. "Sasha," I say, "look at the time." But Gramatsky is hooked. He says, "Borya, let's keep playing!"

"Fine with me." I'm just killing time in Sierra Leone, looking after a diamond mining prospect—I've got nowhere special to be tomorrow morning. I say, "Same stakes?"

He says, "No, let's raise the stakes. Let's play for a hundred bottles per game." He's thinking he can win his two hundred bottles back in just a few hands.

Well, I go on a winning streak and before long, he owes me nearly a thousand bottles. Now Gramatsky decides he's not even going to go to the fucking airport. He'll fly the next day. Or the day after. He doesn't care anymore. It's getting dark at the pool, and the winter rains are going to come, so we go up to his suite. We're drinking cognac and gambling all night long. When you're deep into a game, serious gambling, eight hours or ten hours—it just flies past.

By the time we decide to call it quits, the sun is up, it's around eight in the morning. Gramatsky owes me 12,500 bottles of Cordon Bleu cognac. Back in 1986, at fifty bucks a bottle, that's well over six hundred thousand bucks.

We're wiped. We both crash and sleep until late in the afternoon. Then we wake up and go get something to eat at the hotel restaurant. Marat's girlfriend, Natalia, was sitting there, Volodya Davidson as well. I can't remember everyone, but it's a whole bunch of Russians. We order food, some more drinks, and he starts telling everyone about our card game.

"WHAT A NIGHT!" Gramatsky said. "I owe Boris 12,500 bottles of cognac. But instead of all that liquor, you know what I'm going to do? I'm going to invite Borya and all of you for dinner at the most expensive restaurant we can find."

"Sasha!" Boris said, glowering across the table. "Did you lose to me or not?"

"I lost."

"Then you've got to pay everything you owe—down to the last bottle."

"All right, Boris, I'll get you the 12,500 bottles. But I'm not paying full price. I'm going straight to the Martell factory in France and buy them in bulk, wholesale, dealers' cost."

"What's the fucking difference? Go wherever you want and buy them at whatever price you want. But make sure that those 12,500 bottles appear at my house."

"Okay, okay," Gramatsky said, smiling. "Will we drink them together?"

"No problem," Boris said. "But do you think you'll live long enough to drink as much as you want with me?"

GREAT FORTUNES WERE BEING MADE in Sierra Leone in the mid-1980s, and great fortunes were being lost.

"There was also so much corruption in that country, whenever a European businessman came, the locals saw him as a mark," Boris says.

Like this guy Volodya Davidson—a close friend of Kalmanovich. He was starting a gold-buying business in Sierra Leone. Davidson was one of the guys who got duped. I remember it well. They brought gold for him to buy. The first purchase was small, about two kilograms, and they allowed him to make a profit on it. Then they did a bigger deal and they ripped him off—I think Davidson got stiffed for one hundred sixty thousand bucks.

Once while I was at the hotel in Freetown, I met this Austrian guy who was just sitting there crying. "What happened?" I said. He's literally sobbing with his face in his hands. He shipped five containers full of electronic goods and alcohol into Sierra Leone and all five containers simply disappeared from the port. They were impossible to find, there was no one in the government to ask about it. He'd invested everything he had into this shipping operation. His whole business was gone. I felt sorry watching him sitting there, crying about all the money he'd lost.

One of the biggest financial losers in the entire Sierra Leone escapade was Marat Balagula. The alluvial mining prospect in Kono District never became viable due to the torrential nightly storms.

"Eventually the entire dam they'd built was washed away by the rain," Boris says. "Months of work just flushed away. So much time and effort and money put into this fucking operation, but the mines never managed to produce diamonds. Marat's company lost close to $3.5 million once the final accounting was done."

Shabtai Kalmanovich's fortunes would also quickly sour. During a 1987 visit to the United Kingdom, he was arrested by British police for having passed over $2 million in forged checks. He was extradited to the United States, was released on bail, and returned to Israel, where he was charged with espionage. In 1988, he was sentenced to seven years in prison for spying for the KGB.

After the fall of the Soviet Union, Kalmanovich reinvented himself again—this time as an oligarch and a philanthropist. He promoted concerts in Russia by Michael Jackson and Liza Minnelli, owned a chain of drugstores, and purchased the popular Spartak Moscow's women's basketball team.

On November 2, 2009, while being driven in his Mercedes sedan through Moscow, Kalmanovich was shot more than twenty times by unknown gunmen in a passing Lada. He died on the scene. Police said the shooting had all the hallmarks of a professional hit and was reportedly tied to Kalmanovich's shady business dealings.

BORIS HAD BEEN BIDING HIS TIME in Sierra Leone for months when he finally got the highly anticipated phone call from Brooklyn.

"At last, the phone rings and I hear the voice of one of my closest friends in Brighton," Boris recalls. "We've got a guy in Brighton who tipped us off that Vadik was supposed to be at a meeting in a restaurant, and that I needed to fly back over right away.

"I book the first flight I can get to New York. I'm planning to whack Vadik as soon as I see him."

CHAPTER 19

"THIS WAS MY REVENGE"

Within hours of landing at JFK, Boris's tipster gave him all the details about the meeting Reznikov was supposed to attend, right across from the marina, filled with private boats, on the Sheepshead Bay inlet.

We knew the exact time Vadik was supposed to be at this restaurant on Emmons Avenue. My buddy Lenya from Boston was with me—we each packed a .38. We chose the spot for the hit carefully. We stood about fifteen meters away from the restaurant because it was early evening, still daylight outside—or rather half-light—and we couldn't risk being seen by Vadik, even in the shadows. After waiting a while, we see Vadik drive up to the restaurant and leave his car almost at the entrance. He went inside and talked for five or six minutes.

Lenya and me both have our guns out and are ready to start blasting as soon as he gets in the car. But Vadik suddenly runs out, jumps into his Nissan, immediately makes a sharp U-turn, and speeds away against the traffic flow. It happened so fast we couldn't get a clean shot at him.

We found out later that he'd been tipped off that I was in New York, back on the streets, hunting him. Information flows fast among the Russians. We had someone close to Vadik leaking us information about him. And it turned out that Vadik has someone close to Marat leaking him information about me.

We keep looking for a way to whack him, but Vadik is lying low. Nobody has any news. Nobody can predict the timing of his movements. Vadik knows I'm after him. Vadik knows I'll never let this go. This isn't a *job* to me—this is my revenge. I know he's got eyes on me, too. He's looking for a chance to pop me. A mutual hunt, I guess you could call it. Just a matter of who finds who first. Either way, one of us is going to die.

I stayed in New York another week and a half, maybe two weeks. But Vadik never surfaced. And I had other business I needed to handle. There were people in Germany waiting to buy two kilos of cocaine from me. I also needed to make sure Sasha Gramatsky paid me the 12,500 bottles of cognac he'd lost in Freetown. I had plenty on my plate besides taking revenge. I couldn't just sit on my ass in New York waiting for months at a time.

I get on a flight to Germany and I figure sooner or later, I'll get another call, another shot at Vadik. But I was wrong about that.

In the first week of June, I flew to Germany. I sold two kilos of cocaine wholesale to our connection in Berlin for 175,000 deutschmarks, then I set up a meeting with Gramatsky about all the bottles of cognac he owes me. This isn't just collecting a debt—Gramatsky said he'd pay me the full amount in front of a lot of people in Sierra Leone, so I can't let this slide. It's now a matter of reputation.

We meet at a restaurant in Berlin. It's Mishka Zhlob, Gramatsky, this guy Papella, and me sitting at a table. Papella, like Gramatsky, is a big-time gambler. I've got one of my best guys positioned nearby, armed with a knife—he's my backup in case the discussion goes badly.

At first Gramatsky doesn't want to pay. Instead of the 12,500 bottles he owes me, Gramatsky says, "Boris, I can only give you a hundred twenty thousand in cash. Otherwise, my wife says she'll go to the police."

We have a saying in Russian. "When it comes to *fuflyzhniks,* you take whatever they give you. As for the rest, God will be their judge." I accepted the hundred twenty thousand bucks—and Gramatsky promised to make the rest up to me over time. And to his credit, he kept his word.

ONCE VADIK REZNIKOV LEARNED that Boris was in Europe, he made his move against Marat Balagula. There are diverging versions of the confrontation that occurred inside Balagula's popular Brighton Beach Avenue restaurant, Odessa, on June 12, 1986. Most accounts agree that Reznikov entered Odessa, pulled a semiautomatic pistol, and demanded that Balagula give him $600,000—a sum that Reznikov considered due him from a gasoline deal gone wrong.

"This is how Marat told me the story," Boris says.

Vadik pulls out his *volyna* and says that unless Marat pays him this six hundred thousand he'll meet an ugly end. Vadik tells Marat he's got three options. The first is to go to the police. The second is to kill Vadik. The third is to pay Vadik the six hundred grand.

Marat replies, "Vadik, I'm not going to go to the police; I'm not a *musor.* And I'm no murderer, so I'm not going to kill you. Let me think about how I'm going to pay you."

I'm still in Berlin when all this is going down. Marat calls me in Germany and tells me exactly what happened, how Vadik tried to muscle him. Then he says he's going to take this to the *Italyakhas*—meaning Gaspipe. He says it's best if we let the *Italyakhas* solve this matter.

I say, "Marat, if you give it to the *Italyakhas,* believe me, sooner or later, it'll all come out. The *musors* will charge you. Keep this between us! It's a Russians thing. Let me fucking finish him off. I'll fly back now and take care of it."

"We'll see, Boris," he says. Marat didn't call me off—but he didn't give me the go-ahead, either. Basically, he left me in limbo. And right away he went and told Gaspipe and his crew about Vadik threatening him.

Years later, I ended up in the same federal prison with Gaspipe. He told me what Marat said to him. "I'm being muscled by this thug for six hundred thousand—Vadik is gonna kill me unless I pay, and if I get killed, well, our gasoline business together is finished." Gaspipe was a greedy motherfucker, and after Marat put that idea in his head, Marat didn't have to pay a kopek for the contract. Gaspipe was making so much dough with Marat in gasoline, he had to solve this matter on his own.

In 1996, cloaked behind a screen inside the United States Senate, Anthony "Gaspipe" Casso testified in detail about the events that transpired in New York a decade earlier.

"Marat reached out to us and told us what happened," Casso said.

We agreed to meet him the next day. When we went to Marat's house, we found out that he was so scared that he had a heart attack but did not want to go to the hospital. I remember seeing Marat in bed, hooked up to all kinds of machines, refusing his doctor's orders to go to the hospital.

Since Marat was with our family, and especially since he was such a moneymaker for us, this was not just a threat against Marat; this was a threat against the Lucchese family as well. We knew what we had to do.

According to Casso, he relayed the situation to Lucchese family boss Vic Amuso, who sanctioned a hit. It was contracted to Joseph Testa and Anthony Senter, often called "the Gemini Twins," prolific killers once part of the infamous Gambino family crew led by Roy DeMeo.

"We asked Marat and one of his guys to get us some information to identify Vladimir," Casso said. "One of Marat's guys got us his picture and license plate number."

As Casso instructed, Balagula arranged to meet Vadik Reznikov the next day at the Odessa restaurant, on the pretext of giving him the $600,000.

On Friday, June 13, 1986, Reznikov arrived at Odessa, expecting to get his money, and when he realized that Balagula was not going to show, he left enraged. According to eyewitness reports, shortly before 7:20 P.M., Reznikov walked out of Odessa and got into his brown Nissan, which was parked across the street in front of Misha Vax's apartment building at 1130 Brighton Beach Avenue.

A light-green Plymouth sedan carrying Anthony Senter and Joseph Testa pulled up. The ever-wary Reznikov was evidently caught off-guard by the unfamiliar faces of the two Cosa Nostra killers. Testa got out of the Plymouth and approached Reznikov's Nissan, drawing a .380-caliber pistol equipped with a silencer and began firing through the open window on the driver's side.

Reznikov was shot six times—in the head, left side, hip, and leg. He died on the scene.

No arrests were ever made in Reznikov's murder. The case remained unsolved until 1994, when Casso became a cooperating witness for federal prosecutors and admitted his role in dozens of mob murders, including the killing of Vadik Reznikov. In his testimony before the U.S. Senate in 1996, Casso said that after he ordered the successful hit on Reznikov, "Marat didn't have any more problems from any other Russians."

IN THE SHORT TERM, at least, Marat *did* have a problem with Boris Nayfeld, who was fuming in his Berlin hotel room when he learned what had just happened in Brighton Beach.

I was so upset with Marat when I first heard that Gaspipe killed Vadik, I was furious. It was *my* job. But one of my guys says to me, "Well, what's done is done. Good riddance to bad trash."

It was true—Vadik getting killed meant I had one less thing to think about. In the end, it was a positive. Because when Gaspipe flipped, when he started cooperating and told the government everything, by then Marat was doing time in prison for credit card fraud, and the feds tried to pin Vadik's murder on Marat. Marat *also* started talking to the FBI, and if I'd pulled the trigger, who fucking knows? The feds could have picked me up for it, too.

After a while I realized that the *Italyakhas* killing Vadik was a blessing in disguise. But when I first got the news in Berlin, I was so angry with Marat. I shouted: "I wanted to kill this motherfucker—this was *my* revenge!"

—

Boris's frustration about the loss of personal vengeance notwithstanding, the death of Vladimir Reznikov allowed him to maximize his growing power within the New York underworld. At this point, few other Soviet émigré gangsters had the balls to try to challenge him.

And in global affairs, Boris's base of operations would soon broaden far beyond the shores of South Brooklyn as he set up a thriving business with two new partners and made a permanent home in one of the most beautiful cities of Europe.

PART
THREE

PART THREE

CHAPTER 20

THE WALL

After Evsei Agron and Marat Balagula, the most significant criminal partnership Boris Nayfeld formed was with Ricardo Fanchini, a dapper, globe-trotting, bug-eyed mobster later dubbed "the Polish Al Capone."

Born Marian Richard Kozina in 1956 in Katowice to a Polish mother and an Italian father, Fanchini fled to the West in 1977, settling first in Germany before coming to the United States in the '80s. Fluent in Russian, he seamlessly blended into the criminal circles of Brighton Beach, where he was known as "the Polyak," or "the Gypsy," a reference to his part-Romani heritage.

"I met Richard Fanchini in the mideighties—that's when he first appeared in Brighton," Boris recalls. "He quickly made his name as one of the most capable criminals around. He had a mixed Polish-Russian crew. They specialized in what we call 'night jobs.' But not small-time burglaries. Richard and his guys would clean out entire stores. Mostly furs and diamonds."

Brighton Beach in the '80s was a bustling marketplace for thieves selling swag.

If Richard and his crew stole a mink coat that cost twenty-five hundred dollars, he'd sell it for a thousand immediately in Brighton Beach. You always knew when Richard cleaned up on a big fur job, because you'd see half of Brighton Beach walking around in new mink coats.

When we got introduced, we had no business together, we just knew of each other by reputation. Richard was a distinguished-looking guy, always dressed sharp. He was athletic, liked to play tennis. Compared to a lot of our Brighton Jews, he was sophisticated—very intelligent. What was impressive about Richard is how he managed to move around Brighton on his own, never getting caught up in our Russian rivalries and beefs. He was part of the Russian in-crowd without getting caught up in our internal squabbles.

Richard had his hands in a lot of criminal businesses. Around the time we met, his crew started to counterfeit U.S. currency. They were producing fake twenties. I was impressed by the quality and told him, "Hey, it would be nice to get my hands on some of these." He got me about forty thousand dollars of these fake twenties for me, which I sold at a good profit.

When Fanchini got jammed up, I helped him get out of New York. One night in 1987 Richard and his crew are robbing a sporting goods store. They're in the midst of cleaning the place out, their lookout has a walkie-talkie, but he doesn't see the cops arriving. The *musors* catch Richard and his entire crew red-handed, inside the store, take them all away in handcuffs. Richard made bail quickly and while he's waiting on a trial date, he tells me he wants to run away to Europe. By that time, I'd been doing some things with Milik Brandwain both in Europe and Sierra Leone.

I said, "Richard, go to Brandwain. He'll help you get set up in Antwerp."

The Ukraine-born Rachmiel "Milik" Brandwain kept up the façade of a legitimate businessman in Antwerp's Diamond Quarter, but law enforcement considered him one of the principal Russian organized crime figures in Europe, a top money launderer for other Russian mobsters.

Out on bail for the burglary charge, Richard prepares fake documents and takes off for Europe. First to Brussels and then Antwerp. Before long, I get word that Richard and Milik have become business partners.

Credit where credit is due—Richard proved himself just as capable at legitimate business as he was at crime. Brandwain already had a trading company—it had started off small, just clothing and some electronics, but he was also smuggling gold on the side. It was only when Richard Fanchini arrived in Antwerp that the business really took off.

Once I saw how well things were going for them, I flew straight over to Belgium and joined the company as a partner. In fact, it wasn't long before I started to spend more time in Antwerp than in New York.

The import-export company, M&S International, was located in the heart of Antwerp, on the Pelikaanstraat in the Diamond Quarter.

Richard and Milik were the principals. They were the businessmen. They ran the day-to-day import-export operations. I provided the *krysha*—officially, I was the head of security—and had a ten percent ownership stake in the company.

By 1988 and 1989, M&S started to expand enormously. Richard's a guy with a nose for changing market conditions. He always has an instinct for what's about to become popular. For instance, he got us selling the earliest mobile phones—those huge, expensive, heavy ones that looked like bricks—when they were just coming on the market.

In the eighties, electronics technology was changing so fast, and Richard always kept M&S at the front of the action. We sold a lot of electronics to Russian sailors who would come into the port of Antwerp. Whenever a ship from the Soviet Union came in, the sailors bought up our goods because there was such a big underground market for any technology from the West in Russia and they knew they could make good money doing *fartsovka*.

We supplied stereos, TVs, phones, and the earliest personal computers that hit the market. Milik Brandwain had good connections in the Far East, guys with factories in South Korea, so we could buy all the electronics at the cheapest possible prices. We eventually expanded our distribution into Berlin and across Europe.

When I first joined up with Fanchini and Brandwain in Antwerp, no one knew the Berlin Wall was going to fall. And soon. There were still the two zones: GDR and FRG.* We set up operations in Berlin—there were a lot of Russian Jews opening factories and restaurants there. The head gangster over there was a guy called Fima Laskin. He was originally from Lvov and had been in West Berlin since about 1974. I got to know Fima well. We did a couple of robbery jobs together. He had some good rackets going with counterfeit money and icons. They were smuggling Orthodox icons out of the Soviet Union and selling them at a big profit. I didn't realize at this time that Fima was going to become a major

---

* German Democratic Republic, meaning East Germany; and the Federal Republic of Germany, meaning West Germany.

problem for me. But if you were a Russian criminal doing anything in Germany, Fima Laskin expected to get a piece of the action.*

ON NOVEMBER 9, 1989, the Berlin Wall came down. While most of the world was watching the unprecedented celebratory scenes unfolding on television, marveling at the spread of freedom into the Communist bloc, the guys at M&S International saw only dollar signs.

For a trio of criminals—all born behind the Iron Curtain—it was the business opportunity of a generation, if you had the vision of Ricardo Fanchini, the connections of Rachmiel Brandwain, and the muscle of Boris Nayfeld. In the autumn of 1989, there was suddenly a fortune to be made in the supply chains of the Soviet Army based in East Germany, officially known as the Western Group of Forces.

Overnight, the Soviet Army in East Germany became our biggest account at M&S. You have to remember—it's 1989, communism is falling, but there's still a huge Soviet military presence stationed in Germany. No one knows what to expect next. The two zones, GDR and FGR, are in the process of reuniting. Even after the Berlin Wall fell, those Soviet soldiers weren't going back to Russia anytime soon.

West Germany had agreed to help subsidize the transition—there was something like 1.5 billion deutschmarks allocated to keep five hundred thousand military personnel in East Germany, while the Russians were figuring how to get the people and the equipment out of there—find adequate housing and so on.

---

* Efim "Fima" Laskin, dubbed by the German press "*der schöne Zar*" ("the Beautiful Czar"), was one of the original Russian mob bosses active in Western Europe; his criminal history included counterfeiting, drug trafficking, and arms dealing—he was convicted of importing weapons and explosives in Italy and selling them to the Red Brigades terrorist group.

Milik Brandwain had all the right military people in his pocket. The guys you needed to know were certain colonels. The supply officers. Guys in charge of procurement. These colonels were the ones who kept the Soviet Army functioning. They had the authority to purchase on a massive scale. They were supplying the entire Red Army in East Germany with the necessities of daily life. We're talking about half a million military people, *plus* their families.

The Soviet colonels could see that communism was starting to collapse everywhere—not just East Germany—and they were all willing to take kickbacks, to start lining their pockets by doing business with M&S. We got these colonels all set up with Swiss bank accounts.

We split the profit from every transaction. Let's say a pair of socks cost two deutschmarks. We set the price at three deutschmarks. Or four deutschmarks. Or five. It didn't fucking matter. We padded the price and split it fifty-fifty between the supply colonel and us. The same with any item we sold to the Soviet Army. Food, clothes, electronics, cigarettes, liquor. M&S made enormous amounts of money during that transition period in Germany. *Huge.* We weren't the only ones doing this. Half of Berlin rushed in and did the exact same thing.

BY THE LATE 1980s, Antwerp had become an unlikely hotbed for Soviet émigré criminal activity. How did so many thieves and racketeers born in the USSR find themselves in this picturesque Flemish city with a population of less than half a million? One factor was the ease of smuggling narcotics and contraband into Antwerp's seaport, the second-busiest container shipping port in Europe.

But the primary draw, according to Boris, was the bustling trade in precious gems dominated by Orthodox Jews.

"I needed a home base, so with the first real money I got from the company I bought a nice two-room apartment in central Antwerp," Boris says.

Business kept booming with M&S. And the time was fast approaching when Russia would open up, the Soviet Union was about to fall—we could all see it coming, and we were ready to go do business there, too. Eventually we had our M&S stores in Russia, the Ukraine, Latvia, Estonia.

All the stores carrying our merchandise paid us in cash. One of my responsibilities in providing the *krysha* was collecting all the company's money across Europe and bringing it back to Antwerp. Throughout the week, I was on planes, bringing back suitcases full of cash.

While traveling back and forth with the cash from the business, that diamond *schneyer* job I pulled with Igor and Edik came back to bite me on the ass. I went to Sweden to collect the money from our stores there, and when I get to the airport, I've got over a hundred thousand in my carry-on. I land in Belgium and I'm passing through the customs at Brussels airport. I show them my passport. They search my bags and see I've got a hundred thousand U.S. dollars. Right away, they stick me in a holding cell at the airport—no explanation—until a few hours later when these detectives arrive from Antwerp.

One of the detectives says, "Where did you get all this money?"

"From my work," I say.

"What kind of work?"

"I'm head of security for M&S International." I tell them we're an import-export business based in Antwerp, and I'm responsible for carrying this money from our sales in Sweden. They seem skeptical, put me under arrest, handcuff me, and take me with them in the back of their car to Antwerp. I spent the night in an Antwerp jail cell. The next day, one of these detectives shoves a photo in my face and says, "Did you rent this Toyota?" I barely remembered, but, yeah, it was the car I rented for a couple months when we pulled the diamond *schneyer* job.

"Sure, I rented that car—what about it?"

They asked me if I knew anything about a diamond robbery—a rip-off of one and a half million dollars in diamonds. Some Hasidic Jews had been scammed, big-time, and the car rented in my name was seen parked at the scene of the crime almost every day. This rental car agreement was the only link to the unsolved crime. Then they gave me detailed descriptions of Igor and Edik.

"Do you know these men?"

"Yes, I know them—we met in Rome, when I was leaving the Soviet Union back in 1979. Look, I was just their driver. I didn't know anything about a robbery. I was in Antwerp looking for work. They offered me a job, asked me to rent a car to drive them around. Said they'd pay me three thousand dollars a month. I rented the Toyota and drove them to work. I don't know anything about diamonds or any kind of robbery."

Lying to detectives came effortlessly to Boris—but he was taking a risk here, because he wasn't sure who the Antwerp detectives might possibly bring forward to identify him.

I really wasn't sure if anyone had seen me behind the wheel of that fucking car. There were many days when Igor and Edik drove from Brussels to Antwerp alone, without me. I told the detectives, I left for the U.S., asked them to turn in that car back to the rental place. "They must have pulled a robbery using my vehicle once I was in New York."

There were plenty of eyewitnesses who'd seen the car, and the Antwerp Diamond Quarter was covered with surveillance cameras, even back then in the nineteen eighties. Many of the local diamond merchants had seen Igor and Edik arrive in that car.

A detective takes me into this room equipped with a one-way

mirror, tells me to strip to the waist. I can't hear any of this, but some of the Hasidic Jews we'd ripped off are looking at me on the other side of the mirror. None of them ever saw my face, so they all told the detectives, "No, that's not the right guy." Igor and Edik were the only ones they dealt with.

Finally, the Antwerp cops realize they can't pin anything on me. They demand to know where they can find Igor and Edik. I tell them, "No idea." I wasn't lying about that part. "Maybe they're somewhere in Europe. Maybe in America. Like I said, I was only the driver."

The Antwerp cops had no choice but to release me. They had no eyewitness IDs and no evidence tying me to the $1.5 million in stolen stones. And the thing is, at this time Belgian law allowed you to enter the country with any amount of cash, so these *musors* had to return the hundred thousand, which they counted and vouchered and packed neatly in my carry-on bag.

LIFE IN ANTWERP in the late '80s and early '90s was glittering for Boris.

Those are some of the best memories for me—this time spent living in one of the most beautiful cities of Europe. My *krysha* with M&S was bringing me a hundred thousand cash each month. That was the *legitimate* salary. That first year in Antwerp, I bought a black Bentley. Went out to fine restaurants all the time.

Marat Balagula was with us in Belgium for a while—he'd gone on the run from the credit card case. His daughter was living in Antwerp, and after getting convicted on fraud charges in '86, he came over with his girlfriend, Natalia.

Balagula had enough money secreted away that he managed to stay on the run for several years, dividing his time between Belgium, Sierra Leone, and South Africa. "Marat was doing a lot of business in Johannesburg. And he managed to stay free almost three years. That's not fucking easy when the FBI and Interpol are looking everywhere for you. The *musors* finally nabbed him on his way back to Antwerp—Interpol picked him up at the Frankfurt airport. And because he'd gone on the run, when he was sent back to the United States, the judge threw the book at him."

On February 27, 1989, after years as a fugitive, Balagula was arrested in the airport in Frankfurt am Main, West Germany. In December 1989, he was extradited to the United States, went to trial, was convicted, and was sentenced to eight years in prison for the $750,000 credit card fraud.

In November 1992, Balagula was convicted at a separate trial for gasoline bootlegging and given an additional ten years in federal prison.

While passing sentence, Judge Leonard Wexler made a point of addressing the economic havoc wreaked by the educated men like Marat Balagula who had come to the United States as refugees from religious oppression in the USSR.

"This was supposed to be a haven for you," Wexler said. "It turned out to be a hell for us."

Ultimately imprisoned until 2004, after his 1989 extradition Balagula's influence quickly waned. Boris says that he lost all touch with his former friend after Marat's conviction. Balagula would never again play any significant role in the world of Soviet émigré organized crime.

And the unfathomably lucrative gasoline-tax scheme, in which Balagula had played so integral a role, was by the late 1980s beginning to implode.

Michael Franzese, the young Colombo Family caporegime, had been the first major mobster to be taken down for gasoline bootlegging. He explained how it all unravelled for his operation.

The feds had no idea how we were doing it—for years. The FBI met me outside of my office—I had a Mazda agency out in Long Island—and said, "Just tell us how you're doing it—we'll give you a pass." Yeah, right, they'll give me a pass. I said, "I don't know what you guys are talking about. If you wanna buy a car, I'll sell you a car. I'll *give* you one if you want." They got so angry with me at that point: "You don't wanna help us! You're gonna go down!" I said, "Relax, guys, go do your job."

Honestly, the feds didn't have a *clue* until my partner Iorizzo turned snitch and blew the whistle on everybody.

In March 1984, Lawrence Iorizzo, already sentenced to five years and ordered to pay a $1.7 million fine for his role in gas-tax theft, entered the Witness Protection Program and began testifying against Franzese and others in the operation. On March 21, 1986, Franzese pleaded guilty to one count of racketeering conspiracy and one count of tax conspiracy.

"I was sentenced to ten years, and I ended up serving eight and a half," Franzese says. "I had to pay $14.7 million in fines and $5 million in forfeitures."

With Franzese off the street, his original partners immediately felt the heat from other Cosa Nostra crews. In May 1989, the Rumanian-born Michael Markowitz was shot and killed while driving his Rolls-Royce in the Sheepshead Bay section of Brooklyn—police theorized he'd been killed because the mob knew he was talking to investigators about the gasoline business.

"When I left the street, they whacked Markowitz. They'd already shot up Persits, but he didn't die," Franzese says.

Lev Persits was paralyzed after being shot in the back in a November 1987 assassination attempt.* The third of Franzese's Jewish partners, David Bogatin, was convicted of gasoline bootlegging in a 1987 trial but jumped his $500,000 bail and fled to Eastern Europe, setting up the first commercial bank in postcommunist Poland. In 1992, he was

---

* Lev Persits died of natural causes in September 2010.

extradited to the United States, convicted of tax evasion, and given a prison sentence of two and two-thirds to eight years.

During the presidency of Donald Trump, David Bogatin's name was again in the headlines; reports surfaced that in 1984 Bogatin had paid $6 million for five condominiums in Trump Tower on Fifth Avenue, a deal so flamboyant that Trump personally attended the closing. While he was a fugitive from his tax-evasion case in Europe, as Wayne Barrett first reported in the *Village Voice,* New York State prosecutors seized the five apartments in Trump Tower after concluding that Bogatin had purchased them to "launder money, to shelter and hide assets" as well as using them on weekends "for parties."*

WHEN HE WASN'T ENGAGED in his own prodigious bouts of partying, most of Boris Nayfeld's time in late-'80s Antwerp seems to have been spent smuggling bags stuffed with cash—both real and counterfeit— through the major airports of Europe.

"One afternoon I get a call from Fima Laskin, telling me to come to Berlin to pick up five hundred thousand dollars of counterfeit U.S. currency. We've got a buyer at thirty cents on the dollar in Sierra Leone—all we need to do is deliver the bag and he'll give us two hundred thousand real dollars for half a million counterfeit. It was Misha Sheferofsky and me who were supposed to carry in this money."

Mikhail Sheferofsky was a Moscow-born mobster who later changed his surname to Sater. His son, born Felix Sheferofsky, now known as Felix Sater, was a senior adviser to Donald Trump, a convicted felon whose name figures prominently in the Mueller Report as a link between the Trump Organization and Russian organized crime.

---

* Wayne Barrett, *Trump: The Deals and the Downfall* (New York: HarperCollins Publishers, 1992).

I carry the half million in counterfeit from Germany to Holland, give it to Misha Sheferofsky to take to Sierra Leone via London. Everything was set up in advance. Once Sheferofsky gets to Freetown, he's supposed to be led through a VIP line at the airport—the one used by politicians and diplomats—bypassing the customs agents. Sheferofsky flies from Amsterdam to London, but due to bad weather his flight gets there late, he misses the connection, needs to get a hotel in London, wait for the next flight to Sierra Leone.

At Gatwick the customs controls were heavy, they find the half a million dollars in his bag and demand to know where he got the money. Sheferofsky tells them he sold some diamonds in Amsterdam and needs to take this cash to Sierra Leone to buy more stones. Bad luck—the agents closely inspect the bills, see that they're fakes, and Sheferofsky gets busted. He ended up doing a couple years for trying to carry that counterfeit money into Sierra Leone. It was a completely fucked-up score, but even still, after he got released, Fima Laskin would keep Sheferofsky around, using him for one little job or another.

As our M&S business kept growing, I held on to the apartment in central Antwerp but decided to buy a villa just outside the city. It wasn't a huge villa, but the location was perfect—in a quiet suburb called Edegem. Angela was coming to visit a lot—eventually she came over to live. She brought our son Ilyusha, who was three years old. He started kindergarten, learned to speak Flemish. Angela fixed up the villa. She filled the place with expensive Belgian furniture and fine Russian artwork. Before long we set up a pleasant family life there in Edegem.

But once my wife, Valentina, found out about this situation, she arrived in Antwerp. Without any warning. She came to see me specifically to have this talk. She says, "Boris, I know you have a lover and a child, but don't destroy our family." We talked about everything frankly, without anger. She wanted an answer from me, but I left it

without an answer. Open-ended, I guess you'd say. I wanted to keep
Valentina and my family in New York and have this other life—my
second family—in Antwerp with Angela and my young son.

It meant having to travel to America often. By then Valentina
and I had a big house on Staten Island—that's where I lived when I
was in the U.S. Meanwhile, Angela stayed with Ilyusha in the villa in
Antwerp.

At this time, my daughter Alesya was about seventeen and she'd fly
to see me in Antwerp. I'd take her shopping and buy her whatever she
wanted at the boutiques in the fashion district. She got to see Brussels
and Paris and Berlin. Whenever Alesya came over, I spent time with her
in the apartment and then I'd go spend time with Angela and Ilyusha in
the villa.

It was complicated to split myself between these two families and
two homes, flying between New York and Antwerp. It became quite
a headache, honestly. Juggling a wife, a mistress, two sets of kids—
well, that takes a lot of time and energy. Between providing the *krysha*
for M&S and all my other rackets, I was constantly traveling, carrying
money through airports. Looking back on it now, I'd say it's better not
to have anything to do with women when there's serious work at hand!

THE CAT WILL EVENTUALLY GET a downpour of the mice's tears.

The old Russian proverb kept ringing in Boris's ears.

Valentina confronting him in Antwerp had—momentarily—
brought him face-to-face with the reality of his wholly unrealistic domestic arrangement.

Besides a wife and a mistress—two lavish homes, two disparate
families—Boris was juggling a dizzying array of criminal activity in
Europe.

With Marat Balagula now extradited and facing decades behind bars, the pipeline of cash from the fuel-tax scheme in the United States was about to dry up; for Boris and his crew, Balagula was indeed the "golden goose" behind the unimaginably profitable gasoline racket.

Yet even as the legitimate import-export trade at M&S was bringing in millions annually, in 1990 Boris decided to add another file to his criminal portfolio.

International heroin trafficker.

CHAPTER 21

CHINA WHITE

My introduction to the drug business came in the mid–nineteen eighties, actually," Boris recalls.

Long before heroin, I started smuggling cocaine into West Germany. I had a guy who could get us coke at fifteen thousand bucks per kilo in Brooklyn. The price of cocaine in New York is always fluctuating. When the *musors* make a big bust, the price per kilo spikes. When there's too much cocaine on the streets, the price drops.

I had mules who carried into West Germany on their bodies. Sometimes I'd fly over to Germany on the same plane with the mule, but I'd never sit in the same row, and obviously never carry the stuff myself. I could sell one kilo for a hundred thousand deutschmarks wholesale. Approximately fifty-five thousand U.S. It was not a bad business. Even after the paying the mules ten thousand per kilo, it was profitable enough.

But Boris found he couldn't compete with the larger, more established cocaine rings already active in Western Europe. "There were guys in Holland who could get each kilo for three or four thousand from the source. That's the proper price for cocaine if you bring it yourself from Latin America into Europe. Since I had no connection in Colombia or Bolivia or Mexico, the cheapest I could find was fifteen grand per kilo from a Russian connection in New York. For me, cocaine was nowhere nearly as profitable as the heroin business would become."

THERE'S A STRIKING DEGREE of cognitive dissonance when you listen to Boris talking about his role as a major heroin trafficker in the 1990s: on the one hand, he expresses utter contempt for the junky, the *narkoman;* on the other, he makes no apologies for the fact that he was personally responsible for flooding the streets of New York City with shipments of pure heroin.

"For me, narcotics was just another business," Boris says with a shrug. "Heroin was another commodity. I never retailed it, I only sold it wholesale. Pure. Uncut. I never dealt with the *narkoman* on the street. For me, it was strictly supply and demand. A demand already existed. I was the supplier. I figured if I wasn't bringing it in, someone else was going to."

IT'S THE OLDEST RATIONALIZATION in the drug business.

If I don't sell this junk, someone else will.

Nonetheless, the older generation of Soviet émigré criminals in Brooklyn like Evsei Agron wanted nothing to do with drugs.

"Only a few Russians in the early eighties were selling heroin—guys like Monya Elson," Boris recalls. "Their product was from Turkey, smuggled in from Germany. Turkish heroin was not good quality. The best heroin in the world at this time came from Thailand. China White. That's what Richard Fanchini was able to buy—directly from the source."

For Boris, Ricardo Fanchini was, once again, the trailblazer. In addition to the purity of the product, Fanchini set up an ingenious smuggling system within the legitimate importing business of M&S International.

"I got into the heroin business strictly as an investor," Boris says.

One day Richard comes to me and says, "Boris, if you put up some cash, you'll make a great profit." I knew that Richard and his crew were moving heroin, I knew they had a profitable operation, but I didn't yet know all the details.

I put up ninety thousand, and yes, I made quite a good profit. That was the extent of it. Once the business at M&S started to take off, once we were bringing in a lot of legitimate income, Richard says, "Boris, I don't want to do this anymore. I'm getting out." He'd made plenty of cash from heroin already—millions and millions.

He says, "Here are my people, here's my operation, why don't you take over?" He transferred his connections, and I started to use these people to smuggle heroin to America. From that moment on, I was running the heroin business with those same Polish guys who worked with Richard.

The operation worked like this. We'd send one of our trusted Polish guys to Thailand to do the buying. He'd fly to Bangkok, where Richard had an established network of people with pure heroin. We could get a kilo of China White in Thailand for between $5,000 and $7,000. Once our guy checked the heroin for purity, he'd normally buy twenty to thirty kilos at a time. This was the most dangerous part of the operation. In Thailand if you get caught buying heroin, it's the death penalty. They hang you over there. But these Poles didn't give a shit. The Polish guys working for Richard had balls.

The next step was to buy TV sets. And at the time, Japanese and Korean TVs were cheap in Bangkok. Unscrew the back and you could fit two or three kilos of heroin inside a television. Remember, they were much bigger and bulkier than TVs today. There were cavities inside next to the cathode-ray tube and the wiring. Each of our shipments would be ten TVs loaded up with twenty to thirty kilos. The TVs were repackaged in their original boxes, looking brand-new, then imported via M&S International into Poland.

Warsaw was always the hub of the operation, the transit point. Bangkok to Warsaw to New York: that was our triangle.

The televisions packed with heroin arrived at Warsaw-Okecie Airport, where they were examined by Polish Customs. M&S International was already importing large quantities of electronics from the Far East for sale in Europe—stereos, radios, computers, televisions—so nothing seemed suspicious about these ten TV sets with kilos of heroin inside.

Back then, there were no scanners that could detect what was inside a TV. Unless a customs agent took apart the TVs, he'd never find the heroin. So now we've got twenty kilos of pure heroin in Warsaw waiting to be smuggled into the United States. The Poles take out the heroin, reassemble the TV sets, put them back in their boxes, and we sell them at a profit—as we would with any other M&S electronic product.

My day-to-day manager was a close friend, Dima Podlog—a guy who I could trust with everything. Dima's the kind of guy who would never in his life do anything improper. Dima looked for guys willing to transport heroin. He was managing all the sales. From New York, Dima sent mules to Poland—mostly Russians, a few Israelis—and they transported the heroin on their bodies. The transfer was always done in hotel rooms. Each mule would be met by the Polyaks, the heroin brought to the hotel already prepackaged in smaller units of between 200 and 400 grams. These packets would be flattened and smudged all over with fresh-ground coffee. A drug-sniffing dog can't pick up the scent of heroin because of the smell of coffee.

Then the packets were strapped to the body of the mule. We smuggled only in the wintertime when they could wear bulky clothing— it's nearly impossible for a mule to smuggle heroin on his body in the summer months. The mule would have no problems boarding at the Warsaw airport because at this time there were no body X-rays.

The system worked so well because Poland wasn't on the DEA's radar. Our mules weren't arriving at JFK on flights from Bangkok or Bogota or some other drug hotspot. Who the hell is expecting a pipeline of pure heroin coming into the United States on commercial flights from Warsaw?

For bringing two kilos of heroin successfully to Brooklyn, I paid each mule ten thousand. If they brought more than usual, say three kilos, I paid them fifteen thousand. The all-in cost to us, factoring in the transportation to Poland, the flights and hotel, delivery to America, was about twenty-five thousand.

My heroin was selling in the range of $120,000 to $140,000 in New York. If a twenty-kilo shipment cost us $500,000 all told, we could sell it wholesale for between $2.4 and $2.8 million. That profit wasn't all mine, obviously. I split it fifty-fifty with my Polish partners. This heroin was of such good quality, the retailers could cut it about four or five times and make millions. I didn't want any part of that—cutting it with whatever bullshit they use—I only wanted to deal with the pure product.

My constant headache was that I didn't have a direct connection to wholesale purchasers. Richard wouldn't turn over his buyers to me. He was very cagey about that. He turned everything else over to me, but not his buyers. I knew he'd been selling to the *Italyakhas*, but he wouldn't tell me who. Think it's easy to unload that much fucking heroin? We're talking twenty or thirty kilos per shipment. There are very few guys able to lay out a couple million in cash to take twenty or thirty kilos of China White off your hands.

My one lead was this *Italyakha* that I got through Grisha Luydoyed. I won't name him—he's still alive, still in the streets. He's a guy with a good reputation. He was born in Sicily. The *Italyakhas* in the U.S. would call him a "greaseball." I came to meet him at his house. He was wearing an ankle bracelet, out on bail while awaiting trial for a drug case. He says, "Boris, you see my fucking bracelet. I can't do anything. I can't even give you the name of anybody, God forbid. They're watching me all the time."

I talked it over with Dima and we say, fuck it, we've got no choice but to start distributing on our own. This was our one big weakness in the operation—we could bring twenty or thirty kilos from Bangkok to Warsaw to New York, but we could never unload that shipment quickly into one set of hands. And if you don't have one big wholesale buyer, then you need to take the risk of selling smaller amounts, a kilo or two at a time to various people. Then there's a good chance that you'll sell to the *musors*. The DEA have all kinds of informants and undercover agents, working to make smaller buys on the street.

I warned my guys constantly to be careful. "Don't go looking for buyers on your own!" I wanted Dima to control all the sales. Whenever I talked to Dima on the phone, we used a code which we'd switch up often. We wouldn't try to sound too innocent—we knew the *musors* could be listening—but we'd make it sound like we were talking some another racket like, say, prostitution.

I'd call from New York from Europe and say, "Dimka, I'm sending you two women. Both of them are married. They're looking to make some money as escorts. Just make sure they don't get gonorrhea."

That meant, "I'm sending over two mules, each one is carrying two kilos, make sure they don't sell to the *musors*."

When you're a successful criminal, when you're running a strong operation, of course, there's a constant battle with the government—all day long you're trying to hide what you're doing from the *musors*. The rules are simple. It's their job to catch you. It's your job to outsmart them.

But until you start making serious money you don't realize that there's an even bigger danger out there. Guys no different from you— criminals who see you're doing well and start scheming how to take your slice of bread away from you. So many wolves are hiding in the shadows! Guys you think are your friends, but really they're just waiting for the chance to kill you and snatch what's yours.

IT WAS PRECISELY just such a case of jealousy, territoriality, and greed, Boris maintains, that precipitated an ugly dispute with Efim Laskin, the Berlin-based mob boss.

Fima Laskin knew how well I was doing. Not just with my heroin operation. He saw the kind of money we were making at M&S. He knew about our deals with the Soviet Army. He knew that I'd always be carrying a lot of cash whenever I was in Berlin. Sometimes I'd have as much as two million deutschmarks from our M&S stores in Germany. Just in one weekly pickup.

Fima had his nose in everything. He knew I'd fly into Berlin once a week to collect the cash from sales and personally take it to Antwerp. Fima comes to me with a plan. He says I should leak him the info on my pickup schedule in Berlin, then he and his crew will organize an armed robbery thirty minutes prior to me getting there to take the money.

I said, "Fima, are you crazy? I'm a partner in M&S. I'm one of the owners. You want to rob the company and rob *me* as well?"

"Don't worry, Boris," he says. "After the heist, we'll share the money fifty-fifty."

I turned him down flat.

I told him, "Fima, don't play such games."

He took my refusal as a deadly insult.

Boris didn't yet realize just how grave an insult this was, nor the lengths Fima Laskin would take to exact his revenge.

CHAPTER 22

OLD NEW YEAR IN PARADISE

By 1990, with Evsei Agron dead and Marat Balagula imprisoned, Boris Nayfeld had emerged as the dominant Russian organized crime figure in the United States. But his ascension to the top roost in Brighton Beach was about to be challenged by a former friend named Monya Elson, sparking what is still regarded as the bloodiest era in Brooklyn's Soviet émigré underworld.

"For me, the war with Monya Elson started when I was celebrating the Old New Year at the Paradise," Boris recalls. "If things had gone the way these fucking snakes planned, I'd have been blown to bits that night."*

---

* Old New Year, also known as Orthodox New Year, is a holiday celebrated by many Russians on January 14. Although the Soviet Union adopted the Gregorian calendar in 1918, the Russian Orthodox Church continued to use the Julian calendar, leading to two separate celebrations and the famously oxymoronic greeting: "*Starym Novym Godom!*" or "Happy Old New Year!"

The storied feud between Boris Nayfeld and Monya Elson seems less of an outright *war* and more a series of double- and triple-crosses, spectacularly botched assassination attempts—as well as a few gruesomely successful ones—ranging from New York to Los Angeles, Munich to Moscow.

"The strange thing about it is, I'd never really had problems with Monya before that night," Boris says. "In the beginning, in the early days in Brooklyn, Monya and me, we were fine with each other. We sometimes had meals together and found ourselves part of the same mix.

Monya is a Moldovan. He's from Kishinev. Once he landed in the U.S., Monya got introduced to Evsei. I noticed that Monya always went out of his way to become close to Evsei. But Evsei knew Monya's worth; he didn't think much of Monya. They did a few things together, but Evsei wouldn't let him get really close.

He was always a *schvitz.** He wanted to play a role as if he had spent half his life inside. But his true story is this: he served in the Soviet Army as a tank man. Then he worked in Kishinev as a bus driver. He was never a *blatnoy*. He never spent time in a Soviet prison. But having hung around a few real criminals, Monya picked up the language and manners.

You're not born a criminal, of course. You become one. In America, Monya began diving into anything where there was a chance to make money. There wasn't an area that he didn't try to find his way into to make a buck. He did *schneyer,* burglaries, robberies, sold that poor-quality Turkish heroin.

Once we were all in L.A. Our crew went out to the West Coast to extract money from someone—we ran into Monya and were all together at a table in a Russian restaurant. This was Evsei, myself, my cousin Venya, Monya, and Mishka Zhlob.

---

* *Schvitz*—from Yiddish for "sweat," can also mean a "braggart."

Mishka Zhlob was a *vor v zakone* from the old school. Back in the Soviet Union, Evsei and Mishka Zhlob had worked together as part of the same pickpocketing crew. By which I mean, they did *konka* together. They reconnected in New York after emigration. Mishka Zhlob was originally from Odessa; he'd done more time in prison than Evsei. Much more. Many people in America knew Zhlob as a thief in law, a well-respected criminal from the Soviet days.

But if Evsei was cultured, witty, good at handling people, could converse on any topic, Mishka Zhlob was—well, it's unlikely he graduated from high school. He was a loud and crude, a criminal first and foremost. Zhlob was condescending—he'd always find a way to remind people of his high status among the thieves. Lots of people just avoided him. You know that type? They're off-putting, abrasive, simply unpleasant to be around. As much as people loved socializing with Evsei, they *hated* socializing with Mishka Zhlob.

In any event, we're out in L.A., and Monya Elson is at our table, and for whatever reason, Monya is running his mouth about the Russian prisons. He starts talking about the Central, one of the harshest prisons in the Soviet Union.*

I'll never forget how Mishka Zhlob stopped Monya in his tracks.

"Young man!" he shouts. "What system is in place at that prison?" Well, Monya had never been in the Central and, of course, doesn't know how to reply. He answers, "A round one."

"A *round* one?" At that point Mishka Zhlob says, "Listen, young man, I know you've never been to the Central. Shut your mouth and never again say you've been there!"

---

* Vladimir Prison, often called the Vladimir Central or simply the Central, is a maximum-security prison in Vladimir, Russia. Built in 1783, it was the largest prison in the USSR.

IF HE HADN'T BEEN A *BLATNOY* in the Soviet Union, Monya Elson certainly established himself as an ambitious young criminal in Brighton Beach's underworld of the 1980s and 1990s. In 1984, he was convicted in Israel for cocaine trafficking and served six years in prison. When he returned to Brooklyn in 1990, he was listed on the books as an employee of the Rasputin restaurant, a popular establishment owned by Alex and Victor Zilber, two prominent gangland figures in Brighton Beach. Elson quickly assembled a crew of enforcers and gunmen dubbed "Monya's Brigada," engaging in extortion, drug dealing, armed robbery, and murder for hire.

A lot had changed in the Brighton Beach underworld since 1984. With Evsei Agron dead and Marat Balagula now serving a twenty-one-year federal prison sentence, Monya Elson made no secret of his intention to take over the perch as the top-ranking Russian organized crime figure in New York. And by December 1990, he saw one obstacle blocking his path: Boris Nayfeld.

On January thirteenth, 1991, we're celebrating the Old New Year at the Paradise in Sheepshead Bay. I'm with Angela and some other friends like Dima Podlog. It was a nice party—good food, drinks, dancing. Nothing suspicious. Except that twisted *kozyol* Misha Sheferofsky—the guy who got busted with the half-million counterfeit dollars Fima Laskin gave us—he keeps buzzing around my table, saying "Boryek, how about taking me along in some business?" I told him, "Misha, stop angling for an invitation. I'm not taking you along in anything. I've got my business and you've got yours. Now get lost!"

Meanwhile, the whole time we were partying inside, my Lincoln Town Car was in a parking lot across from Paradise, and someone was crawling under it in the darkness, planting a grenade under the fuel tank. The guy also ran a Bickford fuse cord to the exhaust pipe. When I was driving home, the heat from the exhaust pipe was supposed to light the cord, and the fuse would activate the grenade.

Once the party was over, I left with Angela and Dima. I dropped Dima off at his place in Brooklyn, then took Angela home—she still lived with her parents in Starrett City. I dropped her off, went home to Staten Island, and parked the car there at my house. In the morning, Valentina took the kids to school in the Lincoln. In the meantime, I was sleeping off a hangover. That afternoon I drove into Brooklyn to my friend Zyamochka, on Brighton Fifth Street. I got there and parked the car across from this elementary school, went upstairs, and we started to play cards.

So we've been playing clabber for a few hours when Valentina calls me at Zyama's. She's at her job—working as a nurse at Coney Island Hospital. She sounds upset, tells Zyama she needs to talk to me. Some cops had called her at the hospital—the Lincoln was registered in her name and they tracked her down. "Boris, I just got a phone call from the police!"

"About what, Valya?"

"They said they found a bomb under the Lincoln. Go to the car— the police are still there with it."

I get the hell out of Zyama's, straightaway, leaving behind my .38, in case the cops frisk me. It was dark outside, and I had no idea what had happened during the afternoon. They'd closed down the streets. Cop cars were all over the place.

Someone who worked in the school, a security guard, spotted the fuse dangling under my Lincoln. He got down on his hands and knees and saw the grenade taped to the gas tank. The first war with Iraq was going on and people were on edge about possible terror attacks. So this security guard called the police. They evacuated the entire school. All the children and teachers had run out. They evacuated everyone who lived on the street, too. The NYPD bomb squad came and disarmed the grenade. The Lincoln was still parked there; both the trunk and the hood were left open. All these cops were surrounding it.

I walk over and very calmly tell them, "This is my Lincoln. Please tell me what's going on here."

They tell me to come to the Sixtieth Precinct house. I call up Dima Podlog—his English was good and I wanted him there to translate exactly what the *musors* were saying. A bunch of detectives and FBI agents were already there. They tell me, "Boris, we know who you are. We know what you do. Someone's trying to send you a message with that grenade."

A *message*? I knew it had nothing to do with sending a fucking message. Whoever planted the grenade was trying to take me out. The thing is, when we were out partying at Paradise, I'd parked in an unpaved lot with a lot of bumps and potholes, so as I pulled out, the fuse got knocked loose. Detached from the exhaust pipe. The cops kept fishing around wanting me to tell them if I had enemies who would want me dead. I told them, no, I couldn't think of anyone. Anyway, if someone had a problem with me, I was capable of handling it myself.

WITH BORIS'S COUSIN VENYA IN PRISON, with Ilya Zeltzer murdered, his most trusted muscle was now a fierce-eyed Georgian-Jewish gangster named Shalva Ukleba, a.k.a "Shaliko," a widely feared gunman whose father had been a *vor v zakone* in the Soviet Union.

I'm not waiting for the *musors* to find out anything. Right away, I start my own investigation. I grab Shaliko and together we drive around Brooklyn, trying to get to the bottom of it. I tell Shaliko: "First, we need to find out who's been buying *limonkas*." In Russian we call an

American grenade a *limonka*. A lemon. We went to see Borya Rezany,*
he was the most likely seller. We find him and I say, "Rezany, I know
you sell lemons, tell me who's bought them recently."

It took some running around before we unraveled the whole trail,
but it turns out this guy Rajik recently bought two of the lemons. Now
it's starting to make sense: Rajik is a Russian Jew who emigrated to
Israel when he was young, served in the Israeli Army, and we heard
he was experienced in mine laying and working with all sorts of
explosives.

Shaliko knew this Rajik well. We go and find him right away.
"Rajik! Where are the lemons?" I've got my .38 out, ready to shoot him
if need be. Rajik says, "Okay, I bought two, but I tested one out. I blew
it up on the beach. I wanted to make sure the lemons were working. I
still have the second one. I can show it to you."

I looked at Shaliko. We weren't sure if Rajik was lying to us—we
suspected he was—but he stuck to his story and managed to divert the
suspicions from himself.

Boris and Shaliko kept their ears to the street, sifting through rumors for who else might have been behind the grenade-planting job.

It's impossible to keep any secrets in Brighton Beach. Before long, we
start hearing that it was Monya Elson. People keep saying, "Monya sent
someone to plant the *limonka* on Biba." Makes sense. Because ever
since he came back from Israel, it was well-known that Monya took on
contract jobs from whoever.

Monya thought he could come back to Brighton after six years
away and take everything over. Since he'd been back, he'd started a lot

---

* *Rezany*—nickname meaning "Scarface." *Limonka* refers to a "lemon-shaped"
fragmentation hand grenade, like the famous Mk 2 grenade.

of beefs. He'd made a lot of enemies. At this time, in early 1991, his main beef wasn't with me, it was with Slavik Ovoschnik.

Vyacheslav Lyubarsky, a.k.a. Slava Ovoschnik, was a forty-nine-year-old racketeer, jewel thief, and heroin dealer who'd reportedly run afoul of Elson in a diamond deal gone bad.

On March 3, 1991, Ovoschnik was shot in the buttocks while in the hallway of his fourth-floor apartment building in Brighton Beach. Monya Elson was suspected of ordering the shooting, but no one was ever arrested or charged.

Then on May 14, 1991, in the middle of the afternoon, Elson was shot at point-blank range in front of the Café Arbat on Brighton Beach Avenue.

"People think that attack on Monya was my doing," Boris said.

But Slavik Ovoschnik ordered that hit. It was payback for Monya shooting him. Slavik paid a black guy to take out Monya. The guy walked up, got really close, and shot Monya five times in the stomach. But Monya struggled with the guy and knocked the gun away. Monya was badly hit. It was surprising that he lived, actually. But the doctors did surgery at Coney Island Hospital and managed to save him. He had a bunch of internal damage. They had to cut out one of his kidneys.

I came to visit him in the hospital, saw the state he was in. I kept pretending I wasn't aware of anything. I kept pretending I didn't suspect him of planting the lemon on me. Yet I already knew that he was my enemy. I knew that a war had already started between me and Monya.

For now, at least, the war remained undeclared.

Boris Nayfeld and Monya Elson played out a charade of friendship for months—exchanging feigned smiles and bald-faced lies.

At the hospital, I kept acting like everything was fine between us, I expressed my sympathies, wished Monya a speedy recovery. But I knew that the minute he recovered—*if* he recovered—I was going to fucking whack him.

This is even talked about in the Jewish law: if you know someone who wants to take your life away, you should beat them to the punch, and it won't be considered a sin.*

WHEN MONYA ELSON WAS FINALLY DISCHARGED from Coney Island Hospital, recovering at his home on East Sixteenth Street in Sheepshead Bay, Boris decided to pay him another visit.

I figure the best strategy for now is to keep Monya close. That way he won't suspect that I'm getting ready to take him out. I go to Monya's place with Dima Podlog. Monya knew we were always looking for ways to unload our product. We give Monya a package of thirty grams to sell. We were chatting in his place for a while. I remember Monya showing us a machine gun, a silencer, some counterfeit money. He says, "No problem, Biba, I'm going to help you sell this stuff."

After that, I also went and met with Slava Ovoschnik. He sometimes sold his own heroin—and he was looking for more. He knew my stuff was top quality. We worked out the terms of him moving some of my product. Knowing that he was in the middle of his own war, I asked him, "Slavik, do you want to get rid of Monya?" He tells me, "Of course." I say, "Well, if I find someone to take care of him for you, how much would you pay?"

"I'd pay forty thousand," Slavik says.

---

* Boris is loosely paraphrasing a passage from the Babylonian Talmud: "If someone comes to kill you, get up early in the morning to kill him first."

"Fine, it's in the bag."

I left Slava Ovoshnik's place feeling good: Slavik would help me unload some of my heroin, and he'd also be the one to pay for the hit on our mutual enemy.

Right before going to Europe, I meet with Monya one more time to talk about the heroin deal. I was trying my best to keep him close, but he must have picked up on my suspicion. "Boris," he says, "if anyone anywhere says *anything* about me, don't believe it. I'm not involved in any move against you."

He assured me he wasn't. That only confirmed to me that he was.

As I'm getting ready to fly to Belgium, I decide it's time to take out a contract on Monya. I went to another one of the guys who was moving heroin for me, Sasha Presaizen—we called him "Babushka"—who owed me $220,000 for two kilos.

I say, "Babushka, have you got someone to do a job? I'm putting a contract out on Monya." Sasha Presaizen tells me, yes, he's got a guy named Slepinin who used to be special ops in the Soviet Army.

I've never heard of this guy Slepinin. I don't know him personally. But when you're taking out a contract, that's for the best. You don't *want* to know too much. You always want to create some buffers, some insulation, between you and the guy pulling the trigger.

BY EARLY 1992, with the Soviet Union freshly broken up into fifteen separate nations, there was a brand-new wave of criminals arriving in Brooklyn.

"When I left the USSR in 1979 it was nearly impossible to get a gun," Boris says. "You couldn't even get a small pistol. We all carried knives. Now, back in Russia, weapons were for sale everywhere. Kalashnikovs. Rocket launchers. Trityl. Everything the Red Army had in stock was for sale. There was a complete breakdown of the old criminal code. Total lawlessness. From 1991 to 1994, in Russia, a human life was worth nothing. This was the time when the first killers for hire emerged. If someone needed to be taken care of, there were many guys with combat experience willing to hire themselves out to do the jobs."

Aleksander Slepinin was one of the more imposing mob mercenaries to arrive in Brooklyn. Six foot five, three hundred pounds, Slepinin was a heavily tattooed forty-four-year-old whose résumé, in addition to Special Forces training, included expertise in a variety of martial arts and time in a Soviet prison camp.

I ask, "Babushka, how much would your guy want?" He tells me a hundred thousand. "Okay," I say, "you owe me two hundred twenty for the two kilos, just knock a hundred off for the contract, and you'll owe me one twenty." He says, "Fine, it's a deal."

"But listen," I say, "I need this done while I'm over in Europe. I'll give you one month. If you don't take him out within one month, the contract is off. I'm going to come back and take Monya out myself."

I get over to Belgium—I'm there in Antwerp less than a week—when Monya calls me from New York. He says, "Boris, guess what? I've found the guy who planted the lemon on you!"

"And?"

"And it'll only cost you a quarter* for me to get rid of him." I tell him, "Monya, I don't need the guy who *planted* it. I need to know who gave the contract!" He says, "All right, if you don't want it done, then—"

"Don't lay a finger on him," I say, and hang up.

Not even a week later, Monya calls me again. "Boryek, when is your birthday?" he says. I tell him, "October." He says, "I'm giving you an

---

* $25,000.

early present: I'm going to get rid of that guy. Free of charge." I say,
"Monya, didn't you hear me the first time? Leave him *alone*! I need to
talk to this guy. If you take him out, I'll never get to the bottom of who
ordered the contract!"

Well, a few days pass and Shaliko calls me in Antwerp telling me that
Rajik got shot. Monya and his crew drove up to Rajik's car and started
blasting him with a machine gun. Rajik drops down inside the car and
pretends he's dead. But he's just wounded in the hand. Rajik finds his
way to a hospital and gets himself stitched up.

Obviously, Monya's trying to cover his tracks—he's trying to get rid
of anyone who can tie him to the lemon, who can confirm the whole
story. I'm in my villa in Antwerp and Shaliko tells me, "Boris, I'm
sitting here with Rajik. Turns out when we were doing our investigation
about the lemons, he lied to us. He admits it *was* him who planted the
lemon on you." I say, "Fine, tell Rajik I'm going to fly over soon and
we'll talk in person." Shaliko says, "No, he doesn't want to meet with
you. He's scared." I say, "Fine, just pass him the phone."

Rajik comes on the line and, yes, he's afraid. Afraid of me, afraid
of Monya. He says, "Boris, believe me, I didn't want to do the job, I
didn't attach the lemon properly on *purpose*—so that you wouldn't get
blown up."

I knew that he was lying. I only survived because I'd knocked that
fucking Bickford fuse loose in the bumpy parking lot. "Well, the fact
that it didn't explode means nothing," I say. "But if that's your story, all
right, that's your story. You didn't want it to explode. Rajik, what I need
to know is this: Who gave the contract? Who sent you?"

"It was Monya," he says.

CHAPTER 23

THE WAR

With Rajik's help, we start working backwards and piece it all together. Monya accepted the contract, but it originated with Fima Laskin in Germany. Fima held a grudge against me since that time I turned him down on his suggestion to rob M&S together. He decided to send that snake Misha Sheferofsky over to New York. Sheferofsky was the messenger, the middleman, relaying the proposal to Monya that they kill me.

It made sense to me now why Sheferofsky was buzzing around my table on Old New Year's Eve at Paradise, pestering me that we should do some business together. While Rajik was outside planting the lemon under my Lincoln, Sheferofsky was there to have eyeballs on me the night I was supposed to die.

They figured, if they get rid of Biba, they can completely take over. Fima Laskin can take over everything I've got in Europe, my *krysha* operation at M&S—he'll replace me and provide protection to Milik and Richard. And Monya can take over my heroin operation in America.

Yes, I was angry. I wanted revenge. But it also made sense to me. It's part of the criminal life. People see a crew with a strong leader, a crew making good profits, and they start scheming to remove that leader and to take over his businesses. Guys like Fima Laskin and Monya Kishinevsky* figure they can kill a boss, then simply step into his spot and reap the rewards. It's a dangerous game, though, because there will always be people inside a crew who know who did it and why. When all's said and done, there's always going to be payback.†

Unlike the Mafia, Russian organized crime has no prohibition against killing a boss. Without a "commission" or overarching body to enforce rules, any position of leadership is extremely precarious. The life of a boss is always at risk.

A few weeks later, Monya's *brigada* struck. At 1:20 a.m. on Sunday, January 12, 1992, Vyacheslav Lyubarsky, his wife, Nellie, and their twenty-six-year-old son, Vadim, were coming home from a night out at the National restaurant when they were ambushed. In the hallway of their apartment building on Brighton Eleventh Street, a gunman dressed all in black approached from the shadows of an alcove. Slava and Vadim were armed with unlicensed guns—a .38 revolver and a semiautomatic pistol—but were apparently caught unaware.

The assassin shot each man multiple times, killing them, leaving Nellie Lyubarsky screaming but unharmed. He quickly escaped and was never apprehended.

---

* "Monya Kishinevsky" refers to Monya Elson—Monya from Kishinev, Moldova.

† Mikhail Sheferofsky, a.k.a. "Mihail Safer," died of natural causes on November 2, 2012.

"That hit was organized by Monya," Boris said. "He had this relative Oleg—well, I don't know if he was really a relative, but he called him a nephew. Oleg was Monya's main triggerman. Later on, after this Oleg had himself been killed, Monya pinned all the murders he was ever charged with on him. You know, because dead men tell no tales."

The double homicide received widespread media attention: The *New York Times* reported on the Lyubarsky murders as an illustration of the escalating mob-related crime wave rocking the Soviet émigré enclave of Little Odessa. The NYPD had no leads, and for years the investigation went nowhere. It wasn't solved until 1995, when Monya Elson was charged in a federal indictment for ordering the murders of Slava and Vadim Lyubarsky.

THE TIME WAS GETTING SHORT. The month deadline was nearly up; Boris Nayfeld was waiting at his villa in Antwerp, growing frustrated that he still hadn't heard a word about the contract on Monya Elson.

I'm about to fly back to New York and I figure, why spend a hundred grand, when I can take care of the job personally? I get Sasha Presaizen on the phone: "Call your guy and tell him that the contract is off. It's taken too long. I'll handle it myself."

Presaizen tells his guy Slepinin, that I've called off the contract. Slepinin turns around and calls Monya, saying, "There was a contract put out on you. I'll sell you the information." He asks Monya to pay him fifty grand and Monya agrees. Slepinin says, "Bring the money tomorrow and I'll tell you who put out the hit on you."

On June 23, 1992, the bearlike Aleksander Slepinin was parked in his Cadillac Seville on a quiet residential street in Sunset Park; despite his reputation as a veteran assassin, Slepinin seems to have been wholly unprepared for the vicious double-cross to come.

> Slepinin's sitting in his car when Monya and his guys show up with the fifty grand. Once Monya flashes the money, Slepinin tells them all about the contract, that he got this job from Sasha Presaizen, and that it was me, Biba, who'd put a hit on Monya.
>
> But now that Monya's got the information, he figures, why spend the fifty thousand bucks? It's easier just to whack this fucking guy. The story we all heard is that before they shot him, Slepinin begged for his life, told them he had small children, but Monya and his guys just laughed and whacked him anyway.

Police found Aleksander Slepinin slumped in the front seat of his Cadillac, shot three times in the back and then finished with two bullets to the head. Once again, no arrests were made until 1995, when Monya Elson was indicted and charged with Slepinin's murder.

THE END FOR EFIM LASKIN, "the Beautiful Czar," who'd reportedly ordered the hit on Boris Nayfeld, was even more gruesome. On September 27, 1991, Bavarian police officers found the body of fifty-two-year-old Laskin sprawled on the hood of his red BMW 850i in the parking lot of a Munich swimming pool. One German news account described it as a "bestial crime." Witnesses reported a struggle in which several attackers had savaged Laskin with knives, stabbing him in the neck and chest eleven times, piercing his heart, liver, kidney, and intestines. Official reports were that the former amateur boxer had bled to death. Investigators suspected that Laskin had fallen "victim to a power struggle within the Russian mafia."

It was not until 1999 that an arrest was made: Aleksander Timoshenko, a.k.a. Aleksander Bor or "Timokha"—a thief in law from

Gomel, Belarus, and a close associate of Boris Nayfeld, was apprehended in Munich in connection with Laskin's murder. Police had found traces of his DNA at the crime scene; a bloodstained handkerchief and wig had been left behind by Laskin's assailants.

Prosecutors maintained that there were at least two other accomplices present during Laskin's murder.

Boris Nayfeld has long been suspected of involvement in the murder of his erstwhile friend, though he was never charged, and he has always denied participating in the hit on Fima Laskin. "God punished him," Boris told me.

In 2003, a Munich court sentenced Bor to life in prison for the murder of Laskin. In his defense, Bor claimed to have been present but not a participant at the 1991 "altercation," which he called a "spontaneous killing"; he pointed the finger at two accomplices, both of whom were now, conveniently, deceased. Bor's life sentence was overturned on appeal, and in a second trial he received thirteen years.

Released on parole in 2006, he returned to Russia. In January 2014, in Moscow, Bor was charged with drug possession and on camera, to members of Russian law enforcement, he categorically denied being a thief in law. Such a renunciation is a capital offense by the strict code of the *vory*. In May 2014, as he was exiting his Mercedes to attend church in a tony suburb of Moscow, the fifty-year-old Bor was murdered by an assassin who ran up to him from behind and fired several close-range shots from a pistol.

"When I flew back to America from Antwerp, I hid out at my friend Magadan's apartment in Brooklyn," Boris said.[*]

---

[*] Alik Magadan, real name Oleg Asmakov.

I waited for Shaliko, to locate Monya. As soon as Shaliko gave me a signal, we would make our move. Our plan was to kill Monya and his entire crew.

But we couldn't find Monya in New York because by then he had gotten the hell out to L.A. The cops were looking for him after the murder of Slava Ovoschnik and his son.

Monya was supposed to be taken out by a contract killer while he was there in California, but that hit also got completely fucked up.

This attempt on Monya Elson's life occurred on November 7, 1992, in Plummer Park in West Hollywood, a popular meeting place for Soviet émigrés. Elson and the gunman struggled over the semiautomatic pistol; in the fracas, the assassin managed to get a shot off, but only wounded Elson in the arm. At the hospital, Elson gave detectives a fake name and said he'd been shot while fending off a mugger who wanted to steal his Rolex watch.

"The hit man ran up on Monya and had a clean shot," Boris says.

He pulled the trigger, but the gun jammed. The firing pin got caught in the lining of his jacket.

So Monya goes to hospital to get stitched up, and two days later, when he's supposed to be picked up by his friend, a different hit man, an Armenian, crawls under the car to plant an explosive, but this time, the detonator goes off early and the Armenian's hand gets blown off.

After that, my war with Monya went back and forth for at least a year, both of us trying to take each other out. Honestly, whatever else I was doing—handling the heroin business or working for M&S in Europe—I never stopped trying to kill Monya.

THEN, during one of his frequent business trips to Russia for M&S International in late 1992, Boris Nayfeld learned that Elson had put an enormous bounty on his head.

> Monya knew I was in Moscow and he got in contact with this Balashikhinsky* group leader named Seryoga Boroda. He placed a $500,000 contract with Boroda to have me taken out while I was in Russia.
> And he might have got me, too. But one of my very good friends was Rafik Svo, a powerful thief in law, who was also close with Seryoga Boroda.

In the early 1990s postcommunist Russia, Sergei Kruglov, a.k.a. "Boroda" ("the Beard"), and Rafael Bagdasarian, a.k.a. "Rafik Svo," were two of the most high-profile criminal authorities in the Moscow *bratva*.

> Seryoga Boroda immediately gives Rafik Svo a tip-off. He says, "Listen, Rafik, your friend that's visiting here from New York, you better let him know there's a contract out on him." He gave Rafik all the information, and Rafik passed it on to me.
> "Who took out the contract, Rafik?"
> "Monya Kishinevsky."
> "For how much?"
> Rafik tells me, "Half a million."
> Now, I'm skeptical. Sounds far-fetched. I'm thinking, "That figure's awfully high." I was aware someone could order a hit on me while I was in Russia, but I didn't think they'd pay half a million.
> A couple of weeks go by and Rafik comes and tells me, "Boris,

---

* "Balashikhinsky group"—refers to gangs from Balashikha, a suburb of Moscow.

Monya has upped it now. He's offering a million to take you out. And he
wants it done quickly."

Naturally, for that kind of money—a million bucks—someone's
going to accept the job. Doesn't matter if Monya will really pay it, that
million-dollar figure sounds magical to most people. So now I'm wary.
Watching my back all the time.

One night, we're driving to one of our stores—M&S had five stores
in Moscow. Besides clothes and electronics, we sold lots of luxury
items. I'm with a girlfriend and my bodyguard—he's driving us in a
Mercedes 500 sedan. I wanted to pop by and pick up some Rémy
Martin XO cognac and chocolates to take back to the apartment. Our
store was located not far from the Kremlin. There was a construction
site across the street, surrounded by a fence.

As we're driving closer, we get caught up in some heavy traffic. It's
about eight o'clock, and the traffic slows to a crawl as we get closer to
Red Square. For some reason—I still can't explain it—I changed my
mind. I suddenly had a bad feeling about going to the store. "Fuck it,"
I said, "this is taking too long—just turn the car around." My driver
made an immediate U-turn and went back to our apartment. The
next day Rafik Svo found out about the snipers waiting for me in the
construction site. Had I got out of the car at the store, no doubt, the
two guys would have shot me dead.

I didn't know it, of course, but there were two assassins armed
with machine guns in the darkness, hiding behind the fence. They
were laying in wait for me. As soon as I arrived, they were supposed to
open fire.

Just a few days after that attempt, me, Rafik Svo, and Petrik—another
thief in law—are riding in Seryoga Boroda's Mercedes. Suddenly, a call
from Monya comes in. Boroda answers it on the speaker, and we all
hear Monya asking: "Well, what's happening with our acquaintance?

How much longer until the job gets completed?"

Boroda says, "It's extremely hard for me to get close to him because he hangs with thieves in law."

At that, Monya says: "I don't give a *fuck* about these thieves in law. To me, any street cleaner capable of pulling the trigger is more important than a thief in law!"

There was silence in the car. I looked at Rafik Svo and Petrik. Since these thieves in law were sitting in the car and overheard the entire conversation, I figured this was surely the sentence for Monya.*

BUT MONYA ELSON WOULD PROVE to be a remarkably resilient target. The third attempt on his life came on July 26, 1993, as he was coming home with his wife, Marina, and his bodyguard, Oleg Zapivakmine.

In the middle of the afternoon, Elson's black Lexus pulled up in front of his redbrick apartment at 2553 East Sixteenth Street in Sheepshead Bay; a white Oldsmobile screeched to a stop. Two gunmen opened fire—one wielding a Streetsweeper 12-gauge shotgun and the other an Uzi. Monya was shot in the back, thigh, and left ankle, Oleg Zapivakmine, wounded in the stomach, returned fire with his pistol.

Marina Elson was hit the worst: she took cover behind some garbage cans—likely saving her life—and was shot point-blank with shotgun pellets in the face, throat, and chest.

According to court documents and a report in the New York *Daily News*, the unsuccessful assassination attempt had been orchestrated by Igor Grafman, owner of the Metropol restaurant, and one of Boris Nayfeld's closest associates. The alleged shooters were Alex Magadan and Boris Grigoriev, the Oldsmobile driven by Slava Konstaninovsky—one

* Implied death sentence.

of a pair of Ukrainian twins, known in the underworld as "the Brothers Karamazov."

Two months later, on September 24, 1993, Oleg Zapivakmine was shot and killed in front of his Brooklyn home while changing a tire on his car. The execution-style murder has never been solved.

Marina Elson required reconstructive surgery on her face; after she recovered from her wounds, Monya Elson left the United States, relocating his operations to Fano, Italy, where he was reputedly under the protection of powerful Kiev-born mob boss Semion Mogilevich, a.k.a. "the Brainy Don."

Immediately after the shooting, in 1993, according to the FBI, Elson vowed a vendetta against his would-be assassins: "He said that his revenge will not occur in the United States but will happen somewhere overseas."

—

Later that year, Boris Nayfeld was himself overseas—busily stockpiling military-grade explosives in Poland and drawing some unwanted scrutiny in Belgium.

"In December 1993, I went to Warsaw to do a munitions deal when I learned I was being watched by the *musors*," Boris recalls. "I came to Poland to buy a suitcase with ten remotely controlled explosive charges. These charges can be attached to the bottom of a car, then detonated from a distance. Each charge contained a hundred grams of trityl. I paid just over ten thousand bucks for the explosives. But while I was in Warsaw, I got the tip-off from Belgium: 'Boris, there's surveillance on your villa. Watch out!'"

CHAPTER 24

THE *MUSORS*

I learned I was being watched just by chance. When I went to Poland, the M&S offices in the Diamond Quarter got burglarized, and the thieves got away with a small safe with about fifteen thousand dollars inside.

Our manager at M&S was a Belgian guy by the name of Frank. Frank gets introduced to a girl who's part of the police investigating team, they go out for a few drinks, dancing at a disco, and then she says, "Wanna see something?" She takes him back to some special room in the Antwerp police department and shows him a video screen. Frank immediately recognizes that the camera is locked in on the front of my villa, showing all the comings and goings.

All the time I was in Germany and in Poland, I had friends of mine, thieves in law, staying at my villa. Whenever I was in Belgium, various criminal friends of mine like Rafik Svo, Timokha, Petrik—they all used to come to visit me.

Now, I realize I need to get them out of my place. I've also got to get this suitcase of explosives inside and hidden in the secret storage area where I keep my guns. As I'm driving up to the villa, I'm staring out the window, trying to figure out where the fuck a camera might have been positioned. Finally, I spot it: inside the second-story window of the villa across the street. There's a specially built casement concealing the camera. As I drive by, I catch a glimpse of a bearded guy behind the window, watching my villa's entrance. Turns out to be a special undercover unit of the Belgian police, not regular cops. They rented out that villa, pretending to live there, filming everyone coming and going.

I drive on without stopping and drop the car off at the M&S company garage. Then I take a taxi home and tell the thieves in law staying at my place that they needed to leave because I'm under surveillance and, at any moment, the cops might be at the door and every one of us will be fucking arrested. My friends pack up and leave immediately.

When you're a criminal, being tailed by strange cars or having your house under surveillance simply comes with the territory. I make sure that all my weapons and the explosives I bought in Poland are securely stashed away, so I figure it's safe to fly to America for New Year's.

When I get to America, I don't go straight home to New York. Valentina was with the kids at the apartment we had in Miami Beach, so I make a connection straight to Florida. I spent New Year's there with my wife and kids, then I came back to New York City on January fourth. My passport was about to expire, and I needed to renew it before I could fly back to Belgium.

Even though my villa in Antwerp was being watched, I thought it was just routine surveillance, not connected to the *musors* in America. I didn't believe that the DEA was on to me.

IN FACT, BY EARLY 1994, the Drug Enforcement Administration had pegged Boris Nayfeld as a "high-ranking member of Russian organized crime" and powerful international heroin trafficker. Special agents working out of the DEA's New York office were waiting for the most opportune moment to pounce. For more than two years, the DEA and prosecutors in the Southern District of New York had been using undercover agents, confidential informants, and court-authorized wiretaps, methodically building a case on Boris Nayfeld's drug-smuggling operation.

"It all started to fall apart for us when two of our mules got busted at JFK," Boris recalls.

These two guys Grisha Luydoyed recruited for us. I used to give Luydoyed two thousand dollars for every mule he recruited. Well, Luydoyed—being a fucking idiot, besides being greedy—recruits two mules who are junkies.

They fly to Warsaw to buy furniture—Luydoyed owned a couple of furniture stores in Brooklyn—and they come back with four kilos of pure China White strapped to them. It's a nine-hour flight from Warsaw to JFK—you think a couple of junkies carrying four keys on their bodies are going to resist the urge to get high? They go into the bathroom right on the fucking plane and start shooting up. Of course, a flight attendant sees them getting high, nodding off in the middle of the aisle, and when the plane lands, she turns them in.

They were decent enough guys, actually. They weren't snitches. They were just junkies. They kept their mouths shut and took their sentences: one got five years in prison, the other got seven. I helped them out—I gave their families money to pay for the lawyers. But the *musors* found business cards on them linking them to Luydoyed's furniture business. Now the feds are looking for heroin coming on flights from Warsaw. And they're also watching Luydoyed.

Then another of the mules that Grisha recruited, this kid— Moysil, Moysin—I forget his fucking name! The fatso greasy one who testified—fuck! *Moysif!* Yes. This kid Moysif runs into the *musors*. He sells directly to undercover DEA agents.

Boris is referring to Alexander Moysif, a twenty-four-year-old, part-time limousine driver who made several heroin sales to an undercover DEA special agent named Louis Cardinali. The DEA also had court-authorized wiretaps on calls between Moysif and Dima Podlog, allegedly talking about heroin using code words like "potatoes" and "baby formula." The investigative trail led to three Sicilian-born heroin dealers—Calogero Badalamenti, John Romano, and Giuseppe Genna—with reported ties to New York Mafia crime families, who were buying product from Moysif. In April 1992, thirteen arrests were made, including Dima Podlog and Alexander Moysif. "Now the *musors* have Dima and Moysif and these greaseballs. As always, they work their way up the ladder. When they come looking for Grisha Luydoyed, he goes on the lam—he flies to Europe. They caught him trying to cross the border from Hungary to Rumania."

In September 1992, Grisha Roizes was arrested in possession of heroin in Rumania and held in a jail cell there. "This DEA agent flies over to Rumania and he flips Grisha Luydoyed right away. I mean, Luydoyed didn't even put up a fight. He immediately gives the DEA everything they needed to bring down our whole operation."

"IN DECEMBER OF 1993, I made my last shipment of heroin," Boris recalls matter-of-factly.

Not from Warsaw. I sent it from Belgium. I've got four kilos with me at my villa in Antwerp. I tell one of the guys working for me, "Why don't you fly over to New York with this stuff? If you bring in these four kilos, I'll pay you $20,000." Well, he smudges coffee all over the heroin packages, to ward off the dogs. Four kilos. That's too much to tape to your body, so he packed everything into a carry-on bag.

He later told me what happened when he landed at JFK. Because of the mules who've flipped, the DEA was closely watching this flight from Belgium. They let the passengers off only five at a time. Everyone's told to place their carry-on bags on the floor and a dog runs around, sniffing everything. This guy told me his heart dropped into his heels when one of the dogs started sniffing his bag—but the strong smell of coffee masked the heroin. He went through customs without problem and got the heroin into Brooklyn. I gave him his $20,000, but it was the last shipment of heroin we ever got through—those were our final four kilos.

That January of 1994, even though Dima and a bunch of our mules had been arrested and charged, I still didn't feel the walls closing in. I didn't know Grisha Luydoyed was cooperating. I didn't think the DEA knew about me. Dima insulated me completely. I thought, well, if I lay low, if I don't move any more heroin for a while, they won't be able to connect the operation to me. I also figured if the feds had a solid case, then why didn't they arrest me in April 1992, when they brought in Dima and Moysif and that bunch of Sicilians?

I go into Manhattan and get my new passport, then I buy a ticket to Brussels. I was planning to fly back to Belgium on January twelfth. But as I'm getting ready to leave home, I start getting a strange feeling. Something's definitely wrong outside my house.

I'm looking out my bedroom window and see a couple of cars I don't recognize driving by. My place in Staten Island is just half a block from this huge nature preserve. It's not a through street. But that morning I notice a couple sedans heading toward the park that morning, and I keep waiting for them to come back. They never do. I'm thinking, Okay, this is strange: who's hanging out in the fucking nature preserve in the middle of winter?

I'm already feeling edgy as I walk out of the house, put my luggage in the trunk, and get into the car. Valentina is at the wheel. She's driving me to JFK. As soon as we pull out, all these cars race up and block the street. Sirens, shouting, DEA agents jumping out of their cars telling me not to fucking move—I get out of the car, they frisk me, cuff me, and put in the back of one of the DEA agents' cars.

Once I'm arrested, they take me to the DEA office in Manhattan. The agents tell me I'm suspected of being in the narcotics trade and right away—without having a lawyer present—they start asking whether I want to sign a deal offering to cooperate. At that time, cooperation was out of the question.

"Fuck no—I'm not going to sign anything," I tell them. As far as I'm concerned, they've got zero evidence of my involvement with drugs. I'm being charged with conspiracy to distribute narcotics under the RICO Act. They give me my charges to read. The papers list the names of people who I've never had any dealings with, whether drug related or any other sort of criminal activities. Of the seven or eight people listed in the charges, I knew maybe two.

Dima Podlog was managing things for me—I didn't want to know any of the names of the mules. I didn't want to know the names of the buyers. I'm sitting in the DEA headquarters, saying to myself, "This is a frame-up. These *musors* are trying to pin things on me that I had nothing to do with. It shouldn't be too hard for a good defense lawyer to smash their accusations to pieces."

The problem was my understanding of the American jurisprudence system was based strictly on what I'd seen in the Hollywood movies. Somebody gets indicted, charged, arrested—then they hire these big-shot lawyers to defend them; the lawyers cross-examine witnesses and persuade the jury to acquit.

I was looking at the American justice system through rose-colored glasses. I figured that since I never got caught red-handed in possession of drugs, there were no photos or phone calls, no direct evidence linking me to drugs, it would be difficult for the government to prove this case.

I was badly fucking mistaken. Only much later did I realize why. In America, unlike Russia, you don't need to be caught red-handed. You don't need to be caught in the act. The only thing the government needs is for a couple of people to get arrested, agree to cooperate and testify against you in front of a jury, and that testimony alone can put you away for many, many years. It was the first time I was hearing about big conspiracy cases—the RICO laws. Prior to that, I didn't know fuck all about RICO.

As the agents are taking me over to MCC, I'm saying to myself, "I don't think they have a case, but if I have to do some time—fuck it, I'll do some time. I'm no stranger to it."

Boris arrived in the high-rise federal lockup in Lower Manhattan known as the Metropolitan Correctional Center (MCC) on the afternoon of January 12, 1994.

When I got to MCC it was really overcrowded at the time. The MDC* in Brooklyn was under renovations, and ever since [Rudy] Giuliani began his war against the Mafia, the federal jails in Manhattan and Brooklyn were filled with *Italyakhas*.

Once I got to the seventh floor of MCC—the general population floor—I met many of the *Italyakhas* I'd known since the gasoline business in the mideighties. An underboss, some lieutenants, a few soldiers. We reminisced about the good times in gasoline, all the money we had rolling in, split fifty-fifty between Russians and Italians. They always invited me to dinner. These guys would make their own spaghetti and sauce. Good cooks. And they had good advice. The

---

* Metropolitan Detention Center in downtown Brooklyn, the other major federal lockup in New York City.

Italyakhas knew so much more about the system than me: the defense lawyers, the prosecutors, the judges, the different federal prisons. One thing they kept telling me was not to rush to hire a lawyer. Why? One of them says, "Because lawyers are people who hold nothing holy. The only thing holy to a lawyer is fucking money!"

One morning I get called downstairs to see a lawyer. "What's going on?" I ask the guard. "I never called for a lawyer." But these defense lawyers all read the newspapers closely. When I got arrested, it was all over the news that this Russian mob boss was accused of running an international heroin-trafficking ring from Thailand to Poland to New York. I go downstairs and see this Jewish lawyer. He's about seventy-five years old. Maybe older. His hair is dyed dark brown and he has a big, bright smile of white teeth. "Boris, trust me—I'm the only lawyer in town who can help you beat this case."

I ask him, "How much would it cost?" He tells me, "Up front, it will cost you $80,000 to retain me. And once we go to trial, of course, there will be separate payments."

"Okay, I'll think about it."

When I get back up to my floor, I talk it over with the *Italyakhas*. I tell them the lawyer's name. They all start laughing at me. "Boris! Of course, he wants eighty grand up front," one of the *Italyakhas* laughs. "Boris, that fucking guy's dying of cancer—he won't live long enough to represent you at trial."

MCC was so overcrowded, they kept moving all of us around. Upstate to Otisville, back to MCC, back up to Otisville. You'd spend three or four months in Otisville, then be taken to MCC again to work with a lawyer, face new charges, and so on. On top of everything, preparations go so slowly it's possible to spend two or three years waiting inside MCC prior to trial. At one point, with all this shuttling back and forth, I ran into Dima Podlog—not in Otisville, but at a federal jail out on

Long Island. Dima had already been inside for about twelve or fifteen months.

Dima told me that the feds had offered him a deal of seven years if he pled guilty, but he refused. He said, "No, Boris, we're gonna win this."

Dima was wearing the same rose-colored glasses as me at first. He went to trial and a lot of our former mules went to trial as well, even though none of them were caught red-handed. None of them were busted while in possession of drugs. The government case was based solely on two or three guys who started to secretly cooperate with the DEA.

On April 27, 1993, Podlog was convicted in the Southern District of New York of conspiracy to distribute narcotics. On October 5, 1994, he was sentenced to serve a term of twenty-seven years in federal prison.

Our Dimka, instead of getting seven years by pleading guilty, ended up getting twenty-seven years after losing the trial. Meanwhile, the guys who pleaded guilty and cooperated, like Grisha Luydoyed and this fatso Moysif—he was the government's main witness against Dima—they all got released.

The big stroke of luck for me was this long stretch—more than six months—I spent in Otisville. I started to talk to a bunch of our mules and other guys who'd been sentenced already. They were the first guys to teach me how the federal system worked. I'd never met these mules—Dima buffered me from all that. One was an Israeli named Adam—in Russian we call him Adik.

Adik and another mule come over to me while we're walking the yard. Adik says, "Boris, we need you on the outside—we need you back on the street."

I tell him, "How the hell am I supposed to get out on the street? I've been locked up for fucking months. I don't know if I'm in the world of the living or the dead. I don't even have a court date. I don't know when I'll go to trial—"

"Trial? What *trial?* Forget that word!" Adik says, "Boris, ninety-nine percent of the time, the feds win at trial. You don't go to trial, you negotiate. You give the feds something they want, then they cut your time." I'm walking along, shaking my head. The feds have been pressuring me to give up my cousin Venya and my close friends. I keep telling them no way. This guy Adik stares at me and says, "Listen, Boris, have you got an enemy?"

I laugh. "Of course, who doesn't have enemies?" These mules haven't been living under a rock. They know all about my war with Monya Elson.

"Here's what you do—you get your lawyer to write a letter. You offer to give them your enemy."

"How does that help me?"

"Have your lawyer make a proposal to the government. Say you won't give up anyone close to you, but if they want Monya, you'll testify that he tried to kill you and you tried to kill him. Offer that to the government. If they want Monya bad enough, they're going to work out a deal with you."

Around the same time there was another guy I met up in Otisville—his name is Roberto Alcaino. A Chilean Jew. He was the top money launderer for Pablo Escobar in the U.S. When I met him, he'd been inside for many years already. He'd taken a plea in this big cocaine case out in California in the 1980s. If he'd gone to trial and lost, he would have got life, but by pleading guilty and cooperating he worked out a deal for fifteen years.

Roberto says, "Boris, you've got to negotiate. You can't beat the feds at trial—*no one* ever does—but you always work out a deal if you give them something they really want."

I saw what happened to Dima. I didn't want to go to trial, lose, and

wind up with a sentence of thirty years, forty years, life. I wanted to
see the streets again before I was eighty fucking years old. I just had
to figure out if what these guys told me was true—if you could cut your
sentence by giving up information on your enemy.

By THE MID-1990s, the code of silence was breaking down within most
ethnic organized crime groups: high-ranking mobsters who would never
have spoken to the feds were now cutting deals, negotiating plea bargains with prosecutors, and offering to be cooperating witnesses instead
of spending long terms in prison.

Cosa Nostra's once-sacrosanct oath of omertà, first breached by Joe
Valachi in the 1960s, had been utterly shattered in the early 1990s when
high-ranking mafiosi like Alphonse "Little Al" D'Arco, acting boss of
the Lucchese crime family, and Sammy "the Bull" Gravano, underboss
of the Gambino crime family, cut highly publicized deals to cooperate
and testify against fellow mobsters for the government.

Things were no different with Russian organized crime. Hardened
gangsters, raised with the ethos of the *vorovskoy mir,* criminals who'd
always scoffed at the idea of cooperating with the Soviet state, began
offering information and testimony to U.S. federal prosecutors in exchange for reduced prison time.

This sea change among the Russian mob initially surprised U.S.
authorities; for decades they'd believed that criminals from the USSR—
men who'd endured the hardship of Soviet prisons and draconian threats
from the KGB—would neither crack under police questioning nor betray each other: too great was the stigma of being labeled a *kozyol* or a
musor.

But by the mid-1990s prosecutors found that Russian mobsters, like
almost all other organized criminals in the United States, were willing to
provide whatever information was necessary to get themselves out of jail.

BORIS NAYFELD HAS ALWAYS RATIONALIZED his decision to cut a deal and cooperate with government as a continuation of the unfinished war with Monya Elson. To hear Boris tell it, talking to the prosecutors was a smart and strategic chess move. His feud with Monya Elson could continue in the U.S. justice system, using prosecutors and defense counsel as proxies rather than hit men armed with grenades and machine guns.

I get transferred back to MCC and I talk with my attorney, David Schoen. "Tell the prosecutors I'll confess that I'm guilty of trying to kill Monya Elson," I say. "Monya planted a grenade under my car. I take responsibility for all assassination attempts on Monya. If this information is suitable to the government, I'm prepared to testify against Monya if it come down to it."

My lawyer wrote the letter. We stated specifically we'd only give them Monya Elson. They knew Monya was hiding out in Italy. If they got their hands on him, I said, I would testify against Monya. If the prosecutors had said, "No, that's not good enough, Boris, we want information on your close friends, too," I would've refused. I would've gone to trial, even though I was looking at thirty to life if convicted.

In the U.S. federal court system, this cooperation agreement is known as a 5K1.1 motion, an official letter that prosecutors write on behalf of defendants who have provided "substantial assistance" so that the judge may impose a lesser sentence. Since the terms of Boris Nayfeld's 5K1.1 agreement are sealed, there's no way of knowing for certain how much assistance he provided the DEA and federal prosecutors.

But over the years, various legal experts and Russian underworld figures have scoffed at the idea that a defendant could offer such narrowly defined cooperation, testifying "only against an enemy."

"Not squealing completely is like being half pregnant," an unnamed organized crime figure told a reporter for the BBC Russian Service when asked about Boris Nayfeld's claims.*

"I didn't help the feds put one guy in prison besides Monya," Boris insists. "When I got out, all my close friends were still free. The feds put a lot of pressure on me to give up all the guys close to me—Venya, Kadik, Igor—but I refused. I didn't betray a single friend. No one from my inner circle. I only gave them Monya."

On March 8, 1995, Elson was arrested in Fano, Italy, and extradited to the United States in April of that year to face charges of murder, attempted murder, extortion, and conspiracy.

Facing the prospect of serving life inside a federal prison, Elson, too, would soon agree to cooperate with the United States government.

* Vladimir Kozlovsky, "Biba and the Mountain of Heroin: The Last Boss of the Russian Mafia in New York," BBC Russian Service, July 28, 2017, https://www .bbc.com/russian/features-40749471.

CHAPTER 25

FAIRTON

While waiting to testify against Monya Elson, Boris Nayfeld was
sent to the Federal Correctional Institution (FCI) Fairton in New
Jersey.

"Fairton is a small federal camp, with a free-standing building that
houses guys who agree to cooperate with the government, to testify as
witnesses, or guys who are already in the Witness Protection Program,"
Boris says.

Compared to prison in the Soviet Union, well, Fairton is a fucking
paradise. Every day the food was excellent. You could eat anything
and as much of it as you wanted. We had a good gym and a backyard
with a basketball court and a bocce court. And there were so many
interesting characters—Italian Mafia bosses, Latino drug traffickers,
black gangsters who decided to snitch on their gangs. Talking to these
guys for hours, I can't say I was ever bored.

We even had wine! There were these lifers, guys who'd been there
for eighteen or twenty years already, they used to squeeze fresh oranges

and make wine, then bring it around and pour it into our coffee cups. I'll never forget this one lifer who'd been there for something like twenty-four years already. He comes around to my cell acting like he's in charge of the welcoming committee. "Boris, if you need anything, just let me know," he says. "Wait, are you getting kosher?" I told him no.

"Don't worry," he says, "now you will."

He wrote a letter to the warden, passed it to me and I gave it to the CO. They jumped right on it: "You're Jewish and you're *not* getting kosher?" They started to give me kosher food, and packages of matzos and grape juice on a weekly basis. I drank the grape juice on Shabbat eves.

I asked this lifer his story. Turns out he was a pilot, back in the Vietnam War, when they were smuggling heroin inside the coffins of dead soldiers. There was even a movie made about it. Later he was a pilot for the drug cartels in Mexico. He ended up in a state prison where some guys were trying to blackmail him. He made a shank and stabbed two guys dead. Facing the death penalty, the feds came to him and said: "If you help us, we guarantee no death penalty." He flipped and started to cooperate with the government. I think he gave them some U.S. Army general who was involved in the drug smuggling in Vietnam.

Another guy at Fairton when I first got there was Carlos Lehder, one of the leaders of the Medellin cartel. He was preparing to testify against Manuel Noriega, the president of Panama. His mother was German and his father a Latino, and he was demanding to be transferred to Germany after he testified. Nobody in Fairton liked him—everyone said he was gay. Who knows? He always stood off by himself—never socialized.*

---

* Lehder, the logistical mastermind of Pablo Escobar's multi-billion-dollar drug empire, was said to be responsible for 80 percent of the cocaine that arrived in the United States in the 1980s.

The ground floor at Fairton had a cell block for those guys who'd been there a long time, and the top floor was for the new arrivals like me. My cellmate was a guy who was in for bank robbery. Such a strange guy. He always wore sunglasses. Day and night. It's always dark in the cell, why wear sunglasses? Every weekend he'd watch auto racing on our TV. He could spend five hours straight watching races in his sunglasses without moving. He was in prison for thirteen years already and had finished his cooperation with the government and his release date was coming.

I was counting the days to his departure. Once he left, I was going to take the lower bunk. The federal prisons at this time allowed the inmates to have porno magazines, and my cellmate collected about two dozen of them. He made them into albums. Every night, inmates would rent these magazines from him for a pack of cigarettes, or a couple of dollars.

Finally, the day comes for him to be released. He flat-out refuses to leave. "Boris," he says. "I'm not going anywhere. I'm staying right here." I say, "What do you mean? You're going free!" I really didn't care what the fuck he did with his life, to be honest, but I wanted him gone. I wanted to take his lower bunk. The COs had to threaten to sedate him and drag him to a train station before he'd go. Then he starts to carefully pack the albums of porno mags. I'm staring at him. "What are you taking those old magazines for? You're going to be free, in the real world, there's real women out there."

"Boris, I don't want any real women—I'm used to these ones now." He waves one of the magazines in my face. "*These* are my women!" They had to drag him out of Fairton against his will. A peculiar guy. I sometimes wonder if he was ever able to function when he got back into the real world.

After a few months, I get transferred downstairs into a single cell. That was considered the main privilege of seniority within this unit. You get privacy downstairs. Privacy—probably the most valuable commodity in an American prison: a single wooden bed, a wooden table, your own color TV.

In a Russian prison, you're constantly thinking about hunger, how not to starve to death. In a U.S. prison, you're thinking about who gets to control the channels on the color TV. Anyway, downstairs, that's when I met a lot of *Italyakhas* from the different crime families. In the neighboring cell to me was a guy called Little Al, a boss from Staten Island. He'd been there for a few years already. He was testifying in a lot of big cases that were in the news.

Alphonse "Little Al" D'Arco," the acting boss of the Lucchese crime family, was the highest-ranking Cosa Nostra member to ever turn government witness when he flipped in 1991. D'Arco is considered the first boss of one of the major Mafia families to cooperate and testify for the government, and his surprise defection proved instrumental in convincing other high-profile mobsters, like Sammy "the Bull" Gravano, to break the Mafia oath of omertà. D'Arco's court testimony helped convict dozens of high-ranking mobsters, including Colombo boss Victor "Little Vic" Orena, Bonanno consigliere Anthony Spero, and the most powerful mobster in the United States, Genovese boss Vincent "Chin" Gigante.

"Little Al and I became good friends," Boris says.

We often went for walks in the backyard, played bocce, worked out together. He got the nickname Little Al because he was short. There were some younger Mafia inmates who also cooperated on various cases and when we'd go out for our walks, they'd make fun of him, saying, "Hi, midget!"

"You see that, Boris?" he says. "Out on the streets, when I was a captain, when I was a boss, they'd bring me money every day, and they'd kiss my ring. Now they call me midget."

Little Al told me a lot of stories about how the Italian Mafia really operates. He said that years ago the *Italyakhas* used to work together, actually like a family—but things changed. "Now it's *tutto per me*," he'd say. Everyone was out for himself—it was totally egotistical. He used that phrase a lot: "*Tutto per me!*"

He said that his own crime family betrayed him, they were going to kill him. He feared for his own family—by that I mean, his *personal* family—and they drove him into a corner and that's why started to cooperate.*

One day when we were walking the yard he told me how the *Italyakhas* murdered one of their own people and they told Little Al that he needed to dispose of the body. He had to dismember the corpse and to get rid of it, clean everything up. It was an education for me. He told me how he first joined the family, became a soldier, a captain, an underboss. Then he kept going up the ranks to become the acting boss and the feds were able to pin six murders onto him.

Little Al told some good stories. I don't know if all his stories were *true* or not, but they were interesting. Talking to him for hours every day improved my English.

He was also a good artist. He'd show me his pencil drawings. "What do you think of this one, Boris?" They were quite Chagallian. Totally reminded me of Chagall. But for whatever reason he would always put skulls, corpses, images of murders at the bottom. I thought he was a bit hung up on that theme—all the dead bodies and blood and skulls. I figured there was probably something wrong with him psychologically. Some abnormality or deviation in his personality. But I liked his drawings. And I was sorry when Little Al got moved out of Fairton, because by then we'd become very good friends.

---

* D'Arco believed that the Lucchese family had marked him for death, a threat that extended to his wife and children as well.

After Little Al was transferred out, another prominent Lucchese mobster—one who D'Arco had given evidence against, Gaspipe Casso—came to Fairton in June 1994.

Toward the end of my stay, Gaspipe was also there in Fairton. When we saw each other, we talked about Marat Balagula and everyone who was into gasoline with us, those good times we had, making millions stealing from the government. We talked about how he ordered the hit on Vadik Reznik before I got a chance to get even with that motherfucking snake. Gaspipe had flipped by the time I saw him, he testified against almost all his friends, and was going into the Witness Protection Program. He wanted to get out the same way Sammy the Bull did.

I didn't mind reminiscing with him about gasoline, but I noticed that the *Italyakhas* themselves did not like Gaspipe. They all steered clear of him. The other *Italyakhas* told me that if a guy brought, say, a half-million bucks to Gaspipe to buy into a business, Gaspipe would simply kill the guy, pocket the half million, and forget about the business. Everyone in Brooklyn knew Gaspipe had a lot of blood on his hands. Something like twenty-five murders. Even by their standards, the *Italyakhas* considered Gaspipe vicious and untrustworthy.

As did the U.S. Justice Department; Casso was thrown out of the Witness Protection Program in 1997 after prosecutors alleged that he'd been bribing guards, assaulting other inmates, and testifying falsely under oath. Instead of a reduced sentence and relocation with a fictitious identity, having confessed to dozens of homicides, Casso was sentenced to 455 years in prison without the possibility of parole—the maximum sentence permitted under sentencing guidelines. He died in prison in Tucson, Arizona, in December 2020 due to complications arising from COVID-19.

BORIS NAYFELD MAINTAINS that it was difficult to reconcile his notions of the code of silence and noncooperation with police, which he'd
learned as a young criminal in Belarus and in Brooklyn, while being in
a WITSEC unit filled with mafiosi and narcotraffickers who'd flipped.
The biggest internal dilemma he faced was the stigma of being housed
in such a protected unit at all: among the general population of federal
prisons, WITSEC units are derisively referred to as "cheese factories."

Of course, every high-ranking organized crime figure at Fairton
had his own justifications for why he'd gone, overnight, from "stand-up
guy" to "super snitch."

Perhaps Little Al D'Arco best captured the changing ethos in organized crime with his line *tutto per me.* The WITSEC unit at Fairton
was filled with self-serving opportunists, master manipulators out to
save their own skins and do as little prison time as possible—and Boris
Nayfeld was clearly no exception.

"To be in a unit like that, a place full of protected witnesses, of
course it made me uncomfortable," Boris says.

There were interesting characters, the conditions were good, excellent
food, and so on, but to me the most horrifying thing was thinking that
I might have to testify against someone. Even if that someone was my
enemy. For months while I was at Fairton, the government was prepping
me for a situation where, if Monya was to go to trial, I'd be ready to
testify against him.

But even as I prepared to testify, I said, "There's no way Monya will
ever have a trial. Once they catch him, the first thing that he'll do is
cooperate." I knew that fucking snake would never risk going to prison
for life. And he wasn't facing a single life sentence. He had three
murders on his plate. Slavik Ovoschnik and his son. Also, the contract
killer Slepinin. I knew Monya would start ratting out everyone, even his
closest friends, instead of going to trial. And that's exactly what he did.

To this day, Boris insists on drawing a distinction between himself and turncoat mobsters like Little Al D'Arco, Gaspipe Casso, and Sammy "the Bull" Gravano. Although he willingly cooperated and gave testimony to lesson his prison sentence, Boris quickly returned to the Brighton Beach underworld and never asked for government protection.

"There was an article in the *New York Times* about two Russian mob guys who cooperated but declined to go into the Witness Protection Program," Boris says. "It was myself and Monya."

WHILE WAITING for his time to testify, Boris faced a looming judgment day in his ongoing domestic drama. While locked up, it became patently obvious that he could no longer juggle two families—his legal wife, Valentina, and his mistress, Angela.

Fairton isn't a long drive from New York City, and Angela came to see me on visitations. After Ilyusha was born, I promised her that we would get married if she waited until I got out of prison. She would bring little Ilyusha. I told her, "Wait for me. When I get out, we'll get married." I promised that I'd get a divorce from Valentina.

Then when I told Valentina I wanted to get a divorce she also came to see me on a visitation. She knew all about Angela and Ilyusha, of course—she'd already flown over to Antwerp to talk to me about it. At Fairton she said, "Boris, we still have a family. I understand that there can no longer be love between us, but think about our family, think about our children." She said, "Let's not divorce. I'll keep my eyes closed. It's okay for you to have lovers and do what you're doing, but don't destroy the family."

"You know what, Valya? I won't be able to live like that. It's best if we divorce. You should go and make your own life."

Although later on, at our divorce hearing, Valentina was yelling that

I was a bandit and a murderer, I can honestly say she was a completely normal person, a good wife and mother. She tried to save the family. I destroyed it.

MEANWHILE, the only woman for whom Boris had ever expressed unwavering devotion, his grandmother Riva Nayfeld, died on October 23, 1997, while Boris was locked up in Fairton. "The worst day I ever had in prison was the day I learned my grandmother died. Even though Mama was ninety-five, and in a nursing home, her death was a huge shock, a big blow to my conscience. For my whole life, she'd replaced my mother for me. I loved her very much."

Boris asked for "compassionate leave," accompanied by U.S. Marshals, to attend his grandmother's funeral on Staten Island. He was denied. "I was upset when they turned down my request to attend the funeral. All that stuff you see in the Hollywood movies, when guys get released from prison for a day with Marshals to go to the funeral of a loved one—it's bullshit. At least, in my experience. Doesn't really happened. Because no one cares.

The day I learned she'd died, I sat there remembering everything she'd done for me and Gena. When I was locked up during my first term in the *zona* at Bobruisk, once or twice a year, the Soviet authorities allowed us to have a private visitation with family. Despite being ill and weak, Mama would take the train from Gomel to Bobruisk, then walk about one and a half kilometers, hauling food in bags, so she could spend three days with me at the private visitation room at the prison.

After the Soviet doctors told us she was going to die any moment in 1979, she lived nearly twenty more years in New York. She loved America. She stayed the whole time with my brother, Gena, and his wife—until the very end, when she had to go to a nursing home. As for me, she didn't know everything I was into. She knew I was doing criminal things—I mean, there was no hiding that. She read stories about me in the Russian-language newspapers. But I never told her exactly what it was I was doing. As best I could, I protected her from trouble and didn't want her to worry because of me.

I would have loved to see her just one more time. At least to give her one last kiss. Everyone locked up in Fairton with me could see I was upset. It was a tough time. As we say in Russian, it was a time "to gather your willpower into your fist." All I wanted was to get drunk. I wanted a bottle of good cognac, but I had to make do with that sweet wine the lifers made from oranges.

The first thing I did when I got released, I went over to the cemetery on Staten Island, placed a stone on her grave, talked to her. That was the least I could do. Every year, if I am a free man, I go there on the day of her *yahrzeit,* along with my brother, Gena—the *bratva*—and we spend a day at her grave.

For months at Fairton, I kept asking, "Well, when am I going to testify already?" Finally, I phoned my prosecutor and asked, "I've been inside for more than four years now. When is Monya's trial going to happen?" Finally, the prosecutor said, "Forget about it. Monya is not going to trial. He's made a deal. He's cooperating. You don't have to do anything else, Boris—just hold tight, you'll get your sentence."

Monya started to cooperate with them and sold out everyone who worked for him. The one clever thing he did was to pin the murders on the person who was no longer alive—his supposed relative Oleg—as if it was only his doing, not Monya's. And that's how it works in the U.S. system. Monya got his sentence, and I got mine.

Despite being charged with three murders, attempted murder, extortion, and a host of other felonies, Monya Elson's sentence was comparatively light—only seven years—and law enforcement authorities confirmed that Elson, like Boris Nayfeld, had provided "substantial" cooperation with their investigations.

Before I got arrested, Monya knew that sooner or later I would pop him. Or maybe, if I slipped up, he would have popped me. He came pretty close when I was in Moscow that one time. Monya's a very lucky guy not to have gotten killed. But I'm also a lucky guy.

When I was being brought in before the judge to get my sentence, my lawyer was standing there, the DEA agent who worked my case, the prosecutor. My sentence ended up being the time I'd already served, the four years and four months I'd been inside already, plus I had to do five years of probation. I said in front of everyone, "You know what? It would have been a pleasure to spend another four years inside if only I'd popped Monya!"

"Four years?" the DEA guy says. "Boris, you have no idea how lucky you are that you didn't. If you'd killed Monya, you'd never have seen the streets again. You'd be doing life right now."

PART
FOUR

PART

FOUR

CHAPTER 26

KRYSHA

When he was released from Fairton in May 1998, Boris Nayfeld paid lip service to the terms of his federal probation, but it wasn't long before he was back in the streets: he quickly launched a new racket providing *krysha* in the Russian-controlled prostitution business, gathered a young crew of Georgian thugs around him, and was accused of orchestrating a high-profile contract killing in the heart of Antwerp.

When I got of prison in spring of 1998, I didn't go outside for about half a year. But I needed to start making some money. One of my first calls is to Milik Brandwain in Antwerp. As far as I was concerned, I still had my ten percent stake of M&S International.

Brandwain picks up the phone and I say, "Milik, the company has been operating while I was on the inside. My ten percent share from those four years is due to me."

Milik snaps, "What ten percent are you talking about? I *lost* business because of you!" Supposedly, M&S had filed for bankruptcy while I was inside. And Milik was trying to say that the news of my arrest and conviction for heroin trafficking had hurt his reputation.

We go back and forth for a bit, then I say, "All right, so you're not going to give me my rightful share? I'm not going to argue. Milik, I'll leave it in God's hands."

"What are you saying, Boris?"

"God will decide which one of us is right and which one is wrong."

I hang up on him. I tell Angela, "If Milik calls, tell him I'm not around. Tell him I'm in Europe."

Milik calls right back. "Why is he hanging up on me? Pass the phone to Boris." Angela tells him, "Boris is in Europe."

I can't travel anywhere without permission of my probation officer and the judge, but I don't want Milik to know that. I want to give him a scare.

About a day went by and Milik's wife, Galina, calls to talk to Angela. Galya and Angela were friendly. Galya's upset, says Milik filed for divorce from her, he's involved with some young woman and supposedly he's doing a lot of cocaine with her.

ON JULY 17, 1998, the forty-nine-year-old Rachmiel Brandwain was walking in a parking lot in Antwerp's Diamond Quarter, not far from the M&S International office.

A lone gunman wearing a mask approached from behind, shooting Brandwain seven times with a pistol—six times in the torso and the coup de grâce shot to the head. He died on the spot. Police said the crime was most likely a professional contract killing; no one has ever been arrested for the murder.

Detectives in Antwerp and Interpol agents immediately considered Boris Nayfeld the prime suspect.

"Since Milik was also involved in devil knows which other affairs—

over the years he'd managed to piss off a lot of people—I wasn't too surprised to hear that he was killed in broad daylight in Antwerp," Boris says.

Because I'd been one of his partners, because we had an argument about my share of the company, the police accused me of having something to do with his murder. About two weeks after he was killed, agents from Interpol flew in from Belgium. They had a meeting with my probation officer in Brooklyn, and they said they believed that it was me who killed Brandwain.

I came down to Court Street in Brooklyn to see my probation officer. These two Interpol guys were there, one in uniform, one in plainclothes, asking me questions about Milik's murder. I hadn't left the country. I didn't have permission to travel out of the state, let alone to Europe, without clearing it with probation and the judge. Not to mention, I didn't have any money! I was still trying to get back on my feet after being in prison.

My probation officer says, "How could Boris have done it? He was in America. He couldn't fly anywhere." The Interpol agents ask a few more questions, and my probation officer says, "I can assure you Boris wasn't in Belgium." Which was the truth—I hadn't left my house in months. The Interpol guys left and flew back to Belgium.

A few weeks later, I call up Milik's widow. Galina was in the process of settling up Milik's estate, liquidating the M&S company holdings.

"Galya," I said, "I know Milik didn't agree, but I believe there's something due to me. After all, I have a ten percent ownership of the company."

She said it was fair that I should get something for my ten percent share—she offered me two options, a store in Odessa and one in St. Petersburg. I'd never been to the one in Odessa, but I knew the one in St. Petersburg. I'd been there often. It was located centrally, very close to the Moscow Railway Station. It was a good-sized store, about one hundred eighty square meters—a high-end supermarket and had a good clientele. Anyway, I chose that store and had to work out with my probation officer to allow me to travel to St. Petersburg.

I wanted to sell it immediately. At the time, it was valued at about two hundred seventy thousand dollars. I needed the cash because I owed people money from before I was arrested in 1994. When the DEA locked me up in '94, all my cash was out on the streets. I hate carrying debts. When the time comes for me to die, my dream is to not owe a single kopek to anyone. I wanted to immediately sell this store just to settle the debts. But I had no idea how crazy the criminal situation had become back in Russia.

As soon as I tried to sell it, it turned out some Pitersky criminals had falsified a bunch of documents and made it look as if there had been a corporate takeover and the store no longer belonged to me. With those fake ownership documents these crooks were in the process of selling the store. This kind of thing was happening all the time in the late 1990s in Russia. I had to try to stop the sale quickly. And I knew I'd have to get to St. Petersburg personally if I was going to figure out what was going on.

"THE TERMS OF MY PROBATION said that I didn't have the right to meet with other criminals," Boris remembers. "But I've been a criminal my whole life. Who else do I *know* besides criminals? So after about six months of staying in the house, I started to go back out to Brighton."

It wasn't long before Boris was again trading on his violent reputation for settling disputes and his particular criminal forte: "money extraction."

While in Brighton, I was approached by this woman named Tanya who ran a massage parlor. There are many of them around New York and New Jersey. It's usually an ordinary apartment or storefront office where young Russian women provide sexual services—obviously not just massages—running on a twenty-four-hour basis. In the Russian community, these brothels are all operated by women. We call them *mamkas.*

Well, this woman Tanya approaches me and tells me she used to run a large massage parlor along with another *mamka* named Irina. Tanya suspected Irina had been stealing from the business—pocketing money during her shifts. It costs a hundred to a hundred fifty bucks per session, depending on what the client wants specifically. If he wants something extravagant or unusual, naturally, the price goes up. Tanya installed hidden cameras to see how many clients came in and out, and caught Irina stealing red-handed. They decided to part ways, and Tanya said Irina had to pay back the $30,000 she stole. Irina asked for a bit of time to settle up and then decided to stiff her. That's when Tanya approached me and asked for my help.

"Okay, I'll take care of it," I tell her. "However, you're aware that with money-extracting jobs, we take half."

She says, "That's fine. Fifteen to you and fifteen to me."

I accept the job. This ex-partner of hers, Irina, was getting ready to open up a new place in New Jersey. It was a ground-floor office complete with a front desk and five private bedrooms. There was a bigger client base in New Jersey than Brooklyn. This wasn't like the massage parlors in Brighton—typically just Russian girls. She also had Chinese and Filipinas. However, for whatever reason everyone's always drawn to the Russians.

Tanya gave me Irina's address. At this time, I was starting to put together a new *brigada.* Since the collapse of the Soviet Union, there were so many young Georgian guys newly arrived in the U.S. Guys in their twenties from the former Republic of Georgia. They were unemployed and looking for work. Strong, hungry young guys who wanted to live the criminal life. Also a few young Russian guys had formed around me, kind of a new young crew I was trying to educate about criminal matters.

I take two of my Georgian guys and drive out to New Jersey and got there early in the morning. We're waiting until we see Irina arriving at nine to open up. The moment she inserts the key into the lock, I'm right behind her—I give her a push and all four of us are inside—Irina, me, and my two young Georgians. It's completely dark, she's scared, but when I tell her I want to talk to her about a business issue, she pulls herself together, turns the office lights on.

"What's the issue?" she says. I tell her, "You owe your ex-partner thirty big ones. You must pay." She glares at me. Defiant. "I'm not going to pay! I don't owe her anything! And who are you?"

This angered me. I quickly grab her by the throat with one hand and start to press. I keep pressing until her face is red and she's gasping for breath, then I let go. "Never mind who the fuck I am! Either you pay within one week or this new place of yours will never open up for business."

Irina suddenly changes her tune. "All right, I'll pay. I'll pay. But I have a boss, I need to sort it out with him." I tell her, "Fine, you sort it out with him, but pay within a week, directly to Tanya. Don't look for me!"

About four days go by and Tanya calls. "Mikhailych,* they want to meet up with you to talk about the thirty thousand." I was afraid this Irina had involved the *musors*. I said, "Who wants to meet and talk?"

Tanya said it was Irina's new partner, or boss, whatever—some guy

---

* For Russian speakers, one of the less formal ways to address a person you know well, have a lot of respect for—is perhaps older than you—is to use the patronymic name only. One of the many nuances of Russian is that even the patronymic can take on a diminutive form: in the case of Boris Mikhailovich Nayfeld, this becomes "Mikhailych."

she reported to. The guy's name was Sasha Sapozhnik.* When she said that, I laughed, "Is that right, Tanya? I guess I've been away too long—now *shoemakers* have become criminals—fuck! No problem. Fine, I'll meet with this shoemaker. Where and when?"

He wanted to meet me in Brooklyn, at one o'clock the next afternoon. In the Italian section, Bensonhurst, at a nice restaurant.

Again, I take two of my young Georgian guys along. We walk into the restaurant. My guys sit down separately and order some coffee. I walk over to the table. To my surprise, this *Italyakha* is sitting at the head of the table. Good-looking guy, about forty-five or fifty years old. He's wearing a sharp suit, a black mock turtleneck, hankie sticking out of the breast pocket. Two younger *Italyakhas* are sitting on each of his sides. His muscle. Also, a Russian guy who I don't know. Turns out to be Sasha the Shoemaker.

I stare from face to face. "Listen, what's going on here? Which one of you wanted to see me?" The well-dressed *Italyakha* stands up and says, "Boris, don't you remember me?" I tell him, "No, I don't remember you." Then he says, "I used to be very friendly with your boss."

"My boss?"

"Evsei," he says. "He once gave me a nice gift—a tin of black caviar."

I said, "Look, are you here to talk to *me* or Evsei? Because if it's Evsei, you can go talk to him in Washington Cemetery. He's been there a long time now."

He says, "I'm here to talk to you, Boris." Now I sit down at the table. He tells me his name is Patsy or Patty or Pasquale—I can't remember, to be honest. He says, "Ask around the streets about me, Boris. Everyone knows me here."

"I'm not interested in who you are," I tell him, "but I *am* curious to

---

* *Sapozhnik* is Russian for "shoemaker."

know why you're here. You came to tell me about Evsei giving you a can of caviar?"

"No," he says, "our Russian friend"—he points at this Sasha Sapozhnik—"says he owns a massage parlor, and you're getting into his business, demanding money from one of the madams . . ."

Now I feel my face getting hot. I stare at this *Italyakha*. "Let me ask you a question," I say. "Did you ever see Russians coming into the Italian community to collect money? Did you ever see Russians getting involved in business problems between Italians?"

He thinks it over and shakes his head no.

"Then why are you are meddling in Russian business? You looking to start a war? Then declare it. We can go to war *now*."

He says, "Relax, Boris. No one's here to start a war."

"This is a *Russian* beef. A money issue between *Russians*. It doesn't concern you." I turn to Sasha Sapozhnik, speaking in Russian so the rest of them can't understand.

"You fucking snake! You think *he's* going to solve your problem? *Kozyol!* Listen to me—because you brought in an *Italyakha,* you're going to pay double! The debt was thirty thousand bucks. Now you owe *sixty*."

I get up, nod to my Georgian guys. "You have one week," I tell Sasha Sapozhnik, and we leave.

Exactly one week later I hear from Tanya that she got the sixty thousand. She settled up with me for my end, the thirty grand. And after that the word spread among the other *mamkas:* "Biba can put you under his *krysha*."

That's how I found myself in the prostitution business. All these *mamkas* start asking me for *krysha*. I put one of my Georgian guys in each massage parlor. They worked in shifts, so we covered the places twenty-four hours a day. Each guy got a hundred bucks from the *mamka* for providing security. On top of that they got tips—well, sexual favors. The Russian girls would give them a good time without charging.

—

Around this same time, we start hearing stories about some Russian boxer, a professional fighter, who's going around beating up and robbing the girls in various massage parlors. He always comes in the middle of the night, has sex with the girl and pays one hundred fifty for the session, but when the girl goes into the back room where they keep the stash, he follows her, strikes her, and then grabs all the money—all the daily receipts for the massage parlor. He already robbed a few girls of more than five thousand each. All told, he stole something like fifteen grand.

All the *mamkas* are now really afraid of this boxer. They're fucking terrified. I've got all my crew on the lookout, in case he tries robbing one of the places we're protecting.

It's a weeknight—I think a Tuesday—and I'm sound asleep in my house on Staten Island, and the phone starts ringing at about three A.M. It's my young Georgians. "Mikhailych! We've got him—the boxer! We're holding him here. We caught him trying to rob one of our places."

I'm half asleep. I tell them: "Break him. What the fuck are you holding him for? Stop talking to me and *finish* him."

"He says he'll pay back everything he stole. He'll pay back fifteen thousand. He's got five thousand cash in his apartment, and he says his trainer will help him repay the rest."

I start fucking laughing. "You think he's going to pay back a *kopek*? Do me a favor. Don't bother me anymore and just pound the shit out of him." I hung up the phone and fell fast asleep.

At eight A.M., they call again: "Mikhailych! Can you come by here?"

"What the fuck? Fine, I'll be there soon."

When I get to the massage parlor—it's a large apartment in Brighton—I see my three hammerers standing there. They've all got baseball bats in their hands. In an armchair is this young guy, the boxer. He's been roughed up bad but he's still kind of smirking as I approach.

Without breaking stride, I whack him hard across the cheekbone. I also pull out my switchblade and plunge it straight into his thigh. He starts yelling, "I'll pay back the money! Don't kill me! I have money at home, I'll pay everything back. I'll get you the fifteen thousand!"

I pull my knife from his leg, turn to my guys, and say, "What's the point talking to this piece of shit anymore? Can't you see he's lying? He's not going to pay back anything. Not *one* kopek! Finish him. Then chop him up and bury the pieces."

I'm not sure who got more scared, my young Georgian guys or the boxer when he heard me say he was going to be chopped up. As I was leaving, I hear the guy begging: "If you guys take me home right now, I'll pay back everything . . ."

About an hour later, these guys take the boxer to his apartment, and the minute he gets inside, even though he's beaten up pretty bad, stabbed in the leg, he manages to give them the slip. He gets inside, quickly locks the door. My young Georgians stand there banging away. Banging and shouting for God knows how long. By the time they figured out what happened, the boxer was long gone. He climbed out a back window to the fire escape and disappeared completely from Brighton. No one ever saw him again. To this day, I don't know if he's dead or alive.

When my young Georgians called me up to tell me, I started laughing again. I've been collecting money long enough to know when someone's going to pay me and when they're not. But it didn't matter that they let him escape. The word spread fast that we'd taken care of the boxer who was beating and robbing the girls. Even more *mamkas* approached me to get under my *krysha*.

MEANWHILE, as Boris was trying to arrange for the sale of the M&S store in St. Petersburg that he'd been given by Milik Brandwain's widow, a Western Union telegram arrived unexpectedly from Moscow. "This telegram says that my mother—Ekaterina Petrovna Mironova—is on her deathbed. The doctors say she's only got a few days left, and I need to fly over to Moscow immediately if I want to see her. I go straight down to Court Street in Brooklyn and talk to my probation officer. Then my lawyer goes and presents the telegram and a letter to the judge. The judge gave me permission to travel to Russia for thirty days in order that I could see my mother one last time, and in the event that she died, they said I could stay and bury her."

The last time Boris saw Ekaterina Petrovna was in 1993, prior to his arrest for heroin trafficking. "I was in Moscow taking care of some business—it was during all the problems with Monya Elson—and I stopped by her place to see how she was doing.

My mother lived in a small town called Klin, about sixty kilometers outside of Moscow. Before she retired, she'd held the position of Regional Community of Consumer Cooperatives chairman in Klin. And as a Communist Party member, and a woman with a significant position in her industry, she'd lived fairly well: she and my stepfather, Valentin, had a three-room apartment, a Volga* complete with a garage.

When I came to see her that last time in '93, she was ill, and I could see that her health was quickly deteriorating. She would get confused. It was Alzheimer's, I think. She'd leave the apartment and it would take days before someone would find her. She couldn't remember where she lived after she stepped out of her apartment.

I spoke to my stepfather. "How can you let her walk out of the apartment alone? Can't you see it's not safe? Hire a lady, an aide, someone to look after her."

---

* The Volga was a full-size Soviet sedan, one of the most esteemed vehicles in the USSR. Driven by many members of the Soviet *nomenklatura,* the Volga became something of a cultural icon of the Communist era.

He says, "Oh, that would require money to hire a woman."

My stepfather was a retired military officer—he'd been a pilot during the war. He came from a good family. His dad had also been a military officer and used to teach courses at the nearby tank academy. I hate to call him a drunk, but my stepfather loved his bottle. In any event, he was living on a pension and complaining about not having enough money.

I gave him cash to hire a woman to be a home attendant. Someone to be there, as a sitter, to look after my mother. I gave him five thousand rubles. Back then, it was enough money to hire some good help. Regardless of what kind of a mother she was, she was still the one who gave birth to me. Simply because she decided not to go for an abortion and gave me life, I considered it my duty to keep helping her somehow, as long as she was alive.

I went back to New York and I kept sending money for her to be looked after. I would send about three hundred bucks. I did everything I could to help her financially, even when I was in prison four years. When I couldn't send money, there was this friend of mine in Moscow who had a factory—he used to send a care package once a month. A box full of sausages, meat products, and he'd deliver it directly to her address.

After that telegram arrived, the judge granted me thirty days to be in Russia, but by the time I land in Moscow, I learn that my mother has died. She hadn't been buried yet; she was still in the morgue when I arrive in Klin. I paid the priest to perform a funeral service. She was Russian Orthodox. I gave the money for the funeral service. The people who used to work with her at the Collective, they put together a cash collection to pay for the wake.

At the cemetery, as she was already being interred, I was approached by an elderly woman I'd never seen before:

"Boris Mikhailovich? I know you are Ekaterina Petrovna's son. There's a lot I want to tell you about your stepfather." I'm standing there in the cemetery, listening. This woman turned out to be the wife of my stepfather's brother. She starts telling me, "Boris Mikhailovich, we know you've been giving money for your mother to be looked after. Yet you're not aware of many things."

I said, "What sorts of things?" She tells me, "Did you know that Valentin Vasilievich has a second family, right here in this town? Whenever you sent money, or groceries—everything you sent—he gave it all to his second family."

Turns out, my stepfather never hired a home attendant. He never gave my mother any of my money or packages. This old woman told me more stories about my mother wandering in the streets, disappearing for days or weeks. Once, she went missing for fifteen days and was found unconscious in a hospital, without any ID, all bruised and beaten up. Everything I sent to take care of my mother, my stepfather simply gave it to his second family. At the end of her days, nobody was looking after her.

I said to this old lady, "Well, she's gone. What can I do about it now?"

My mother had no savings but there was a three-room apartment and the Volga—there was a small inheritance. I said, "You know what? I'm not interested in getting anything from her. If you give me your word that you will look after her grave, then I will get a notary to sign over my part of the inheritance to you. Whatever is due to me will be yours, but just give me your word." She says, "Yes, I promise you, Boris Mikahilovich, I will look after her grave."

I needed to take photos of the funeral to show the judge back in New York, to prove that my mother had actually died and that I'd been there to bury her. I did all that, we went to see a notary, and I waived my inheritance rights in favor of this old woman, the wife of my stepfather's brother. I signed the waiver that I gave up claims to the inheritance.

Boris vividly remembers standing at the grave of the mother he says he never loved, thinking about how she abandoned him when he was three years old, how she'd shown up suddenly when he was a teenager in Gomel; how he'd gone to live with her and his stepfather for a year in Norilsk, north of the Arctic Circle, and now finding out that all the money he'd sent to help had been spent by his stepfather on his second family. His gaze hardened as he realized that Ekaterina Petrovna, too, had been abandoned in her fragile final years.

"Well, as far as I was concerned, the only mother I had, the only mother I loved, was already buried in Staten Island," Boris says.

But since Ekaterina Petrovna gave life to me, it was my duty as her son to bury her properly. I had to give her the last honor I was obliged to give as a son. Now, I'd completed my obligation.

As I'm leaving the funeral, my stepfather calls out my name—he was kind of wobbling because he was pretty drunk at the time. Valentin comes over to me and says, "Boris, don't abandon me. Please! If you abandon me, I'm going to perish." It was clear he wanted me to keep sending him the money and food parcels each month. He had no clue that his brother's wife had told me the real story about him giving it all to his second family.

I stood there, staring right through him. "You're seeing me for the last time in your life," I said. Then I got in my car and left the funeral. I never had any more dealings with my stepfather. He died not long after my mother—the bottle that he loved so much finally killed him.

CHAPTER 27

OLIGARCHS AND GANGSTERS

The Wild Nineties. That's how the decade is invariably referred to in Russian by most who lived through it—a time of sheer chaos and lawlessness. No one was fully prepared for the anarchy unleashed as the massive, tightly controlled Soviet State economy turned suddenly into a Hobbesian free market. Pandora's box had opened: everything was up for grabs. Every corner of the world's largest country* was being privatized.

Entire industries were being sold off under a rigged voucher system that brought untold billions into the hands of a few. It was the era of the oligarchs and gangsters. Alongside the newly minted billionaires and millionaires came the ascendance of what the Russian sociologist Vadim Volkov called "violent entrepreneurs." Few Russians trusted the

---

* At 17.1 million square kilometers, Russia is geographically the world's largest nation, comprising roughly 11 percent of the earth's landmass.

police or court system, and mobsters like Boris Nayfeld stepped into the breach to provide *krysha* to businessmen, protection that often allowed most enterprises to function.

"During the 1990s, after communism fell, it was difficult to conduct business in Russia without a *krysha*," Boris recalls.

> In fact, I would say it was impossible. If you tried to come in and do business without a *krysha*, it was guaranteed that some organized crime group would extort you.
>
> There was such an explosion in criminal activity; new criminal groups were popping up all over. Everyone wanted to make easy money. All sorts of businesses were being leaned on. All sorts of businessmen wanted protection.

Boris quickly spotted the criminal possibilities in the economic chaos; to that end, he set up a meeting in New York with a powerful *vor v zakone*, Vyacheslav Kirillovich Ivankov, known as "Yaponchik"— "Little Japanese"—due to the Asiatic shape of his eyes.[*]

Born in Georgia in 1940, Ivankov, a former youth wrestling champion, made a name for himself in the Moscow underworld as a thief and racketeer. In 1982, Yaponchik was convicted of robbery, possession of firearms, forgery, and drug trafficking. He was sentenced to fourteen years and was reportedly crowned a *vor* while in the infamous Butyrskaya prison.

He arrived in the United States in March 1992. The U.S. Embassy in Moscow had granted him a travel visa, despite his extensive criminal

---

[*] Many Russian criminal nicknames are crude references to physiognomy. Ivankov's nickname seems to have no relation to the original gangster who went by that name, the legendary Odessa-born Jewish racketeer Mishka Yaponchik—see more on page 321.

history and reputation as one of the most ruthless *vory v zakone* active in Russia. Ivankov's two-week visa rather ludicrously claimed that he was planning to work in the film industry in the United States.

The reasons for Yaponchik's move to the United States have remained mysterious for decades. In 1993, the Russian Ministry of Internal Affairs advised the FBI that Ivankov had come to "manage and control Russian Organized Crime activities in this country." There were sensationalized media reports that Ivankov had recruited "combat brigades" led by an ex-KGB officer and composed of more than two hundred "former athletes and Special Forces veterans of the Afghanistan war."

"Forget that bullshit," Boris says.

This is the true story. When Yaponchik came out of prison in 1991, he had a lot of enemies in Russia. Guys were trying to kill him—he wasn't safe there, so he came to the United States. Not with a crew—he came by himself. And like any of us, he started looking for ways to make some money in America.

When Yaponets* first arrived in America, I was over in Belgium. For the first little while, Yaponets was living at the house of our friend Lyonya Usaty in Brooklyn. The same Lyonya who had been Evsei's driver in the Soviet Union, the same Lyonya who called me at the *banya* to tell me Evsei had been killed.

The criminal community in Brighton who'd known Yaponchik in Russia collected some money—I don't remember how much, as a kind of welcoming start-up fund. Of course, they also paid all kinds of deference to him.

---

* Like many other gangsters, when speaking about Ivankov Boris often alternates between the nicknames "Yaponets" ("Japanese") and "Yaponchik" ("Little Japanese").

Boris arrived back in the United States from Europe with a potentially lucrative business proposal for Ivankov, but he needed a formal introduction.

Once I get back to New York from Antwerp, I call up Lyonya Usaty. I say, "Lyonya, it would be nice to sit and talk to Yaponchik." He says, "Okay, Biba. Come on over." I drove out to Lyonya's house on a weekend. Before that day, I'd never seen Yaponchik or socialized with him. But we knew of each other. Lyonya Usaty introduced us, we greeted each other, sat down in Lyonya's living room and started talking business. It was immediately a warm relationship.*

I gave Yaponchik my proposal. "Slava, now that the Soviet Union has busted wide open, all these Russian Jews who emigrated to America, Canada, Europe, Israel—these Jewish guys who've been living well, making money, all over the world—they're eager to go back to do business. They understand how things work in Russia. They've got connections built up since the Soviet times."

Yaponchik sits there, nodding. "Naturally," I said, "every Jew investing in the former Soviet Union is going to need people from the criminal environment to provide *krysha* so that they don't end up getting the Cossack treatment."

Yaponchik smiled. "You're right, Boris," he says. "Let's do this together." So Yaponchik and me made an agreement to jointly provide a *krysha* to Russian Jews who wanted to return and not get extorted or have their businesses taken away from them by criminals.

---

* In June 1996, Leonard Lev, a.k.a. "Lyonya Usaty," was arrested and charged with having helped arrange a fraudulent marriage that would allow Ivankov to avoid deportation from the United States. Later that year, Lev was convicted at trial in the U.S. District Court for the Eastern District of New York of "conspiracy to defraud the United States government"—his 1998 appeal of this conviction was dismissed—and he was sentenced to five years probation and ordered to pay a modest fine.

I already had one guy asking me for a *krysha*—his name was Anatoly Potik. Later on, in 2015, this same Potik was going to turn out to be nightmare for me—a disaster! But at the time, in 1992, I was trying to help him out with protection. Potik had some manufacturing business in Tashkent and transported a lot of cash. He needed people to back him up, and, if necessary, sort out disputes at the criminals' level. Yaponchik said, "All right. I know what to do. Since I'm here in America now, let's give this to my son."

Right away—this was, I think, the late spring of '92—I flew over to Moscow. Yaponchik's son came to a meeting with me and Anatoly Potik. We were surprised at first because Yaponchik's son was—well, he didn't have the face of a criminal. He was young and polite and spoke in a quiet manner. Potik whispers to me, "Boris, *this* is my *krysha*? Who did Slavik give me?"

I tell Potik, "Don't worry. This is Slava's son. Start working with him. And keep in mind that his papa is behind him."

Before long, Yaponchik and me were giving *krysha* to a lot of Jewish businessmen who approached us about coming back to Russia. At the time, I couldn't stay in New York or Moscow for long, because my main business was in Belgium. Things with M&S were booming. The heroin business was still going strong. Yaponchik and me kept talking on the phone. Then I got arrested by the feds in '94. And Yaponchik got arrested by the feds in '95. He did his time in the U.S., then was shipped back to Russia and had a lot of problems. First, he was on trial for murder in Moscow. Then he was shot. Unfortunately, I never got a chance to meet Yaponets again.

IVANKOV WAS ARRESTED BY THE FBI on June 8, 1995, charged with the extortion of $2.7 million from an investment advisory firm known as Summit run by two Russian businessmen, and in June 1996 he was convicted and sentenced to ten years. After being released from U.S. prison, Ivankov was deported to Russia in July 2004 to face charges that he was involved in a 1992 double homicide of two Turkish nationals. He was acquitted by a Russian court in 2005 after a trial that lasted only a day.

On July 28, 2009, Ivankov was shot while leaving a Moscow restaurant. A sniper rifle was found abandoned in a nearby parked vehicle. He lingered in a hospital for seventy-three days and died on October 9, 2009. His grand funeral attracted hundreds of gangsters representing criminal syndicates from around the former Soviet Union.

THROUGHOUT THE WILD NINETIES, former citizens of the USSR who returned to do business without a *krysha* quickly learned about the cutthroat realities of postcommunist Russia.

Not long after I got released from prison, I got an unexpected call from an acquaintance named Lyova Sadesky. He was part owner of this factory in St. Petersburg that made sausages and meat products. Lyova says, "Boris, I want to give you a present—you know, the factory I've got in Piter? My end is yours now. You've got my twenty percent."

There were five partners, all Russian-Jewish guys who'd been in the U.S. but came back to do business in Piter after the fall of the Soviet Union. I thanked Lyova Sadesky for his generosity, accepted this gift of twenty percent, but I understood there was something funny going on here, some part of the story Lyova wasn't telling me. I mean, who just *gives* away twenty percent in a profitable business?

After burying my mother, I decide to travel from Moscow to St. Petersburg. I'm still on probation, and who knows when I'll get permission to come back to Russia? I figure I might as well take care of a few of my business affairs. I set a meeting with the other four partners in this factory. All of them had lived in America, and they knew my name from Brighton.

Right away they tell me, "Boris, we caught Lyova stealing—and he has to exit the company kopek-less."

"I don't know anything about his stealing. But his twenty percent is now my twenty percent. I'm your partner. Are you trying to break the deal and throw me out? Go ahead. We'll see what happens."

They said, "Boris, no, we're not throwing you out. We want you as our partner. Your share is twenty percent. But for the twenty percent we'd like you to provide us with a *krysha*." Now it all makes sense why Lyova Sadesky was so generous, why he wanted to give me his share of the company. Not only was he accused of stealing, but some local criminals are extorting the business, running it into the ground.

The other owners of the factory tell me that these two Piterskys keep coming around once a month demanding five thousand dollars. They show up at the plant carrying machine guns. As if that isn't enough, they load up their cars with about a thousand bucks' worth of sausages as they're leaving. These owners—my new partners—are scared: "Boris, these thugs threaten us by saying that if we don't pay, they're going to shut down production. Or worse."

"Okay, I'll take care of it." I said, "I'll provide the *krysha*."

But now I've got a problem. In order to provide a *krysha,* people need to know you're around—they need to know that if they mess with your business, there'll be consequences. It helps if you're actually in the country. And I don't have much time left in Russia before I'm in violation of my probation. Luckily, I learned that Ded Khasan was in St. Petersburg—he was applying for a new passport, because he'd lost his old one.

Aslan Usoyan, a.k.a. Ded Khasan—"Grandpa Khasan"—was a Kurdish Yazidi mobster, born in Tbilisi, Georgia, in 1937; by the midnineties he was considered the most influential thief in law in the former Soviet Union, an elder statesman of the *vory v zakone.*

My friend Rafik Svo had been a business partner with Ded Khasan. By this time Rafik was dead—he'd been killed in jail in Moscow in 1993. But because of their close relationship as *vory,* I was quickly able to set up a meeting.

We met on the street in central St. Petersburg. And it was a nice day for walking around the city. Ded Khasan and I hit it off—just as with Yaponchik, it was immediately a warm, friendly conversation. I told him straightaway, "Khasan. I have a piece of this meat processing plant. These Pitersky guys are coming around, making threats, showing up with machine guns, taking whatever they want. I'm now providing the *krysha,* so they can't be coming to this plant and making demands—not when I have a piece of it."

Ded Khasan asks me who these guys are. Well, they left a business card with their names on it. They were connected to some *deputaty*—some local officials in Piter. I handed Ded Khasan the business card.

Ded Khasan smiles. "Oh, I know who this is. Forget it, Boris. They're good guys. I'm going to have a talk with them. They won't come around again."

And just like that, he ended the shakedown. That's the kind of authority Ded Khasan had at this time in Russia. Those Piterskys never showed their faces at the plant again. At the end of our walk Ded Khasan says, "Boris, what are you doing over there in America? Come back to Russia. I'll give you a piece of turf where you'll be able to make some serious money."

"Khasan, I can't. I'm still on probation in the U.S. I'm only here for a few weeks to bury my mother."

For Boris, it was an enticing offer from the high-ranking *vor*. At the time he could see that the prospects for providing *krysha* in the former Soviet Union were seemingly limitless.

After my four years in prison in the U.S., bit by bit, I'm starting to get back on my feet. I've got the *krysha* with the *mamkas* in New York. I'm providing *krysha* to Jewish businessmen in Russia. And I'm looking forward to the day when I'll be finished with my probation and can reconnect with Ded Khasan and do some business together. Unfortunately, just as with Yaponchik, I never got the chance.

Within a few years, Ded Khasan found himself caught up in one of the bloodiest internal wars among the *vory v zakone,* a conflict with another Georgian crime boss, Tariel Oniani, or "Taro." Ded Khasan and Taro battled over control of criminal rackets and the lucrative construction contracts in Sochi, the Black Sea resort that was preparing to host the Winter Olympics in 2014, and their conflict led to numerous murders.

Ded Khasan survived one assassination attempt in 2010 but was killed by a sniper's bullet as he exited a restaurant on Povarskaya Street in Moscow on January 16, 2013.

CALLING ON THE HIGHER AUTHORITY of such prominent *vory v zakone* as Ded Khasan wouldn't work with the other business headache Boris was trying to resolve in St. Petersburg: the disputed ownership of the store he'd been given by Rachmiel Brandwain's widow, Galina.

This wasn't as simple as a couple of hoodlums with machine guns coming by each month demanding $5,000 and a trunkload of smoked sausages.

I spoke to my friends who were thieves in law in Piter. "I've got to straighten something out; these fucking crooks have falsified the registration documents of my store. They're trying to sell it, but I'm the legal owner." The thieves in law checked into it. They said, "Boris, this isn't our doing—and this isn't connected to anyone we know."

You have to understand: At this time, the old criminal code was completely breaking down, By the late nineteen nineties, all the rules were out the window. Normally, when violations of the criminal code occur in Russia, the thieves in law can resolve them. That's what the thieves in law do—they act as judges for other criminals. A respected thief in law can almost always step in to sort out a problem—like Ded Khasan snapped his fingers and stopped those guys from extorting the meat processing plant.

Anyone involved in criminal activity in the streets of Moscow or St. Petersburg—or anywhere in Russia, really—sooner or later, they're going to find themselves in prison. Inside Russian prisons the rules are completely different from the streets. In prison, *everything* is decided by the thieves in law. If someone ends up in a prison for disrespecting the criminal code, there isn't much tolerance. Guys running wild in the streets can get killed in the zone quickly for violations—or for minor indiscretions—committed in the free world.

But since the thieves in law in Piter don't know these fucking guys who are trying to steal my store, that means they're new on the scene, some new *brigada* or "black realtors."* Who knows? I don't have time to poke around to find out who they are. My *vory* friends told me: "It's not us, Boris, so feel free to handle it. Use whatever method you want to take the store back."

---

* "Black realtors": a term coined by the Russian media for rampant fraudsters in the real estate business.

Boris Nayfeld found himself in an unprecedented situation: for the first time in his life, he had to resolve a financial dispute by legal means.

I realize I've got to find a good lawyer who can represent me in court while I'm back in the U.S. finishing my probation. The first guy I call is Marik Tarnopolsky. Yes, the same Marik who helped me and my family move from Albany, the same Marik who tried to stiff me on my diamonds in 1980. He was back in St. Petersburg and I told him that if he helped me out, I'd give him a cut of the sale.

"Marik, hire some lawyers and get some legal action under way! I can't stay here right now." But Marik is terrified. He says, "I don't want to get involved. These guys are going to shoot me, Boris. You want to get me killed?"

Next, I call up Zhenya Ryzhy*, who also worked in the store—one of the managers. I tell him, "Zhenya, can you find a good lawyer to represent me? Let him start working on contingency. Tell him once we can prove in court that it's really my store, that these crooks faked the documents, I'll give him fifteen percent of the sale price."

And then I jumped on a flight back to America so I wouldn't be in violation of the terms of my probation. I could see that this court case was going to take ages. And my time allowed in Russia was running out in a few days. But I left it all in Zhenya Ryzhy's hands.

It took Zhenya quite a while—many lawyers were too scared to get involved—but he finally found this one criminal law professor in St. Petersburg with the Advocacy Office who agreed to take the case. His name was Leonid, a former military prosecutor who was teaching at the university. I thought the situation might take maybe five or six months to play out in the courts. This lawyer spent *years* fighting to take this store back. He was threatened, harassed—it got ugly. One day, while

* "Eugene the Redhead."

Leonid was walking his dog, he was kidnapped, thrown into the back of a car, and beaten up so bad he ended up in the ICU. They almost broke every bone in his body. But I'll tell you something: this law professor had balls of steel, because as dangerous as the case was, he never once backed down.

BACK IN THE U.S., Boris Nayfeld found that his reputation for providing *krysha* was spreading beyond the prostitution business in New York— soon drawing the unwanted attention of federal law enforcement.

"In June 2003, I made this trip to California and that's when I realized that the FBI was sitting right on top of me, digging into my business," Boris says.

What happened was I went to meet up with Roberto Alcaino, the Chilean guy I'd met when I was in Otisville.

I flew into L.A. and met with Roberto. Having been Escobar's money launderer, he still had strong connections in Colombia. He told me he was able to bring in large quantities of cocaine, anywhere in the world we want. As soon as my probation finished, Roberto wanted to travel with me. We were looking for criminal opportunities—ways to smuggle cocaine into the Ukraine and Russia. We start planning to do a test run, bringing a shipment of a hundred kilos of cocaine into the port of Odessa, then we'll see how that goes, develop that business. If the first shipment goes well, we can bring in a lot more cocaine.

Roberto and I wrap up our business, then we go together to meet this *Italyakha*. His name was Joe something. Before I flew to L.A., this guy Kolya Dozortsev—that's Nikolai Dozortsev, who was later my codefendant in my second federal case—asked me to have a meeting in L.A. Kolya and this guy Joe had done some time together in Florida, and he wants to talk to me about the prostitution business.

We agreed to meet at a café, but when this *Italyakha* shows up, he brings a second guy who looks like he's just been at the beach—blond and tanned and wearing mirrored sunglasses. I don't like showing up at meetings with *one* guy I've never met. Two makes me very uneasy.

Me and Roberto sit down at the table with them. I say to this *Italyakha,* "Okay, you want to talk? So talk." He says, "Boris, I've got a big client base here. All these Hollywood types, they want Russian escorts. Everyone out here loves Russian women. I'd like to get some girls out here working for me." I said, "How much do your clients spend per night?" He tells me, "Between fifteen hundred and three thousand bucks."

Okay, that sounds high to me, but this is Hollywood—I don't know the going rate for escorts. I say, "How many women are you talking about?" He says, "About thirty would be nice." I stared at him. "About *thirty?* Do you have any idea how much it would cost to bring thirty prostitutes here from Russia?"

I was strictly providing *krysha* to the *mamkas* in New York, but I understood the numbers. I tell him, "The women need to be flown over from Russia. To start with, you've got to bring them into Mexico. For that, you need to lay out money for passports, airline tickets, hotels, meals—that's more than five thousand bucks per girl. Then add another four to five thousand dollars to smuggle them over the border from Mexico in the trunks of cars. At a minimum you're looking at nine or ten thousand per escort. For thirty women? Go ahead and do the calculations."

The way this *Italyakha* is talking, throwing around big fucking numbers, and the way the blond guy in sunglasses is looking at me, I'm starting to get a bad feeling about this whole meeting. I suddenly decide we should leave. I push my chair away from the table, get up, Roberto gets up, and we leave the place before we even finished our coffee.

A WEEK AFTER BORIS RETURNED to New York, he got a call from Aleksandr Schneider, a convicted arms trafficker with whom he'd done time at FCI Otisville.

Sasha Schneider's nickname is Sobachnik.* That's because back in the Soviet Union he used to train dogs. I've got him managing all my young Georgian security guys—he's handling the details of who works at which massage parlor, their hours, payments, and so on.

Sobachnik says he needs to talk to me right away. "Not on the phone, Boris," he says. He pulls up at my house in his car and we walk into my backyard, by the pool. He tells me the feds were just at his place hassling him with all these questions about me. The FBI guys were saying, "So Biba's in the prostitution business now? Biba's providing protection to massage parlors—now he can bring women from Russia to work as escorts in L.A. and all over the U.S.?" Sasha Sobachnik told them, "No, if that was true, I think I'd know about it. Someone's feeding you bad information."

Turns out the entire conversation that I had in that café in L.A., the feds were listening, because they quoted it back to Sasha word for fucking word. I realize that the meeting in L.A. was a total setup—either the *Italyakha* was an informant, or the guy with him was an undercover fed.

Well, I figure, I got into the prostitution business quickly, I can get out of it just as quickly. I can see that the feds are right on top of me, watching me, harassing my friends. The last thing I need is another conspiracy case to fight while I'm still on probation for my RICO conviction.

Two days later, I gather all the young Georgians working as muscle for me. I say, "Listen to me carefully. As of today, I'm not in the

---

* "Dog lover."

prostitution business. I realize you guys need to eat. You can stay in your spots as security. Provide the protection to the *mamkas*. But this is no longer my *krysha*, I'm *out*. You guys do what you've got to do, just keep the name Biba out of your mouths, understood?"

—

He felt like he'd just dodged the spray of bullets from an Uzi.

Like he'd found another unexploded *limonka* taped to the exhaust pipe of his car.

Knowing that he'd been recorded by the FBI talking—however generally and theoretically—about trafficking young escorts from the republics of the former USSR into the United States, and *still* wasn't charged or under arrest, Boris felt a curious mix of emotions: initial relief, of course, and then a growing sense that he was now nearly untouchable.

Sasha Sobachnik's tip-off was just another indication of Biba's good fortune. He'd long prided himself on having a kind of criminal sixth sense; people often joked in Russian, "That Biba's got eyes in the back of the head."

He'd always had a knack for escaping at the last minute—whether it was from murderous rivals like Vadik Reznikov, Fima Laskin, and Monya Elson, or from the various branches of American and European law enforcement with their constantly evolving techniques of surveillance and complex conspiracy laws.

He'd slipped away again, and the 2000s were shaping up to be a heady decade for Boris Nayfeld. He was about to come into millions of dollars in cash—most of it legitimate.

Post-Soviet Russia—Vladimir Putin's Russia—where Boris was planning to spend most of his time and conduct most of his business, was now a notoriously epicurean playland for those rich and powerful enough to afford to play.

Boris was more than ready to return to a country where the customs, food, mores—and most crucially the language—were second nature.

He was ready to party with good friends in the casinos of Moscow and St. Petersburg.

Ready to invest in Odessa—that seaside city was always the heartbeat of criminal activity, stretching back to the time of the Czars.

It was high time for him to enjoy living the Russian good life he'd long dreamed of since he was an impoverished little kid in Gomel.

But even as he was visiting with his federal parole officer in Brooklyn one final time, preparing the paperwork for his visa to Russia, in all his excitement and exuberance, Boris didn't realize how close he already was to the inevitable crash.

CHAPTER 28

ODESSA MAMA

In early June 2006, Boris got unexpected news from Russia. After more than four years in the court system, there was a verdict in his lawsuit over the store in St. Petersburg.

"The case had been tied up in the courts for so long already, I'd started to wonder if it would ever get resolved," Boris says.

But when the facts were finally presented before the judge, we won the adjudication. This law professor Leonid did some job, despite all the threats, despite being beaten up so badly. It had taken forever, but the court ruled that I was the store's legal owner, and I had the right to sell it.

During all those years the property value had increased so much it was crazy. When Galina Brandwain first gave me the store, I'd been willing to sell it for two hundred seventy thousand. But real estate prices in St. Petersburg had skyrocketed in the years we'd been fighting. Nearly ten times. When I sold, I got $1.9 million. But if I'd only waited a few more weeks—I had no grasp of the real estate situation there in Piter—but had I kept it on the market a few more weeks, I'd have got $2.4 million. I lost half a million by being impatient, but at that point, I was tired of fighting over the fucking store and I just wanted to sell it.

The timing was perfect. I dodged a bullet by getting out of the prostitution business just as the feds were closing in on me. And my probation was finished, so I could come to Russia whenever I want. I got paid the $1.9 million in cash. I ended up giving the law professor three hundred thousand bucks—fifteen percent of the sale. After taking care of the professor and Zhenya Ryzhy, I've got just over $1.6 million. I hired a special armored car and a couple guys with guns to transport the cash from St. Petersburg to my friend's bank in Moscow. As crazy as things were in Russia during those days, moving that kind of cash—anything over a million bucks—I wasn't about to take any chances.

Looking back on that time, that period from 2005 to 2007, I'd call it the golden era—at least, in terms of living the good life. I've suddenly got $1.6 million cash from selling that store. I've got money flowing in every month from my *krysha* operations, and for once I'm not in the middle of a fucking war with someone. All my enemies are out of the picture, either dead or in prison.

Boris's longtime nemesis, Monya Elson, was arrested in March 2006 in a bizarre plot to murder the Brothers Karamazov, the twins Slava and Alex Konstantinovsky, who Elson blamed for the failed hit on him in July 1993 during which he and his wife had been wounded. In the intervening years, the Konstaninovsky brothers had returned to Ukraine and thrived as businessmen; Elson sent a coconspirator named Leonid Roytman to Kiev to arrange the murder of the twins and take over their business empire, which included a large Ukrainian bank. In 2007, Elson pleaded guilty to a charge of conspiracy to commit murder for hire and was sentenced to seven years in prison.

"IT WAS A WILD TIME to be in Russia," Boris says. "People partied like there was no tomorrow. I spent almost all my time in Moscow, St. Petersburg, and Odessa. Everyone in Russia—everyone who had money—was living it up. Central Moscow had so many casinos. At least fifteen or twenty. They've all been shut down now, but at the time you'd see everyone in the casinos. They were the center of all the action. There was so much money whirling through Moscow, legitimate and criminal."

Sasha Gramatsky, the inveterate gambler who'd lost 12,500 bottles of cognac to Boris during that marathon night playing cards in Freetown, Sierra Leone, was now a successful casino owner in Russia.

After the Soviet Union fell, Gramatsky was partners with Otarik Kvantrishvili*—and they had three casinos, one on Begovaya Street in Moscow. He also owned the Tourist Hotel. Gramatsky was always a gracious host. He never once let me pay for anything at his hotel. Whenever I came to one of his casinos, he gave me a credit of forty thousand dollars at the tables. By then he was worth a lot—I'd guess around two hundred million. And whenever I was at his hotel, Sasha always made a point of sending me an excellent bottle of cognac.

---

* Otari Kvantrishvili was a Georgian Mafia leader. A champion wrestler in his youth, Kvantrishvili rose to prominence in Moscow's underworld in the early 1990s; he befriended celebrities and politicians and made a fortune running casinos and sports clubs as well as racketeering operations. He announced he was entering politics in 1993 but was assassinated by a sniper in 1994 while leaving a Moscow bathhouse.

Of all the casinos, I spent the most time at the Shangri-La. I had the gold card and they always took good care of me and my friends—private table, caviar, steaks, lobster, drinks on the house. You'd meet everyone there. Thieves in law and legitimate businessmen. Everyone was at the casinos to gamble and have a good time.

Russia's many ostentatious casinos, which had popped up like mushrooms after a summer rain, seemed symbolic of the new age in the newly liberated country. As a correspondent for the *Independent* observed: "Gambling has been a very visible part of Russian life since the collapse of the Soviet Union, a reckless all-or-nothing game of chance that [seems] to mirror the business climate of Russia itself during its wild transition years."

In Boris's recounting, these nights in Moscow casinos were a nonstop bacchanalia. For men who'd grown up in the Soviet Union, with still-vivid memories of food shortages and luxuries available only on the black market, these were indeed heady times. In just fifteen years the pendulum had swung from one extreme to the next, from deprivation to decadence.

The all-night parties we had had at these casinos—there's no word to describe them. Usually, we had a group of four of five guys at my private table. We'd always invite some young women. Gorgeous escorts. Throughout the night they'd provide sexual entertainment. Sometimes the girls would slip under the table—it was a kind of contest.

A blowjob contest. The girls would give all the guys head and the guy who finishes first wins a prize. Usually, a bottle of fine wine or champagne.

Moscow had the most casinos, but St. Petersburg had plenty, too. During one of my visits to Piter, I came to inspect that meat processing plant I had a twenty percent stake in. We had this one working partner named Mark. Of the five of us owners, he was the only one who spent time at the plant. I came to Piter with a girlfriend of mine, Olga, and we got invited to a night out at a casino owned by my friend Sasha Chelbatsan.

Sasha Chelbatsan is a Chechen—his real last name is Daudov. A great guy. He's blind now—in the middle of a mob war in Piter, some guys threw sulfuric acid in his face and it burned right through his eyes. When the Soviet Union fell in 1991, Sasha Chelbatsan was partners with Vladimir Kumarin, the leader of the Tambov Crew. Kumarin's a big criminal name. They used to call him the "St. Petersburg Night Governor." Kumarin was very close to Putin in the early days. Putin ran the city in the day, and Kumarin ran it at night. Today he's serving time; he got twenty-four years, and I think it is unlikely that he is coming out, not while Putin is still in power. Kumarin knows too much.

Anyway, we arrive at the casino owned by Kumarin and Sasha Chelbatsan. It's just the three of us—my girlfriend Olga, me, and Mark from the meat factory. Sasha Chelbatsan meets us at the entrance, leads us to the upstairs restaurant. Sasha says: "Boris, everything this evening is a present to you from me and my friends. Dinner, drinks— order anything you'd like, it's on me."

I look at this guy Mark. "Hey, you said you know something about wine, right? Order us a bottle, get us some food, I'll be in the casino playing blackjack." I go off to gamble, then they call me when the appetizers and wine are on the table. The waiter opens a bottle of French wine for me to taste. Honestly, I know nothing about wines. I know a good cognac when I taste it, but when it comes to wines, I know fuck all.

He starts to pour a little from the bottle into my wineglass to taste. I tell him, "Fill it up—hey, come on, hurry! I've got to get back to the blackjack." I gulp it down and rush back to the tables. I'm on a winning streak and don't want my luck to turn. They call me back for the main course and dessert and when they bring over the check, my eyes pop out of my head. The tab is more than fifteen thousand dollars. For dinner and wine? For three people? I ask the waiter, "How come it's so high?" Turns out that bottle of French wine cost eight thousand euros—more than eleven thousand bucks. I said "Mark, what the fuck? How could you order such an expensive wine?" He says, "Boris, I didn't realize how much that bottle cost—there were no prices on the menu."

"No prices? All the more reason to ask the fucking waiter!"

Sasha Chelbatsan settled the bill since we were his guests. But I was extremely embarrassed in front of him—I didn't want Sasha to think we were abusing his hospitality. Before heading back to the blackjack tables I said, "Mark! I swear, I'm never taking you anywhere again. Eight thousand euros for a bottle of wine? Who the fuck do you think you are? Royalty?"

Throughout 2007, Boris recalls, the hedonistic carousel kept spinning without a letup. "It was like this almost every night. If we weren't at the casinos, we'd be invited by the oligarchs to wild parties at their mansions in the suburbs of Moscow. I didn't think about saving a fucking dollar, honestly. I spent the money as fast as it came in."

For Boris, the most memorable celebrations were on the balmy shores in the Black Sea. "There's nowhere like Odessa in the summertime. We had rich friends with yachts on the Black Sea. A half-dozen young beautiful call girls were always there. Nonstop partying. If you had the energy, you could do this every night, seven nights a week."

BORIS HADN'T COME TO ODESSA just to enjoy the highlife. By early 2007, with the constraints of probation behind him, he had a chance to fulfill a dream he'd had since his days as a young *blatnoy* in the Soviet Union: making his name in the underworld of Odessa.

Of all the cities in the former Soviet Union, "the Pearl by the Sea" had the longest tradition of contraband smuggling, black marketeering, and fraud. Odessa's gangsters were always considered the most ingenious and sophisticated in the Russian Empire and the USSR.

"Much like Shanghai, New Orleans, and San Francisco's Barbary Coast, old Odessa was both venerated and vilified as a city of sin—heaven for some, hell on earth for others—a haven for smugglers, thieves, and pimps who boasted of their corruption through endless nights of raucous revelry," writes historian Jarrod Tanny in *City of Rogues and Schnorrers*.

"ODESSA MAMA. THAT'S THE NAME we criminals use," Boris says.[*] "Odessa was the premier criminal city in the Soviet Union. It's the premier criminal city to this day. We all grew up hearing the stories of Mishka Yaponchik."

Born Moishe Wolfovich Vinnitsky in 1891, Mishka Yaponchik ("Mikey the Jap") was an Odessa gangster who got his nickname due to his supposedly Asian-looking eyes. He led self-defense groups in Moldavanka, the Jewish ghetto of Odessa, and burnished his legend as a Robin Hood figure during the first decades of the twentieth century.

"Even today, Mishka Yaponchik is a cult hero to many in Odessa," Boris says.

All criminals from the Soviet era know his story. Mishka Yaponchik ran rackets against wealthy merchants and industrialists. He'd come to a merchant and tell him to pay a certain sum to a widow who'd lost her son. He'd say, "Look, if you don't pay, you're going to have big

---

[*] A famous expression is "Rostov Papa, Odessa Mama," referring to the two cities considered the most criminal in the Russian Empire.

problems." And if the merchant refused to pay, Mishka and his men would carry out a raid to get the money.

Mishka Yaponchik made one big mistake: he trusted the Bolsheviks. Yaponchik put together a force of more than two thousand men and they marched to the front lines to fight the Whites. As always happens, the Soviet authority used these people, the anarchists and bandits, and then betrayed them. Once they were done helping the Red Army, Mishka Yaponchik and his people were all executed.*

Mishka Yaponchik lives on in world literature, as the model for Isaac Babel's Jewish gangster, Benya Krik, the dashing "king" of Moldavanka who leaps from the pages of *The Odessa Tales* dressed in a "chocolate jacket, cream pants, and raspberry-red half boots," driving around in a red automobile whose horn blasts the first march from *Pagliacci*.

According to Boris, little has changed in Odessa's underworld in the past century. "A lot of what Mishka Yaponchik was doing back then—his rackets and his banditry—is still going on today in Odessa. As long as there are Russian criminals, the city will always be Odessa Mama."

WHEN BORIS FIRST ARRIVED IN ODESSA, he felt almost untouchable: a jolt of Mishka Yaponchik coursing through his veins. He'd survived multiple assassination attempts—he tallies the number at five—made it through stints in a Soviet penal colony and various U.S. jails and prisons, and arrived in the famed Black Sea port to invest in a lucrative counterfeit-cigarette smuggling operation.

---

* After leading a military unit composed of convicted criminals, anarchists, and university students (the Fifty-Fourth Lenin's Soviet Revolutionary Regiment) and fighting with distinction during the Russian Civil War, Yaponchik was shot and killed under mysterious circumstances in Ukraine on July 29, 1919.

"Richard Fanchini brought Kolya Dozortsev into the cigarette business," Boris recalls.

Richard was, as usual, smart about spotting a profitable illegal opportunity, investing at the start, then pulling his money out before the crime drew any heat. Once Richard pulls his money out, Kolya Dozortsev approaches me: "Boris, do you want to come into the cigarette business with me? I need an investor." Generally, Kolya Dozortsev never invested his own money in anything. He had plenty of dough, but he wasn't the type to risk it. What could I say? I agreed because this counterfeit cigarette business promised some serious bang for the buck. At this time, all over Europe there was a huge demand for American cigarette brands like Marlboro and Camel.

We had the manufacturing operation set up in Odessa—the conveyer belt to produce the cigarette boxes. That's all we needed to produce, actually—the proper packaging. Because we had connections to a factory that made cigarettes with very low-grade tobacco. These were the cheap everyday cigarettes sold in stores throughout the Ukraine.

If we got an order for Marlboros, we'd produce fake boxes filled with the low-grade tobacco, these cheap Ukrainian cigarettes, and only the packaging would be Marlboros. The boxes looked totally authentic. Even if you examined the fine print, you couldn't tell one of our cellophane-wrapped boxes of Marlboros from the real thing.

We had special pallets built with the cartons of cigarettes hidden inside. A Rumanian company covered the transport. They got a share in the business for assuming the risk of getting the cigarettes through the border crossings. They made sure that the right people were paid off so that our shipments didn't have to go through the customs inspection.

We'd get an order from a buyer and then distribute them all over Europe—Belgium, Italy, Germany, Britain. The profit was best in

London. With the taxes in Britain, customers were paying something like seven pounds for a pack of imported U.S. cigarettes.

Beyond his role as an investor Boris was, once again, responsible for providing the *krysha*—securing that the cash receipts got transported back to Odessa safely.

After we'd sold a big order, my task was to pick up the cash from all the sales in Warsaw and bring it back to Odessa. There we'd split our profits according to the shares and reinvest some of the cash to produce more cigarettes. I have to say, counterfeit cigarettes delivered a great return on investment. The profit was comparable to selling cocaine.

THE DOWNFALL WAS INEVITABLE. The version Boris offers is concise. Conspicuously so. Sometime in the summer of 2007, between all his high-rolling at the casinos in Moscow and partying on the Black Sea, he received a routine phone call about the cash flow with the cigarette operation in Odessa.

Kolya Dozortsev calls me up from New York, telling me we've got a problem with the cigarettes. "Boris," he says. "We need eighty-five thousand bucks urgently." He tells me people running the day-to-day operation in Odessa are going on vacation. "We're short on funds, we've got work orders piling up, and we can't stop production."

I phone my banker friend in Moscow. He was always good to me—I could get a loan on short notice, but he was a stickler about the terms. If you told him, "I just need eighty-five thousand for one month—send it straight to Odessa," he'd give you the money, no interest charged, but he'd expect the loan back in thirty days, on the dot, not even one day late.

My friend fronted me the eighty-five grand and we sent it to Odessa, so that the flow of counterfeit cigarettes wouldn't be interrupted. About a month goes by—it's August, I'm in Moscow, and my banker friend reminds me the loan is due back soon. I phone up Dozortsev in Brooklyn: "Kolya, don't forget, in a few days we need to return the money."

He says, "No problem, Boris. Just fly to Warsaw and all the cash will be waiting for you."

Of course, I had no idea that by this time all of Kolya's conversations were being wiretapped and recorded. Or that the DEA would later accuse me of laundering drug money for Richard Fanchini and Kolya Dozortsev. I was talking to Kolya about repaying the loan I'd taken out. It was my *own* money I'd invested in these fake cigarettes. Didn't matter to the feds that I was talking about my own money. From their wiretap recordings, they still charged me in the huge money-laundering and drug-trafficking conspiracy.

BORIS'S RECOLLECTION of what would ultimately become his second felony conviction in the United States can be charitably described as "selective." Filings by prosecutors in the Eastern District of New York paint a considerably more detailed and damning picture of his involvement in an expansive criminal conspiracy.

By mid-2007, according to the DEA complaint, Boris was ensnared in an "ongoing investigation aimed at dismantling an international narcotics trafficking, cigarette trafficking, fraud and money-laundering organization headed by Ricardo Fanchini." The DEA had joined forces with the United Kingdom's newly formed Serious Organized Crime Agency (SOCA), and members of Belgian and Polish police to coordinate an operation to bring down the entire Fanchini organization. Through court-authorized wiretaps, DEA agents recorded hundreds of conversations on phones used by Nikolai Dozortsev and other key coconspirators.

Though his name was largely unknown to the public, the Department of Justice had long regarded Ricardo Marian Fanchini as one of the most significant and sophisticated organized crime figures operating in Europe. After leaving M&S International, Fanchini had a brief, high-profile run as the director of Kremlyovskaya Vodka; he'd worked out a deal with corrupt officials close to Russian president Boris Yeltsin to import a Belgian-made spirit, featuring the Kremlin logo, tax-free into the Russian market. Kremlyovskaya sales took off, and the brand hit its zenith when it was a prominent sponsor of the 1996 Monaco Grand Prix.

But U.S. and European law enforcement claimed that it was a smoke-screen, that Kremlyovskaya was a front company to wash Fanchini's drug-trafficking cash. In 1997, Belgian authorities arrested Fanchini for embezzlement and money laundering; in 2000 he was sentenced to four years in prison for fraud in connection to the bankruptcy of Kremlyovskaya. In 2001, while he was incarcerated, Dutch police raided a ship in port and seized a massive cache of pure MDMA—1.8 million Ecstasy pills weighing 424 kilograms—which they alleged Fanchini was trying to import into the United States.

Upon his release in 2004, Fanchini relocated to London, where he lived under the name Richard Rotmann—the surname of his German-born third wife—and divided his time between an upscale town house in Mayfair and a mansion in suburban Surrey.

Federal prosecutors saw Fanchini as a new breed of criminal-entrepreneur: a gangster for the age of globalization. He jetted around the world with multiple passports and went by a dizzying array of aliases. Besides Ricardo Fanchini and Richard Rotmann, he was known as Jerzy Bank, Riccardo Wojoiechowska, Michael Prokupecz,

Kozina Ryszaro, Richard Ryjwirski, Riccardo Kozina, and Ioannis Skandalis-Themistoklis.*

"PREVIOUS INVESTIGATIONS by the DEA and law enforcement authorities all over the world have succeeded in intercepting and seizing narcotics shipments and prosecuting members of the Fanchini Organization," DEA Special Agent Ryan McHugh wrote in an affidavit filed in New York's Eastern District on October 12, 2007. "However, in virtually every case, Fanchini was able to escape prosecution and conviction by insulating himself with multiple layers of subordinates, coordinating his narcotics operations from foreign jurisdictions that he rotated on a regular basis, and hiding his involvement through the use of false names, fictitious entities and assets under the names of his wives and ex-wives."

By 2007, the DEA claimed that the Brooklyn-based Nikolai Dozortsev was the principal point man coordinating Fanchini's narcotics-trafficking and money-laundering operations in Europe. Dozortsev—aided by his younger half brother, Arthur—was accused of funneling more than $30 million of Fanchini's criminal proceeds into numerous offshore investments, creating shell companies and accounts in the British Virgin Islands, Cyprus, Russia, and Ukraine; and purchasing high-value items such as diamonds, artwork, and a 176-foot luxury yacht, the *Kremlin Princess,* which Fanchini kept on the French Riviera.

Boris Nayfeld's full role in the money-laundering aspect of the operation remains somewhat murky, though the DEA complaint contains

---

* Among his many other aliases, Fanchini was also known—for unknown reasons—as "Warhol."

several wiretap transcripts of Boris coordinating cash pickups with Nikolai Dozortsev—money that the DEA believed was from narcotics sales, not the profits from their counterfeit-cigarette smuggling.

In one transatlantic cell phone exchange, on June 21, 2007, the two heatedly discuss what to do when Boris arrives for a scheduled pickup in Warsaw and finds a huge heap of cash in small denominations rather than hundred-euro notes that would be much easier to smuggle through airport security on his body.

"Kolya, what's with all the small bills?" Boris says. "It's ten boxes! Fuck! What am I going to do with all this cash?" After Dozortsev and Nayfeld brainstorm for a few minutes, Boris figures out a way to bring the bulk cash across the Poland-Ukraine border without going through airport customs: "I'm going by train to Kiev, then by car to Odessa," he says.

According to the DEA's complaint, Boris manages to lug the unwieldy amount of cash successfully overland to Odessa and waits in his hotel room to pass off the drug proceeds to one of Fanchini's key money launderers in Ukraine.

At one point Boris barks at Dozortsev for putting him through all the hassle. "I'll rip you a new asshole for this!"

"It's not my fault," pleads Dozortsev.

The court filings in the Eastern District of New York also make clear that ever since his release from prison in 1998, the DEA had been closely monitoring Boris Nayfeld's activities. They alleged that he was "attempting to form a narcotics-distribution and money-laundering partnership with Roberto Alcaino," and a still-imprisoned Cuban American narcotrafficker named Marcos Cojab, both of whom Boris had met while serving his RICO sentence for heroin trafficking.

Beyond the damning wiretap evidence, the DEA developed a network of informants providing information on Boris's doings. Between April 2003 and May 2004, a confidential source (referred to in the complaint as "CS1") had face-to face conversations with Boris that were dutifully reported to the DEA.

> During their numerous meetings NAYFELD told CS1 that he [NAYFELD] knew nothing about legitimate business. NAYFELD admitted that he had a criminal mind and that crime was his forte. In particular, NAYFELD stated that he had access to unlimited amounts of heroin, cocaine and marijuana. NAYFELD stated that he had vast criminal and political contacts throughout the world but that he most often meets with other criminal contacts in Moscow, Russia.

In July 2003, Alcaino told CS1 that he'd "like to launder $7 million to $8 million per week through Nayfeld," and that he could provide "up to one ton of cocaine for delivery into the United States or Europe."

The dominos began to fall in September 2007 when Rumanian authorities seized a tractor-trailer-load of counterfeit cigarettes being smuggled from Odessa. By then the DEA had court-authorized wiretaps on Boris's Staten Island landline—registered in the name of his wife, Angela Kiperman—as well as Roberto Alcaino's cell phones in California.

ON OCTOBER 2, 2007, WHILE federal agents in the United States and Metropolitan Police in the United Kingdom were busily coordinating the arrest of Ricardo Fanchini, Boris Nayfeld arrived back in New York to coordinate the last-minute logistics of his sixtieth birthday party.

Angela was feting Boris at a catering restaurant called the Passage Palace on Eighteenth Avenue in Bath Beach. Boris delegated all the party's details to his wife but stressed one thing: cost was not a consideration.

"Since I was turning sixty," Boris says, "I wanted my guests to have the best caviar, the best cognac, the best lobster, the best music—the best of everything."

According to the DEA's wiretaps, the birthday party was also seen as the best venue to finalize the prospective cocaine pipeline from Colombia into Odessa:

> NAYFELD stated that if NIKOLAI DOZORTSEV and ALCAINO were both going to be in New York on the 12th for his party, the three men should talk personally. ALCAINO explained that they would have to put a couple of dollars up [front $200,000 for the cocaine], but they would be able to do the 'business' now [start the cocaine shipments immediately]. NIKOLAI DOZORTSEV and ALCAINO agreed to meet in New York to discuss the matter because it was not safe to talk over the phone.

Nine days before Boris's birthday party, news came from the United Kingdom that sent shock waves through Russian mob circles. In the early hours of October 3, London's Metropolitan Police, acting on a request from the United States Embassy, arrested Ricardo Fanchini at his home in Mayfair and began the process of extradition to the United States. (Fanchini didn't contest the extradition and arrived in New York in January 2008.)

Ultimately, the Polish Al Capone would face twenty separate criminal counts including conspiracy to import heroin, cocaine, and MDMA, money laundering, and fraud. The crimes spanned a full decade—1997 to 2007—and ranged over several continents. If convicted at trial, Fanchini was looking at several life sentences.

The bust in London generated considerable chatter on the DEA's wiretaps:

NIKOLAI DOZORTSEV and NAYFELD expressed their concern that Fanchini's arrest was tied to a larger investigation and that they themselves should be worried about being arrested.

Whatever worries Boris felt about his personal jeopardy, they weren't serious enough to cancel the birthday party or put the kibosh on his latest multi-million-dollar narcotics enterprise.

"At the party, we were going to finalize all the details of how to push the first hundred kilos through Odessa, then build up the cocaine business from there," Boris recalls.

Roberto Alcaino flew in from California on October 11, 2007, at 11 P.M. Boris picked him up at Newark Airport in his Bentley. Alcaino was staying at Boris's house on Staten Island and planning to meet a major cocaine trafficker the following morning. Little did he know that the trafficker was also working as a confidential informant (referred to in the complaint as "C12"), who'd already passed on many details of the pending deal to the DEA.

> During calls with C12, ALCAINO stated that the 'Russians' were ready and asked for bank account information regarding where to send the $200,000 . . . C12 subsequently provided ALCAINO with a European bank account that could be used.
>
> On October 10, 2007, C12 spoke again to ALCAINO and asked for a face-to-face meeting in New York regarding the cocaine shipment. ALCAINO stated that he would meet with C12 on Friday morning, October 12.
>
> ALCAINO further stated that he was meeting with the 'Russians' [NIKOLAI DOZORTSEV and NAYFELD] on Friday as well. Finally, ALCAINO stated that he wanted to travel with C12 to Colombia to meet the source of supply prior to the cocaine being shipped.

Friday, October 12, 2007. A balmy fifty-seven-degree evening in Brooklyn as Boris Nayfeld arrived at Passage Palace in his black Bentley. There were more than two hundred invited guests at the party. The cocktail hour featured ice sculptures of exotic animals surrounded by black caviar and red caviar. The champagne was Veuve Clicquot, the cognac Louis XIII. Over dinner, a six-piece band backed up a popular Brighton Beach singer, Misha Botsman, as he belted out Russian chansons.

To some of the guests, the evening seemed more like a wedding reception than a birthday party, especially when Botsman made a dramatic introduction in Russian:

"Ladies and gentlemen, Mr. and Mrs. Boris Nayfeld!"

Angela wore a stunning Versace gown and Boris a navy-blue Armani suit as they waltzed around the parquet floor. Boris flashed a grin—he'd always prided himself on his deft ballroom dancing moves.

"Friends came to New York from almost every state for the party," Boris recalls. "They flew in from Russia, Belarus, Ukraine. The restaurant was packed with family, business partners, criminals. At a party of mine—of course, how could there not be criminals? We had our own security surrounding the restaurant, watching everyone coming and going."

A heavy presence of federal law enforcement was outside doing the same thing.

Not only did the feds have cars sitting outside taking pictures of the entrance, they also installed cameras inside the restaurant to be able to see who sat with who at the tables. Later, one of the feds tells me, "Boris, we didn't want to spoil your birthday party, but we needed to put cameras inside the place—we needed to see all the criminals who showed up."

Well, the *musors* did what they had to do. And we did what we had to do. Of course, we had conversations about our criminal business! I think that's one of the best things that can happen at a party like mine—it's so difficult for the feds to make their recordings while there's so much loud music. At one point, after dinner, Roberto, Kolya, and me are at a table, working out the details about the first shipment of cocaine we were going to bring into Odessa, and the band was blasting chansons in my ear. People were shouting and laughing. I thought, If the place is bugged, good luck to the *musors* trying to understand a fucking word we're saying with all this ruckus!

We were drinking and dancing until about three in the morning. And then we took a break, went home to catch a bit of sleep. We were supposed to go out to another restaurant the next day around noon to do the hangover cure. But we never got the chance to do the hangover cure. Before we could even sober up, the *musors* made their move.

CHAPTER 29

THE LAST PARTY

Boris had, by his own estimate, a dozen out-of-town guests, including Roberto Alcaino, staying at his home on Nevada Avenue in Staten Island. Just before 7:30 A.M. a tactical team of DEA agents smashed open the back door and burst in, guns drawn.

"Everyone's in my house—asleep or resting," Boris recalls.

My cousin Venya and a few others arrived around seven A.M., waiting for us to wake up and go out to the restaurant and continue the party. But then—*boom!*—these fucking feds come crashing in. There must have been fifteen or twenty of them. They've got their Glocks, a few rifles, tactical vests, screaming like maniacs.

One was a Russian-speaking DEA agent. I remember thinking that was interesting: "The DEA's got Russians working with them now?" This guy kept shouting in Russian, "Where's the weapons? Where's the money? Where's the drugs?" In seconds, they've got everybody down on the floor in handcuffs. They keep yelling about guns, drugs, money.

Drugs, guns, money. If anyone even twitched, they'd point their guns and shout, "Stay down!"

We had no weapons or drugs in the house, but they did find a bunch of cash that was given to me at the party. When Russians go to a party, we don't bring wrapped-up presents. It's always envelopes with cash. The gifts totaled about ten thousand bucks. Even though Angela kept telling them it was for my birthday, the feds opened the envelopes, confiscated the cash, and never returned it.

The $10,300 in cash seized from the home of Boris Nayfeld is listed in the superseding indictment's "money judgement," a forfeiture of $300 million which the government alleged was "the gross proceeds" that the defendants obtained as a result of the criminal conspiracy. In addition to the cash the indictment lists a Riva 63 Vertigo yacht; an Aston Martin; a villa in Nice, France; numerous properties in Moscow and Odessa; dozens of bank accounts around the world; and a 2.9-carat diamond taken from the apartment of Nikolai Dozortsev.

ALL THE OUT-OF-TOWN HOUSEGUESTS and Boris's family—shocked, groggy, hungover—were handcuffed and taken outside on the front lawn, as the neighbors gaped on a sunny Saturday morning, while the DEA continued to search the house for evidence.

"They pulled me out of the house first," Boris says.

I was alone, handcuffed in the car with a couple of feds. I was the only one arrested. Well, Roberto was arrested, too, but they took him away separately. He went in a different DEA car to New Jersey.

After I was driven away, the feds kept searching my house. They went through the all the closets, ripped open all the drawers and cabinets. We've got a separate guesthouse out back by the swimming pool—they start tearing it apart. The backyard, too. They dug up the entire property. Looking for guns, drugs, phone bills, whatever they could find to connect me to the case. In the end, they didn't find anything—only the ten thousand in cash that was actually my birthday presents.

The *musors* don't take me straight to MCC—first thing they did was take me to the DEA office in Manhattan. "What am I being charged with?" I ask them. They tell me I've been indicted on two felony counts and that I'm looking at between zero to twenty years on each count. Okay. I shrug. I mean, obviously I want to see what they've got on me. The first charge is cocaine trafficking—actually, it says "*attempted* possession of cocaine." And the second is conspiracy to launder money.

I make bail, meet with my lawyer, realize that the DEA has put together a huge ten-year case on Richard, Kolya, Roberto, me. Right away, I know that they've got my voice on tape talking to Kolya about the money pickups in Warsaw—doesn't matter if I try to tell them I was just picking up my own money, that I was repaying a loan to my banker in Moscow—it's going to be useless to fight them on that charge.

But the real problem I've got isn't the DEA wiretaps. It's Roberto. The morning of my party, Roberto went to meet with some cocaine dealer who came from New Jersey to Staten Island. Thank God I didn't go with him to the meeting. At first, I told my son to drive Roberto in the Bentley. But Roberto said, "It's all right, I'll go myself." If my son had taken him to that meeting, Ilyusha would have been charged in the cocaine conspiracy.

By now, I know how Roberto thinks. We've spent a lot of time together. We hung out in California and he traveled with me to Moscow and Odessa. Remember, he's one of the guys in Otisville who first explained to me how to cut your sentence by negotiating with the feds.

Now I'm one hundred percent sure that he's busy working out a deal with the DEA to cooperate.

I'm sitting there in my lawyer's office going through these charges. The allegations make it sound like me and Roberto are plotting to bring tons and tons of cocaine into Russia through the Ukraine. Sure, we were talking about doing a test run, importing a hundred kilos of cocaine into Odessa, but it was still only *talk*. No money ever changed hands. No cocaine was ever shipped. Okay, fine, we were plotting, but we never actually *did* it.

Still, I know how it played out during my 1994 RICO case. I know how the conspiracy laws can be used to trap you. Roberto can testify that me and Kolya Dozortsev are plotting a massive cocaine business with him. Even with no one caught red-handed, not a single gram of cocaine shipped from Colombia, I know what it means when a guy starts cooperating with the feds. He can talk about things that never took place, things that were only dreamed about, things only discussed in *theory,* and make it sound like a colossal conspiracy: *The Russian Mafia's connected to the cartels in Colombia! They're shipping tons of cocaine from Medellin to Odessa!*

I told my attorney, "Listen, if the feds drop the bullshit cocaine charge, I'll take the money laundering." Our offer suited the feds. I agreed to plead guilty to money laundering and pay whatever fine they demanded. I said to my lawyer, "Just get me in front of the judge so he can give me a sentence—then I'll go do my fucking time."

THE ARRESTS MADE GLOBAL HEADLINES and were trumpeted by U.S. Attorney General Michael Mukasey during a March 2008 speech at the London School of Economics as an example of the kind of international cooperation between law enforcement agencies required to bring sophisticated modern narcotraffickers to justice.

But for all the fanfare of the arrests, in the end, there were few court-room theatrics in Brooklyn. All the defendants quietly worked out plea agreements. Confidential deals were negotiated in the opaque process between prosecutors and defense attorneys that is an integral part of the federal court system and that leaves many details—such as the degree of a defendant's cooperation—filed under seal.

One thing is clear: no one wanted a lengthy jury trial, least of all the U.S. Justice Department. Assistant U.S. Attorney Steve Tiscione admitted as much during the sentencing of Nikolai Dozortsev.

All the accused had been given "generous plea agreements," Tiscione said, in order to "dispose of this case with numerous defendants that would have taken a six-month trial and cost the government an enormous amount of money, since ninety-nine percent of the evidence and witnesses were overseas. [The investigation] spanned several continents. It would have been an absolute nightmare to try the case."

Nikolai Dozortsev pled guilty to one count of money launder-ing and received a sentence of forty-one months in prison. His half-brother Arthur Dozortsev pled guilty to the same count and received probation.

Skillful lawyering by a high-powered defense team led by Gerald Shargel—John Gotti's former attorney—allowed Ricardo Fanchini to plead guilty to a single count of conspiring to distribute 424 kilograms of MDMA seized in the Netherlands, and in November 2008 he was sentenced to ten years in federal prison and ordered to pay a $30 million money judgement.

ON JUNE 15, 2009, Boris Nayfeld came before Judge Charles P. Sifton and pled guilty to one count of conspiracy to launder money in connec-tion with the counterfeit-cigarette operation in Odessa.

"I'd been out on bail for a year and a half by then," Boris says.

At sentencing, the first thing the judge asks the prosecutor is whether or not I've paid the fine—the $150,000 they wanted from me. The prosecutor confirms that I've paid up. Then the judge gives me my sentence. He hits me with five years.

I didn't have to start serving the five years right away—they gave me a few months to put my affairs in order. I was ordered to turn myself in on October fifth, 2009, the day after my birthday.

Boris's attorney received special permission from the judge for his client to attend a sixty-second birthday party in Brighton Beach on October 4 before surrendering himself to the U.S. Marshals Service at noon the following day.

We partied it up at Tatiana, right there on the boardwalk in Brighton. It was more of a farewell than a birthday, honestly. People came to see me knowing I'd already been sentenced. They came to say their goodbyes since I was going off to prison. Doesn't matter if you think, "Well, it's only five years," once you go to prison anything can happen. No one knows if you're really coming home. We partied at Tatiana, had some caviar, oysters, lobster, beef stroganoff. I sipped a few glasses of XO cognac. That's one thing I knew for sure: I wouldn't be tasting cognac for at least five years.

We partied until two or three A.M. I didn't sleep much—my son drove me to MCC and I turned myself in. Straightaway, they stuck me in solitary for more than seven months.

By now, Boris was considered a convicted "high-ranking member of Russian organized crime," so the Bureau of Prisons determined that he should serve his five-year sentence in a correctional facility somewhere in the United States where there were no other Russian-speaking

criminals—until that time he was to be confined alone in an eighteen-
by-twelve-foot cell, having no communications or contact with other
prisoners and no outside visitation.

The extreme isolation of the Special Housing Unit (SHU), which is
used to lock up many terror suspects, has been denounced as violating
basic human rights by Amnesty International. The supermax floors of
MCC are often referred to as "Little Gitmo."

At MCC, the general population is on the seventh floor, but in 2009
they put me into solitary confinement on the ninth floor so that I
couldn't communicate with anyone. The Special Housing Unit—they
call it the Shoe. You're in your cell alone for twenty-three hours a day.
You've got a camera on you all the time. No human contact, except the
guard once a day. When it's time to shower, you've got to turn your back
to the door, put your hands through the little slot—there's a slot where
they pass your food—and get cuffed. The guard opens the door, leads
you out backwards by the handcuffs, stands you against the wall, and
starts the *shmon*.

What's the point of the fucking frisking? You're only wearing a
T-shirt and underwear. In this little anteroom, you extend your hands,
the guard removes the cuffs, and then you can go shower. All this
hassle, mind you, to get to a shower stall that's about two meters from
my cell! Afterwards, you repeat the whole cuffing procedure going
back. It was such a pain in the ass, some days I just refused to go
shower at all.

For nearly eight months at MCC, I didn't get a single breath of
fresh air. I didn't see the sun. The only exercise I got was being taken
to this small room—five meters long and maybe three meters wide.
You're allowed to walk around that room alone for an hour. No fitness
equipment for exercising. I'd just do push-ups and calisthenics and
walk back and forth for the hour.

I'm no stranger to doing time, but solitary confinement for seven and a half months—that's rough. You can go crazy in solitary for too long. Can't watch TV, can't socialize with other inmates, can't play cards or chess when you're by yourself.

Finally, Boris drew a line in the sand.

The warden and some other officer from the MCC administration come around inspecting conditions in all the solitary confinement cells. They ask me if there are any problems.

I say: "Yes, there's a problem—how long are you going to keep me in total isolation?" I tell them, "It's been more than seven months! Send me to the general population floor, otherwise I'll stop eating—I'm going on a hunger strike!" Well, in the end, I didn't have to go on a hunger strike because after eight months—finally—they told me they'd found me a prison in Colorado that had no other Russians.

The only positive about that time in solitary was when this inmate came by with books from the prison library. I wasn't much of a reader when I was younger. Honestly, doing time when you're sixty—or sixty-two—it's a lot different than doing time when you're twenty. Or forty. Your mind is in a different place. At age sixty-two, stuck in the Shoe, I figured the best way to do this time is to spend the time reading. Maybe I could catch up on some of the education I missed all those years I was skipping school, read some of the books Evsei used to talk about.

One good thing about MCC—it has a huge library of Russian books. So many Russians have been locked up there over the years, they've built up quite a collection. Back in the nineties they used to allow inmates' families to mail books, but they've forbidden that now. All the books need to be shipped direct from bookstores. And they need to be paperbacks—hardcover books are forbidden, because supposedly they can be used as weapons.

I wasn't interested in today's stuff, you know, the criminal pulp fiction. I'm talking about the classics. I read the Russian greats: Tolstoy, Turgenev, Isaac Babel. They had some decent Russian history books, too, starting from the time of the Ruriks on through the lives of Ivan the Terrible and Peter the Great.

While I was stuck in the Shoe all those months, the writer I got fascinated with—*completely* fascinated with—was Dostoevsky. A great writer—a genius writer, a very complicated writer. He'd been sentenced to *katorga*—hard labor—in Siberia during czarist times. In exile out there in Siberia he met burglars, bandits, murderers—all the criminal types. He observed the criminal behavior closely and, once he was released from the penal colony, he started writing about it in his novels.

I read all of Dostoevsky's books. All the ones they had in the MCC library, at least. *Crime and Punishment. The Brothers Karamazov. The Gambler.* I *loved* that book.

It's a short novel; very few people read it anymore. It educated me to the fact that Dostoevsky was a gambler—just like me! He became addicted to roulette and had to write the book quickly for his publisher just to pay back his gambling debts. The main character is based on Dostoevsky himself—I have no idea if the English translation is any good, but in Russian it's brilliant.

Then there's *Demons. The Double. Notes from Underground. The Idiot*—that's also a great book, by the way.

Crime and Punishment is probably my favorite—the way he opens up not just the criminality but the psychology of Raskolnikov. The book gives you the true essence of a murderer. In my opinion, Raskolnikov is somewhat abnormal. I mean, on the one hand, he's a merciless killer—hacking the old moneylender to death and also her female servant. On the other hand, he goes about helping a widow who's sick with tuberculosis—or consumption, as it was called back then.

Reading Dostoevsky, I got the feeling he must have lived these experiences, *personally,* that he must have walked down this path. It was almost like he committed these crimes himself. That's genius. For nearly eight months in the Shoe—I'll be honest with you: only Dostoevsky kept me company. Honestly, I couldn't believe how well he understood the criminal mind.

CHAPTER 30

CRIME AND PUNISHMENT

It had been decades since I'd read *Crime and Punishment*. I dug through a box of my old college books and dusted off my Penguin Classics copy after talking to Boris about his marathon reading sessions in solitary at MCC.

I'd completely forgotten that the punishment in the novel comes only in a brief epilogue, after Raskolnikov has made his confession to the two murders; he's sent off to serve eight years of hard labor in Siberia. At first, he feels no remorse or regret; he considers himself to be guilty only of being weak and unsuccessful:

> What is meant by crime? My conscience is at rest. Of course, it was a legal crime, of course, the letter of the law was broken and blood was shed. Well, punish me for the letter of the law . . . and that's enough. Of course, in that case many of the benefactors of mankind who snatched power for themselves instead of inheriting it ought to have been punished at their first steps. But those men

succeeded and so they were right, and I didn't, and so I had no right to have taken that step.

In those controversial final pages, Raskolnikov rejects his own nihilism, embraces his love for the prostitute Sonia, picks up her copy of the New Testament. There begins a new story, Dostoevsky writes, "the story of the gradual renewal of a man, the story of his gradual regeneration, of his passing from one world into another, of his initiation into a new unknown life."

For his part, after eight months in solitary confinement in MCC, Boris Nayfeld was flown out west to serve the remainder of his five-year sentence in the mountains of Colorado. In June 2010, he arrived at the Federal Correctional Institution at Englewood, in the southwestern suburbs of Denver. Situated between several golf courses and parks, with a clear view of the nearby Rocky Mountains, FCI Englewood has a reputation as a "country club" prison. In 2002, *Forbes* magazine ranked Englewood "one of the best places" to do time in the United States.

"Colorado was a low-security zone," Boris says.

To me, it didn't even feel like a prison. All the fitness machines and weights were brand-new. That was my job, by the way. I got paid to run the gym. Honestly, I only showed up a few minutes each day to tell the guys to keep the place looking clean. On Friday, Saturday, and Sunday we had movies in a proper theater. There was a large yard complete with soccer, baseball fields, two large tennis courts, squash and handball courts. Inside, we had pool tables and ping-pong.

They send a lot of the so-called white collars there. The most notable guy doing time with me was the governor of the State of Illinois—Rod Blagojevich. He got fourteen years for trying to sell a workplace in his administration for a million dollars. He's Serbian, but he knows how to speak a little bit of Russian. I used to chat with Blagojevich in Russian every day until one of the other prisoners comes up to me and says, "Boris, be careful what you say to him! Don't you know he used to be a prosecutor?"[*]

In an American zone, unlike a Russian one, since they feed you properly, your main challenge is boredom. "How do I do this time productively?" There were no Russian-language books in Englewood, so I would play chess—we had tournaments every time there was a federal holiday, and I was always champion. I'm no grandmaster or anything, but I'd learned to play at the internat in Gomel. We'd have tournaments and I always won the chess tournaments. You wouldn't get a trophy or an award, just ten cans of Pepsi.

WHILE IN COLORADO, when he wasn't lifting weights or winning chess tournaments, Boris also decided he wanted to illicitly ink his entire life story on his body.

"There were about a thousand inmates in there with me in Colorado," he says.

Only four did tattoos. They were all Latinos and rednecks. Now, in a U.S. prison, the majority of Latinos get tattoos of their families' faces on the chest. I mean, faces of the wife, the kids. It's an initial sign to everyone that you're normal—that you're not gay.

I asked around. The Latinos specialized in tattooing faces, but the white guys, the rednecks, specialized in inscriptions. I decided I

---

* Having served eight of the fourteen years for selling the Illinois Senate seat vacated by Barack Obama, former governor Blagojevich had his sentence commuted by President Donald Trump on February 18, 2020, and was released from FCI Englewood that same day.

needed to ink the words "God Forgive Me" in Hebrew on my belly. I also wanted to have a tattoo of the Torah and the Star of David—well, because I'm a Jew. Not a deeply religious one, but nonetheless a Jew.

I can't read or write Hebrew, so the first step was to get a rabbi to write out the words I wanted. Every Friday in Colorado I attended a Shabbat service. There was a community of about twenty Jews who got together to pray on Friday nights and welcome the Shabbat.

A young rabbi just got transferred to us from New York. Funny enough, he was from Brighton—his parents still lived there. He was about thirty-five years old. I asked him to write the inscription.

"Rabbi, I've sinned a lot," I told him. "I need it to say: God Forgive Me."

"No problem, Boris," he says, and he writes it down on paper in Hebrew.

SEVERAL YEARS LATER, when we sat together, half naked, sweating bullets in a 93-degree Celsius (nearly two hundred degrees Fahrenheit) *banya* in Sheepshead Bay—only a few blocks from where he was nearly fatally shot by Vadik Reznikov in 1986—I found it curious that the massive tattoo Boris has inked across his belly doesn't include the Ineffable Name of God—the sacred Tetragrammaton (*yud-hey-vav-hey*), four letters observant Jews are never allowed pronounce aloud.*

Instead, Boris's tattoo reads *Hashem*—Hebrew for "the Name"—which is how many observant Jews choose to refer to God.

---

* In ancient times the actual name of the God of Israel—which has been anglicized as "Jehovah"—was only uttered once a year, on Yom Kippur, by the High Priest in the temple in Jerusalem.

I took the rabbi's paper to the redneck tattooist. He played around with it and found a book in the library that had the Hebrew alphabet. Evans was an artist—a *real* tattoo artist. You never know who you'll meet in prison! He put the design together in beautiful Hebrew letters. Also, he drew the book of Torah. He drew King David's crown and a pair of lions.

Evans had never met a Jew in his life. He was from Kentucky or Kansas or someplace where I've never set foot in my life—and likely never will. He was doing a bid for bank robbery. He sketched it all out, I came to see the drawing, we negotiated and agreed on a price.

Now, if you get caught getting a tattoo in federal prison, it's no slap on the wrist. Worst case, they can put you in fucking solitary for up to one year. Best case, you lose your phone privileges, can't buy anything in the commissary. And they can dock you fifty-one days from your good time credit. Plus, it can affect your parole—that's if you get caught with a freshly inked and bleeding tattoo.

Well, this didn't scare me. I was in Unit One and I had to sneak over to see Evans in Unit Four. We started the process after lunch. That's the best time. After lunch most of the inmates are gone; some are at their jobs, some out on the yard exercising.

There's no professional tattoo gun in prison, obviously. But Evans had made one as good as the real thing—he disassembled a small fan you could buy in the commissary, took the tiny motor and hooked it up on a melted toothbrush; that motor drove the needle rapidly and with perfect precision. The ink he used was drawn from different ballpoint pens: black, red, blue. It was a very ingenious system.

The big issue is the C.O. patrolling the block, so Evans has his cellmate using a small mirror to see around the corner, and as soon as the officer starts moving towards Evans's cell, the lookout gives the alert—within seconds I've rolled under the bed. The officer looks in and only sees Evans and his cellmate, everything's in order, and then he walks on.

My tattoos were all fairly big pieces, and it took us about four or five sessions to complete—it took longer than it should, probably, because every few hours, I'd have to roll under the bed to hide from the C.O.

Another thing: between sessions, I had to be careful to walk around in a heavy shirt—*always*—otherwise the raw bleeding would be visible. I also had to refuse to shower during the entire time we were making the tattoos. If the authorities can't *prove* that your tattoo is fresh— meaning, done recently inside *their* prison—they have no right to charge you with a violation.

Little by little, I was able to get everything inked on me. Each of my tattoos carries a specific meaning in prison settings. The skulls, the scorpion, the cobra—any Russian criminal can read the tattoos on my body just like you would read a book.

In his old age, Boris returned to that venerable code of the *vor v zakone* he'd first learned at age eighteen inside Colony Number 2 at Bobruisk.

And it's fair to say that in the symbolic jailhouse autobiography inked on his upper body, Boris Nayfeld confesses to far more serious crimes than he was ever convicted of. "Given the kind of activities I've been involved in—I've sinned a *lot*, let's just put it that way. I always have something to ask Hashem to forgive me for. I needed that Hebrew tattoo most of all: God knows I have *so* many sins!"

ONCE HE WAS FINISHED UP with the months of tattooing in Colorado, Boris discovered that he had an affinity for practicing hatha yoga and an untapped artistic talent—best expressed through the fiber arts.

I'd hurt my shoulder and I started taking the yoga classes. I couldn't believe how much it helped with the pain. I still try to practice yoga every day when I wake up—*imagine*!

The air was clean and cold and fresh. The Rocky Mountains were right *there*. When I walked around the yard, I'd see coyotes outside the fence, and sometimes right in our playing fields, I'd watch eagles swoop down from high in the blue sky and catch rabbits or prairie dogs.

Not a bad prison at all, Colorado. I quite liked it. If you've got to spend four or five years locked up, Colorado's a good place to do it.

The best thing I learned out there was crocheting. The prison offered us courses and I chose crochet. I'd make quilts and pillowcases and send them to Angela or my sister-in-law and my niece. Anyone who wanted a quilt, I'd crochet one and send it to them. Crocheting is a great time killer, a great way to do your sentence. And for a person like me, it really helps calm you down psychologically.

In 2014, when he flew back to New York City from his stint in Colorado, Boris was a sixty-seven-year-old two-time convicted felon with no legitimate employment history and, even after three decades in the United States, still rudimentary English skills.

What, then, becomes of an aging, heavily tattooed Russian-speaking Jewish gangster? Boris Nayfeld was never likely to spend his golden years crocheting quilts or unrolling his yoga mat at dawn for vinyasas of cobra and downward-facing dog.

Indeed, it wasn't long before Boris was once again in the news: this time as a would-be hit man who conspired to turn a contract killing into an extortion plot against a shipping magnate in the midst of a scorched-earth divorce.

Department of Justice

U.S. Attorney's Office

Southern District of New York

January 15, 2016

Two Individuals Charged in Manhattan Federal Court with Extortion Plot

Preet Bharara, the United States Attorney for the Southern District of New York, Diego Rodriguez, Assistant Director-in-Charge of the New York Office of the Federal Bureau of Investigation ("FBI"), and William J. Bratton, Commissioner of the New York City Police Department ("NYPD"), announced that BORIS KOTLYARSKY and BORIS NAYFELD were taken into custody yesterday for seeking payment from a victim who they claimed NAYFELD had been hired to murder. . . .

Manhattan U.S. Attorney Preet Bharara said: "As alleged, Boris Kotlyarsky and Boris Nayfeld conspired to extort $125,000 from a victim, claiming that Nayfeld had been hired to murder the victim. Thanks to the FBI and the NYPD, the victim is unharmed and the defendants are under arrest." . . .

NYPD Commissioner William J. Bratton said: "As alleged, this thuggish story seems like a yarn made only in Hollywood. But today, in New York, these two defendants find themselves charged in [a] brazen extortion plot."

Even by the standards of Russian organized crime, the scheme was bizarre and byzantine; the veracity of many of the accusations is still in dispute today.

The version presented by prosecutors in the Southern District of New York is this: Sometime during mid-2015, Boris met with Anatoly

Potik, a sixty-seven-year-old Soviet émigré businessman—the same Potik for whom Boris and Yaponchik had provided *krysha* in the former Soviet Union during the Wild Nineties. At the meeting, Potik groused to Boris about the messy divorce his daughter was embroiled in and, allegedly, put a $100,000 contract out on his difficult son-in-law.

The story was tailor-made for the New York tabloids: the divorcing couple were wealthy Upper East Siders—Oleg Mitnik, a forty-four-year-old Kiev-born "shipping magnate," and his forty-two-year-old wife, Ronit, described as an Israeli "socialite"—embroiled in what the *New York Post* called "one of the most bizarre and bitter" divorce cases in memory. They were feuding over custody of their teenage children and the substantial fortune Oleg Mitnik had made as the president of TRT International, a global freight-shipping company based in Newark. He reportedly also had an $8 million life insurance policy—and had removed his wife's name as beneficiary.

Enter the third in this unlikely trio of conspiratorial Jewish grandfathers born in the Soviet Union: Boris Kotlyarsky—a sixty-seven-year-old businessman, also originally from Kiev, who was introduced to Boris Nayfeld at Chateau De Capitaine, a glitzy bar and grill on Coney Island Avenue in Gravesend known for its lavish Russian-style banquets—and for its popularity among Russian-speaking mobsters. When Boris Nayfeld mentioned the name Oleg Mitnik, Boris Kotlyarsky said, "I know him, he's a good guy."

Who precisely came up with the idea of turning this "good guy" into a target for extortion remains unclear, but in December 2015 and January 2016, Kotlyarsky brokered several meetings at Brooklyn restaurants between Oleg Mitnik and Boris Nayfeld.

Unbeknownst to either of the Borises, once Mitnik heard about the contract on his life he went straight to the cops. All the restaurant meetings were under surveillance by the FBI and NYPD. For the second meeting with Boris Nayfeld, on January 11, 2016, Oleg Mitnik wore a wire. He and Nayfeld spoke for eighty minutes and, according to the FBI's complaint:

> Nayfeld said it was good that Kotlyarsky had intervened on the Victim's behalf. Nayfeld told the Victim to pay him $125,000 to cancel the contract, with $50,000 due by Friday, January 15, 2016.

When Nayfeld and Mitnik met for a third time on January 14, 2016, at Michael's, an upscale Italian restaurant on Avenue R in Marine Park, Mitnik again wore a recording device, and this time his cell phone was wiretapped by the feds. Mitnik said that he wanted assurances that, even after paying the $50,000, he would be safe. Mitnik dialed his father-in-law's number and handed the phone to Boris Nayfeld.

> Nayfeld said aloud, in substance and in part, do not touch the Victim or I will harm you.

Mitnik then wrote a check on his business account, without specifying a recipient, in the amount of $50,000. He handed it to Boris Nayfeld. As Boris was about to leave the restaurant with his son, four FBI cars swarmed in. Again, according to the complaint:

> Nayfeld muttered an expletive and tore up the check. Nayfeld was then arrested.

Kotlyarsky and Nayfeld were both charged with two counts of Hobbs Act extortion. Potik was arrested at JFK Airport with his wife while allegedly trying to flee the country. He was initially charged in the murder-for-hire plot, but those charges were dismissed, and he pled guilty of one count of extortion but did no prison time, since he began cooperating with the government.

Boris Nayfeld immediately began working out a deal with prosecutors, holding Boris Kotlyarsky entirely responsible for the fiasco. "When I ended up in MCC, I found myself on the same floor with Kotlyarsky. 'Borya, you snake!' I said. 'You're the only one to blame for my sitting in here!'"

Nayfeld claims that he found Kotlyarsky hunched over in his cell and sobbing. "I said, 'Why are you crying, motherfucker? What? Has your life ended?'"

Boris Nayfeld claims that he never had any intention of harming Oleg Mitnik on behalf of Anatoly Potik—the U.S. government also now maintains that there was never a genuine murder plot—and that the shakedown was an offshoot of a much more grandiose criminal conspiracy, one right in Biba's wheelhouse of multi-million-dollar "money-extraction" jobs. In the October 2016 indictment against Kotlyarsky, the first count of conspiracy to commit extortion alleges that the two men had agreed to use Nayfeld's "reputation for violence and association with organized crime figures to recover Kotlyarsky's business interests in Russia."

When I was introduced to Kotlyarsky in Chateau De Capitaine, he told me he'd been stiffed for something like twenty million dollars in Russia. I said, "What do you mean 'you've been stiffed'?" He tells me that he had a dry-cargo shipping company, but his Moldovan partner stole it from him. In the late nineties, the feds were trying to put Kotlyarsky away on conspiracy to launder money charges. He ended up doing a little under two years in a camp, but while he was inside this partner stole the company from him.

"No problem," I say, "I'll extract your money. The only thing I need to get is a permit to enter Russia"—I was still on probation from my money-laundering conviction—"and as soon as I can, I'll fly over there and start recovering what's owed to you."

A pipe dream?

Clearly.

Yet I imagine that as Boris Nayfeld mulled over the money-extraction job, he envisioned it as that ultimate gangster retirement plan: *The Last Big Score.*

Had he managed to extract the $20 million from Russia, Boris's 50 percent cut would have set him up to live out the rest of his life in a dacha on the shores of the Black Sea or a gated mansion in the suburbs of Moscow . . .

But they never managed to recover a kopek of the $20 million that was allegedly stolen in Russia. (Kotlyarsky has denied ever enlisting Nayfeld's help in retrieving his business ventures in the former Soviet Union.) "As the saying goes, 'It's better to lose with a smart person than to win with a stupid one.' Well, I wouldn't say Kotlyarsky is stupid—in fact, he's not—but the way things played out, the only thing I 'won' with him was a prison term."

EVEN AFTER THE CRIMINAL CASES WERE RESOLVED, the courtroom drama continued: one new *matryoshka* doll popping out of another. Oleg Mitnik sued his estranged wife and father-in-law for $20 million for emotional distress and defamation. The case was dismissed. Ronit Mitnik countersued, claiming that there never was a murder plot and that her husband had concocted the entire story to gain sympathy and leverage in the divorce proceedings.

The most litigious of all was Boris Kotlyarsky. He still maintains that he is wholly innocent, merely a Good Samaritan who was trying to save Oleg Mitnik's life. Although Kotlyarsky pled guilty to federal extortion charges and was sentenced to a forty-one-month prison term, he later asked the court to vacate his conviction and reduce his sentence, claiming he had received inadequate counsel, been denied access to crucial exculpatory evidence, and suffered duress of being forced, as a sixty-seven-year-old man, to contemplate the prospect of dying in prison. The district court dismissed all Kotlyarsky's complaints as being without merit.

In November 2020, he filed another suit, this time against the U.S. Justice Department, former FBI director James Comey, and former U.S. attorney for the SDNY Preet Bharara, claiming that his civil rights were violated and seeking $250 million in damages. That case is currently pending as of the writing of this book.*

> The sentence, however, was more merciful than could have been expected. . . . All the strange and peculiar circumstances of the crime were taken into consideration. There could be no doubt of the abnormal and poverty-stricken condition of the criminal at the time.
>   —Epilogue, *Crime and Punishment*

If Boris Nayfeld had been convicted at trial of the two counts of Hobbs Act extortion, he was looking at a sentence of several decades of incarceration and would likely have died in prison. But he pled guilty to one count of conspiracy to commit extortion, offered substantial cooperation to prosecutors, and signed a 5K1 letter—the details of which are sealed.

During the sentencing hearing on July 27, 2017, in the United States District Court for the Southern District of New York in front of Judge

---

* The suit alleges that the defendants engaged in "a baseless and malicious prosecution" of Kotlyarsky, a self-styled "hero who blew the whistle on the killer's plot," fabricating evidence that led to Kotlyarsky's arrest "in order to protect an FBI informant: would be murderer, Anatoly Potik."

Katherine Forrest, Assistant U.S. Attorney Andrew Thomas went to great lengths to contextualize Boris Nayfeld's lifelong history of poor decision-making.

"Mr. Nayfeld is obviously a complicated person with a rich criminal history," Thomas said. "He has for most of his adult life been in Russian organized crime. He has involved himself in all manner of illegal activity. . . . I think Mr. Nayfeld recognizes that that existence has led him to lose a significant chunk of his liberty.

"For his entire adulthood, he didn't know any other way and that left him obviously incarcerated multiple times, destitute, and looking for some way to stay on his feet at the time of the charged conduct here." Although he said that Boris was entirely culpable for his role in the extortion plot, Thomas intimated that he was also, to some degree, being exploited; his financial desperation had provided "others with an opening to attempt to take his reputation and leverage it to their collective advantage, perhaps in ways that Mr. Nayfeld didn't appreciate at the time."

Frank Tassone, Boris's defense attorney, described his client as emotionally and financially bereft: "Mr. Nayfeld was living on a Social Security benefit, I think, of $750 a month. He was attempting to seek employment. He was turned down a number of times. . . . I like the word the government used, *destitute*. I think he was destitute not only with regard to the true meaning of the word, but destitute also in spirit and in hope."

Judge Forrest sat on the bench unmoved. She dryly noted that the defendant was no stranger to working out 5K1 deals with the government.

"It's the second time, right?" she said. "This is not the first time. As a practitioner recently said to me, this kind of plea is not a car wash for the soul."

She was less interested in the complicated nature of Boris Nayfeld's personality, or his miserable childhood, than in "whether or not the government believes that this individual presents a danger to society."

"This individual has been involved in very dangerous activity," she said. "I assume his reputation is not unmerited and that his reputation was built upon his conduct, that there was a reason why he was able to utilize that reputation in a credible manner to try to extract a very significant sum of money from someone who believed they were going to be killed. . . . I think the question really for the government is: Are you folks prepared to have this fellow on the street?"

AUSA Thomas replied that, now nearly seventy years old, the danger posed to society by Boris Nayfeld was minimal. "At this point he is removed in time and removed in community connection from the persons [for] whom his reputation is most meaningful," Thomas said. "So I think, perhaps, we are at a moment where the reinforcing cycle of the myth of Boris Nayfeld has probably reached its end."

BORIS HIMSELF TOOK THE OPPORTUNITY to address the court, saying succinctly, without use of a translator: "I would like to apologize to everybody who I did hurt. Maybe I don't have a long time to live because at seventy, I can go at any time. If it's possible, just to die at home."

As she prepared to pass sentence, Judge Forrest wondered aloud about the sincerity of the defendant's contrition and motives for cooperation. "I look at him as a potentially very dangerous man," she said. "I don't have any basis to believe, apart from argument, that the post-arrest conduct is more than a very reasonable strategic decision by the defendant to do that which one would do to get out of jail in a reasonable period of time. . . . What I have to do as the representative of society is to make a judgment about all of the various factors, how dangerous I think Mr. Nayfeld is, despite his age."

In the end, she agreed to a "significant departure" from the sentencing guidelines: only twenty-three months of incarceration; with credit for the eighteen months he'd already been in MCC, Boris would be free in five months. And he would be under supervised release—on probation—for three years.

"But I will tell you, I do this with some hesitation because I am concerned . . . about placing somebody in our community who may not be dangerous to me or to you but could well and truly be lethal to someone else," Judge Forrest said. "I proceed with great caution. I hope [the government] keeps a very close eye on this situation."

AFTER HIS RELEASE FROM MCC, still on probation, Boris applied to the court for permission to travel back to Russia. He presented evidence of a job offer to begin work, on a three-month trial basis, as the commercial director of a mill in the city of Bryansk, 379 kilometers southwest of Moscow, close to the border with Belarus. He would supposedly be working forty hours a week and earning about $30,000 annually.

In his petition he claimed that due to the widespread publicity following his 2016 arrest, "I have become isolated; many people will not socialize with me. I no longer have contact with my former friends." He also told the court that he was under a physician's care for depression, anxiety, and insomnia.

BY LATE 2021, during the COVID-19 pandemic, Boris was living at a friend's spacious house just outside Moscow. His only income is his monthly U.S. Social Security check; he'd finished with his probation, and the position of "commercial director" in Bryansk apparently wasn't for him.

He no longer keeps a residence in New York; whenever he's in the United States, he's a houseguest of his brother, Gena, his clothes and other possessions stored in neatly stacked clear plastic boxes from Home Depot.

Gena Nayfeld, it's worth noting, has *no* criminal record—from the Soviet days or in the United States; after emigration, Gena has been a model tax-paying citizen, working his entire life installing windows and doors.

It's baffling, in one sense, how two brothers—separated by only eleven months, sharing the same biological parents—could have such vastly different personalities and life trajectories, but, in another sense, it's a classic pattern in the complex tapestry of Jewish American life.

Louis "Lepke" Buchalter, the infamous labor racketeer, head of "Murder Inc.," and the only mob boss to receive the death penalty in the United States—he died in the electric chair at Sing Sing Correctional Facility on March 4, 1944—was similarly the black sheep of his family: Louis's brothers Emanuel and Isadore Buchalter were, respectively, a dentist and a pharmacist; and his half brother, the Lithuanian-born Rabbi Charles Eliezer Hillel Kauvar, Ph.D., was a highly respected religious leader, author, and educator in Denver.

As of this writing, Boris was in the process of finalizing his second divorce. He was estranged from all three of his adult children; he'd had no contact with his grandchildren in many years. He was in the twilight of a life that, as he told me several times, had brought him "very few bright days."

And yet, he'd given several interviews in which he'd said he regretted *nothing*, that if he was born again, he'd live his life the same way.

I didn't buy the "no regrets" line.

It sounded too pat, too reflexive, a defensive posture devoid of any of the melancholy I'd sometimes seen when talking to Boris.

Several times over the past year I asked him the following questions:

Was it worth it?

Would you live your life the same way again?

Do you really have no regrets?

He left his answers in the form of WhatsApp voice message monologues, recorded in Russian as he was out walking at five or six in the morning in the suburbs of Moscow.

"If I were given a chance to start again, would I have chosen the same life? That's a very complicated question," Boris told me.

When I was born, in those years just after the war, with the food shortages and few opportunities, it was a very hard time. I understand my father doing what he needed to do, making money "on the left." What he did is not a crime today—it's just business. But my dad went to the gulag because the Soviet authorities wouldn't allow energetic people to try to rise up, to quickly make their lives more agreeable.

My mother was far removed from the criminal world. Initially she was a bookkeeper, and once my father went to the gulag . . . you know, I even understand it now: a young woman with two children is left husbandless, she has to live at her husband's parents' house, a guest of her in-laws, no way of knowing whether her husband will ever return. In the time of the gulag, people like my father not only had to survive on the inside, but also make their way back home. Naturally, I understand that she wanted a different life, and she met another man. However, I don't understand her leaving us behind with my father's parents. Abandoning my brother and I so that she could move on—no, that I will *never* understand.

All right, the only reason I mention it is because, as we say in Russian, I didn't "grow up covered in chocolate." I grew up around regular folks.

IN NOVEMBER 2021, as I was completing the manuscript of this book, Boris's niece on Staten Island found an old black-and-white photograph of her father and uncle as infants in Gomel. On the back of the fragile photograph—about the size of a playing card, spiderwebbed with cracks—their mother penned a short, cramped note in purple ink, addressed to the boys' father, Mikhail, who was serving his sentence of hard labor in the gulag on Sakhalin Island.

The note is dated February 28, 1949, when Gennady was just over two years old and Boris was fifteen months.

> *To our loving father from your two sons Gennady Mikhail[ovich] and Boris Mikhai[lovich]. Remember us, dear father, and don't forget that somewhere you have kids and come back as soon as you can, otherwise it's very painful that our childhood will pass without [our] father. The time that we will spend with you, dear father, will be precious to us.*
>
>

Waiting,

Nayfeld

Her addition of the patronymic—Mikhailovich—a formal way of address virtually never used by Russian children with their parents, is telling: a subtle but pointed linguistic jab. It's easy to see Ekaterina's anger and resentment, but perhaps the note is really a cry for help—the frustration of a young mother left with two small boys in the home of her in-laws, who already disapproved of her not being Jewish. By the time Mikhail Nayfeld did return from his gulag sentence, following his amnesty in 1953, Ekaterina had long since departed and remarried, leaving the boys to be raised by their paternal grandparents.

Ekaterina mailed the photo with the heartfelt children's plea to the gulag in 1949, and Mikhail eventually brought it back with his meager possessions to his parents' home; the delicate photo lay untouched for seven decades in a trunk of Bobeh Riva's that traveled with the Nayfelds to America. It is a vivid reminder of the world of dysfunction, chaos, and confusion into which Gena and Boris Nayfeld were born.

"As a young man, yes, I broke the law," Boris says. "I was a *khuligan*."

I spent three years in the zone, and I made money "on the left." During the Soviet times *everyone* had to hustle. Even today, the old immigrants, the ones who have been in America since the seventies and eighties, those who experienced the KGB and all sorts of police repressions, they all learned survival, learned to make a living "on the left." Not in the "way that was taught by the great Lenin," but in any way possible, just to support their families.

I didn't come to America with plans to be a criminal. I thought I'd brought over enough money—the money that I earned through criminal means in the Soviet times, let's put it that way. I thought that since I'd smuggled out those stamps, if I'd been able to start a business, or buy a taxi, maybe my life would have turned out differently. However, since I came to America and found myself with nothing, and on top of that unable to find work, unsuccessful in all my attempts at employment, I began getting into criminal activities.[*]

You're correct in saying that there haven't been any sweet days. A criminal of my level always has problems with the government as well with other criminals. My survival in America, inside the criminal world, always involved wars.

Even if you make a lot of money and build everything so that it's

---

[*] I can't help but point out the glaring discrepancies here: Boris admits he was regularly stealing from supermarkets during his first weeks in Albany and that with Evsei Agron's help, he *did* eventually recover all the money he'd invested in the counterfeit stamps.

hard for the police or the FBI to catch you, you have to engage in war against them. No, I didn't *kill* policemen—I never wanted to *kill* policemen. However, I always had war on my hands, both with the authorities and with criminals wanting to take both my slice of bread and my life away.

It's a highly complicated life. Yet I came to this life consciously. I knew the rules. In this life, nothing came to me for free.

Would I live it the same way again?

Doug, your question is of a rhetorical nature.

Most likely, if I started all over, yes, I'd have lived the same life. And who knows what a new life may have been like? Perhaps the new life would have turned out even *worse* than the one I've already lived!

If I'd been born, as many are, into a trouble-free family, in a trouble-free time, perhaps my life would have turned out better. That's not important. It's been lived already. That's why I say that I don't regret anything. Because I've lived *this* life, whether it was good or bad.

—

In the four years I've spent talking to Boris, there's one Russian word that's leapt out at me—the word on which almost all of his decisions and motivations hinge.

Выживание.

Vyzhivaniye.

Survival.

It comes up in virtually every context.

Survival. As an impoverished child, during three years in a forced labor camp, as a convicted criminal in the Soviet Union; as a new immigrant in America, during the shooting wars with Vladimir Reznikov and Monya Elson.

Even in his old age, the word "survival" is never far from his lips.

Unlike almost all the other high-ranking mob figures from that Soviet émigré community, Boris Nayfeld managed to survive. But at what cost? Without connections to his children or grandchildren, without much money, without peace of mind.

"In this life," he says, "happiness is only possible when you go out on the ocean, when you're on someone's yacht in the Black Sea, and you know no one can sneak up on you. Only then can you relax. Otherwise, you're always on guard.

"No, it's not a life that's brought much joy. The word 'safety' doesn't exist in my world. You never know who might have put out a contract on you, who might have developed a grudge, who you might have hurt or offended, who might be seeking revenge for things you did twenty or thirty years ago. That's why I always need to stay alert. I can't let my guard down—*ever!* It will likely carry on like this as long as I'm alive because people like me never go into retirement. You stay vigilant until such a moment as God calls you.

"I never expected to live to see seventy," Boris says. "People like me don't expect to live long lives. Even now, there's always someone looking to put me in prison or in the grave. I meet guys in Russia today—younger criminals—who tell me that the things we did in the eighties and nineties are still talked about. For good or bad, our era in Brighton Beach is legendary. I tell them, 'I don't want to be a fucking legend. I just want to die in my own bed.'"

ACKNOWLEDGMENTS

First, I'd like to offer my sincere thanks to the entire team at William Morrow, especially my brilliant editor, Mauro DiPreta. Also, my deep appreciation goes out to Vedika Khanna, Andrew Yackira, Liate Stehlik, Benjamin Steinberg, Kelly Rudolph, Pamela Barricklow, Paige Jesionowski, Dale Rohrbaugh, Aryana Hendrawan, Kayleigh George, Anwesha Basu, Jeanne Reina, Ploy Siripant, and Paul Miele-Herndon.

At 3Arts Entertainment, I'd like to thank the extraordinary deal-maker, Richard Abate, and his entire team, especially Martha Stevens.

At ICM Partners, I'm grateful—as always—for the sage advice of my lifelong agent and friend, Sloan Harris; thanks also to Julie Flanagan, Colin Graham, and Josie Freedman.

At Morgan Creek Entertainment, thanks to David Robinson and Barbara Wall, both of whom provided me with invaluable advice, feedback, and support while I was writing and shaping the narrative of this book.

I could not have completed this complex project—especially during the confusion and turmoil of a global pandemic—without the organizational skills and meticulous work of my assistant, Natalie Robson, or my expert Russian-language translator, S.D.—both of whom were insightful readers of my various rough drafts and willing sounding boards for creative ideas.

Likewise, my daughter, Lena Century, and my mother, Marcia Century, were attentive, perceptive listeners and readers throughout the writing process.

I'd finally like to thank Boris Nayfeld and his various family members for giving me countless hours of their time, recounting, interpreting, and clarifying this most fascinating life story; over the past years, I've come to see Biba as the ultimate *blatnoy,* a Russian-speaking Jewish badman, frightening and fierce, to be sure—but as complicated and colorful, in his own way, as a contemporary Benya Krik.

GLOSSARY

APPARATCHIK—Member of the *apparat,* the administrative system of the Communist Party; a blindly devoted official or follower.

ARTICLE 7B—Medical diagnosis of "psychopathy," which would provide an exemption from compulsory military service in the USSR.

BABI YAR—Large ravine on the northern edge of the city of Kiev, Ukraine. The site of a mass grave of victims, mostly Jews, murdered by Nazi Einsatzgruppen squads between 1941 and 1943. Babi Yar is the subject of a famous 1961 poem by the great Russian poet Yevgeny Yevtushenko.

BANYA—Communal bathhouse. An important part of Russian culture, the traditional *banya* was a steam room heated by a wood-burning stove. Over the years, *banya*s began to include extremely hot Scandinavian-style dry saunas as well as cold swimming pools. One distinctive feature is the *venik* thermal massage, stimulating the body's circulation by whipping or brushing the body with a fragrant bundle of birch, oak, or eucalyptus twigs.

BLACK CASH—Soviet-era term for money made "off the books"—in the black market economy of the Soviet Union.

BLAT—Slang term that became practically ubiquitous in the USSR, most likely originally from Yiddish, meaning the use of personal networks and informal contacts to obtain goods and services in short supply. In the Soviet era, when there were constant shortages of food, housing, and consumer goods, *blat* flourished. A popular folk saying was, "*Blat is higher than Stalin!*"

BLATNAYA PESNYA—"Criminals' song"; a genre of Russian song characterized by depictions of prison life and the urban underworld. Now often categorized as "Russian chanson," *blatnaya pesnya* are steeped in the mythology of Odessa, a city of smuggling and wild excess, a paradise for gangsters and thieves. Popular performers of *blatnaya pesnya* include Willi Tokarev, Alexander Rosenbaum, and Mikhail Shufutinsky.

BLATNOY—Originally meaning "someone with connections," the word *blatnoy* now means a gangster or a "professional" criminal.

BLINI—Thin pancakes, sometimes called *blinchiki*. A staple of Russian cuisine.

BRATVA—"Brotherhood." A common term for Russian organized crime by members of the underworld themselves.

BRIGADA—Roughly equivalent to a "crew" in Cosa Nostra; an informal gang of Russian organized crime figures.

BUR—Acronym for Barak Usilennogo Rezhima, a reinforced high-security barracks within a Soviet prison zone.

CHANSON—See *blatnaya pesnya*.

CHINA WHITE—Reference to high-purity white-powder heroin, originally smuggled by Chinese traffickers from Southeast Asia at the beginning of the twentieth century, in comparison to heroin produced in Mexico, which had a dark brown color and was often described as "Mexican tar" or "black tar." In the 1990s, when Boris Nayfeld was trafficking in wholesale heroin from Thailand to the United States, China White was considered the most sought-after and expensive form of the narcotic.

CLABBER—Trick-taking card game of apparent Dutch origin—where it was called Klaberjass. It uses only the highest twenty-four cards in the deck—ace to nine—and has long been popular within the Russian-Jewish community.

COLONY NUMBER 2—The prison work camp (or "colony") in Babruysk, Belarus, where Boris Nayfeld was first incarcerated at age eighteen.

DEAD SOULS—See *myortvye dushi*.

DETDOM—From "children's house." The Soviet-era orphanage used to house the *besprizornye*, literally translated as the "unattended" or "neglected" children. In the aftermath of the Revolution, widespread famine, and war, there were millions of parentless children in the USSR.

DETSKY MIR, or "Children's World"—Chain of popular department stores for children in the Soviet Union; the first and most famous one was opened in 1957 in the center of Moscow at Dzerzhinsky Square, today's Lubyanka Square.

FARTSOVKA—Soviet-era slang for the illegal purchase of imported goods that were otherwise hard-to-reach or inaccessible for an ordinary citizen of the USSR. Levi's jeans, polo shirts, and other Western-style clothing were in high demand for black marketers, but vinyl records, tapes, cosmetics, and household goods were also a staple of the trade in *fartsovka*.

FENYA—Slang language used among Russian-speaking criminals. Often call the "thieves' cant," it was originally a cryptolanguage, understood only by members of the underworld. Today many fenya words have entered contemporary Russian speech. Its origins stem back to czarist times, and most credit the influence of the port city of Odessa, with its large Jewish population and rich gangster subculture, as many fenya slang terms and loan words come from Yiddish. There are thousands of unique expressions, words with secondary criminal meanings, as well as a rich tradition of criminal ballads, known as *blatnaya pesnya,* sung entirely in fenya.

FUFLYZHNIK—Someone who doesn't pay their gambling debts. Originally strictly used by the underworld, roughly equivalent to the English words "deadbeat" or "welsher," the term *fuflyzhnik* has crept into Russian slang as a "flake" or a "a guy who does not keep his promises."

GOLDINEH MEDINEH—Yiddish for "the golden land," a common way of referring to the United States of America during the peak period of Ashkenazi Jewish immigration—between 1880 and 1924—when more than two million Jews from Russia and Eastern Europe came to the United States.

GRIBENES—From the Yiddish word for "scraps," crisp chicken- or goose-skin cracklings, often served with fried onions. As with other cracklings, gribenes are a by-product of rendering poultry to produce cooking fat known as schmaltz.

GORISPOLKOM—Acronym for Executive Committee of the City Soviet of People's Deputies. In the USSR, the Gorispolkom was the operating arm of local Soviet power in cities, towns, and municipalities.

GOSBANK—The official State bank, which financed the entire economy of the Soviet Union. There were branches in many cities and towns that moved billions of rubles around the USSR, since the economy was nearly entirely cash based. The Gosbank had huge vaults and armed security, nearly impenetrable to robbery.

GPU OFFICER—The State Political Directorate (also translated as the State Political Administration) was the intelligence service and secret police of the Russian Soviet Federative Socialist Republic from February 6, 1922, to December 29, 1922, and of the Soviet Union from December 29, 1922, until November 15, 1923.

GREAT PATRIOTIC WAR—The most common Russian name for the Second World War, specifically the period of June 22, 1941, when Nazi forces invaded the Soviet Union, to May 9, 1945, when Red Army forces captured Berlin. Although the exact death toll remains in dispute, a figure of 20 million people was considered official during the Soviet era. The post-Soviet government of Russia puts the Soviet war losses at 26.6 million.

GULAG—Acronym for Chief Administration of Corrective Labor Camps, a system of Soviet forced labor camps that incarcerated approximately 18 million people throughout their history, operating from the 1920s until shortly after Stalin's death in 1953.

INTERNAT—In the mid-1950s, the Soviet Union developed a mixed boarding-school system for orphans and neglected children, blending education and vocational training with the intention of molding vulnerable children into patriotic proletarians. Nikita Khrushchev called the new internats "schools of the future" at the 20th Congress of the Communist Party of the Soviet Union in 1956.

ITALYAKHA—Slang roughly meaning "big Italian." When discussing members of Cosa Nostra, Boris generally opts for a unique piece of Russian slang rather than the standard word for an "Italian"—*Italyanets*. He'll often refer to an *Italyakha,* or "big Italian," indicating a certain level of respect.

JUVENILE COLONY—In the Soviet Union, a prison camp for those under the age of eighteen.

KALASHNIKOV—Refers to the AK-47 automatic rifle. Known in Russian as the Avtomat Kalashnikova ("Kalashnikov automatic rifle"), it is arguably the world's most widely used shoulder weapon, a gas-operated assault rifle that is chambered for a 7.62 × 39mm cartridge. Developed in the Soviet Union by small-arms designer Mikhail Timofeyevich Kalashnikov, who introduced the most popular version of the weapon in 1947.

KATORGA—Was a system of penal labor in the Russian Empire. After the change in Russian penal law in 1847, exile and *katorga* became common punishment for participants in national uprisings within the empire. Prisoners were sent to remote penal colonies in the vast uninhabited areas of Siberia, where settlers and workers were never available in sufficient numbers, and forced to perform labor under harsh conditions. Fyodor Dostoevsky is one of the most famous names to have been sentenced to *katorga*.

KATRAN—Slang for an illicit casino, often in an apartment or storefront.

KGB—Komitet Gosudarstvennoy Bezopasnosti ("Committee for State Security") was the main security agency for the Soviet Union from March 1954 until December 1991. The KGB, infamous for the terror its very mention inspired in Soviet citizens, was the ultimate incarnation of such preceding secret police agencies as the Cheka, GPU, OGPU, NKGB, NKVD, and MGB.

KHOZYAIN—Used by inmates in a Soviet prison camp to refer to the camp commandant, literally the "owner."

KHULIGAN—As far back as czarist times, the Russian language appropriated the Anglo-Irish word "hooligan" to refer to street toughs and members of youth gangs. By the mid-1950s, behaving as a *khuligan* was codified as a criminal offense. Russian president Vladimir Putin was a member of a *khuligan* gang in 1960s Leningrad. Putin has proudly recalled it as being time well spent in a "street university."

KHULIGANSTVO—Under Article 206 of the Soviet Union's 1960s criminal code, *khuliganstvo* ("hooliganism") included "all intentional acts which grossly violate the public order, and which demonstrate an obvious lack of respect towards society."

KISHKA—In Ashkenazi Jewish cuisine, refers to a once-popular dish of minced meat, rice, vegetables, flour (or matzo meal), and chicken fat stuffed inside the lining of beef intestines. In Yiddish, and many East Slavic languages, the word *kishka* means "guts."

KONKA—A pickpocketing scam, generally on public transit, executed in a team of thieves jostling and distracting the victim, then cutting his or her purse or pants pocket to extract cash. This fenya term, which has the word "horse" at its root, stems from the first horse-drawn tram line in 1860s St. Petersburg.

KOPEK—Roughly equivalent to the English word *cent,* a kopek coin is the smallest denomination within a currency system associated with the Russian economy. The Russian ruble is divided into one hundred kopeks.

KOREN/KORENNOY—From the standard Russian word for "root," describes a unique kind of gangster partnership; two criminal partners are so close, they are joined together at the root. Profits are shared along this structure: even if gained individually, apart from the other *korennye,* money must be shared equally.

KOZYOL (PL. *KOZLY*)—Literally a "goat" (pl. "goats"). In the context of Soviet-era prison camps, it means an inmate who cooperates with the guards and camp officials. The *kozly* form their own distinct caste system within the prisons.

KRYSHA—"Roof" in standard Russian. In the criminal context, *krysha* means protection and patronage. Normally a business will pay a mobster, or other authority figure, a regular fee for protection to come under one's roof, that is, to be protected from the advances from other criminal operations.

KRYTKA—Meaning "lid." In the Soviet era, refers to a self-contained prison reserved for the most incorrigible inmates who systemically violate rules. Prisoners are locked in their cells all day, with no common area for eating or socializing.

KUM—Prison slang for the "head inmate," literally meaning the "godfather." The inmate who interacts directly with the prison administration.

"LEFT SIDE" OR "ON THE LEFT"—See *na levo*.

LIMONKAS—Refers to lemon-shaped hand grenades, like the U.S. Army's Mk 2 fragmentation grenade, first introduced in 1918. Although the grooves and knobs have often been said to resemble a pineapple, among Russian speakers, the slang term "lemon" or *limonka* quickly caught on and stuck.

LOKH—"Sucker." The insult most likely entered fenya slang from Yiddish to mean someone who's easily duped. Now widely used in Russian speech.

LYSY—"Baldie."

MAMA LOSHEN—Yiddish for "mother tongue."

MAMKAS—"Madams," women who run illegal massage parlors.

MILITSIYA—In the Soviet Union, all police forces were known as *militisya*. After the October 1917 Revolution, the Bolsheviks disbanded the czarist police forces and formed All-Proletarian Workers' and Peasants' *Militsiya*. The word *police,* associated with corruption, was replaced in everyday speech by *militsiya.*

MISCHPOCHA—The word for "family" in Hebrew and Yiddish.

MUSOR—In fenya slang, means a "cop." Originally comes from the standard Russian word for "garbage."

MUSORYENOK—A diminutive of the slang for "cop." In other words, "little piggie."

MUZHIKI—Soviet-era term for the "common prisoners" within the prison caste system. Inmates who have committed crimes but are serving their sentences, working as ordered, counting down the days until their release. Unlike the elevated *vory v zakone* or the lowest caste of the *opushchenny,* the *muzhiki* made up the majority of the population of most Soviet prison camps and jails.

MYORTVYE DUSHI—"Dead souls." The phrase comes from the classic satirical novel of the same name by Nikolai Gogol. Gogol's protagonist in *Dead Souls,* Pavel Ivanovich Chichikov, is a nobleman traveling around the countryside buying records of dead serfs from provincial aristocrats to enhance his standing in society, claiming to have more serfs under his name than he could afford. The novel was widely taught in Soviet schools because it mocks the old czarist way of governing the country. Over the decades, the term *myortvye dushi* entered everyday Russian vernacular. As used by Boris Nayfeld, it's roughly equivalent to the American Mafia's concept of "no-show jobs."

NA LEVO—"On the left side." Making money on the black market or under the table. Outside the context of criminal activity, *na levo* can mean having a mistress or an affair outside of marriage.

NARKOMAN—"Drug addict." Generally refers to someone who's addicted to heroin or other opiates.

NARKOMANYUGA—*Huge* drug addict.

NOMENKLATURA—The de facto "ruling class" in the Soviet Union. *Nomenklatura* refers to a category of people within the Soviet Union (at its peak, roughly 1.6 million people out of a population of approximately 250 million), Communist Party apparatchiks who held key administrative positions in the bureaucracy, running all spheres of the USSR's government, industry, agriculture, education, and sports.

OBSHCHAK—Common fund for criminals. The term emerged in the early Soviet penal system and apparently derives from the Russian adjective for "shared," "common," or "communal." It denotes a collective fund, used primarily for the purposes of mutual aid among like-minded convicts. Outside of prison, within an organized crime crew, the *obshchak* is a means by which spoils are divided evenly.

OCHKARIK—Pejorative for someone who wears glasses; roughly equivalent to "four eyes."

ODESSKY—Term for people from Odessa.

OLD NEW YEAR—January 14. New Year on the "old" Gregorian calendar is generally celebrated with more fervor than the more traditional Julian calendar date of January 1.

OKROSHKA—Cold raw vegetable soup, part of the national cuisines of Russia and Ukraine. It is often made of cucumbers, radishes, spring onions, boiled potatoes, eggs, beef, veal, sausage, ham, and kvass, which is a beverage made from fermented rye bread.

OPUSHCHENNY—Meaning "the fallen" or "the lowered-down," the lowest caste within a Soviet-era or Russian prison, including those forced to become *petukhi* ("roosters"), or "passive homosexuals," victims of prison rape, and others degraded to the lowest level of prison society. A kind of untouchable caste.

ORGANIZATSIYA—"Organization" in Russian.

OVOSCHNIK—"Vegetable-seller." The nickname for the Brighton Beach racketeer Vyacheslav "Slava" Lyubarsky, who was murdered with his son, Vadim, in January 1992.

PAKHAN—Boss in the Russian organized crime *bratva*. The word originally meant "chief" or "head." Vladimir Lenin was often described by criminals to be the *pakhan* of the Communist Party.

PALE OF SETTLEMENT—The western region of the Russian Empire, in which, between 1791 and the 1917 Revolution, permanent residency by Jews was allowed and beyond which Jewish residency was by and large prohibited. The Pale of Settlement included modern-day Belarus, Lithuania, and Moldova; large sections of Poland and Ukraine; and relatively small parts of Latvia and western Russian Federation.

PASTUKHI—"Shepherds." Fenya slang used by inmates in a *zona* to refer to the guards.

PEDERAST—Vulgar for "homosexual," from the Greek term *pederasty.*

PELMENI—Dumplings of Russian cuisine that consist of a filling wrapped in thin, unleavened dough. *Varenyky* is the more commonly used term in Ukraine. In Yiddish, the comparable term is kreplach.

PETUKH—"Rooster." In the context of prison-camp culture and general Russian criminal speech, means a "passive homosexual." Extremely insulting.

PIS'MO—Slang for a sharpened coin used by experienced pickpockets in the Soviet era. See *pisatel.*

PISATEL—Russian for "writer." In the underworld, *pisatel* refers to a skilled pickpocket who uses a sharpened coin (*pis'mo*) or razor blade to cut purses, pockets, and briefcases, extracting cash without the victim noticing. In Russian criminal slang, such pickpocketing is called "writing letters."

PITERSKY—Term for a person from Leningrad (in the Soviet era) or St. Petersburg.

PRIKHLEBATEL'—Someone who eats soup or porridge from another person's bowl. A "sponger," "moocher," "hanger-on," or "nobody."

RAZGON—From the Russian word for "acceleration," an elaborate con game of the Soviet era involving crooks dressed in fake police uniforms using the threat of imminent arrest to extract valuables from people engaged in black market activity.

SALO—Slabs of cured pork fat—salted, fermented, or smoked. A popular Russian and Ukrainian culinary tradition. *Salo* is often used as a chaser with vodka.

SHIVA—From the Hebrew word for "seven." The weeklong period of Jewish mourning following the burial of a close relative.

SBERKASSA—Or State Labor Savings Offices. The only version of a personal bank account available to the general public in the Soviet Union.

SCHNEYER—Fenya word, once again originally from Yiddish, for a scam involving valuables like diamonds, gold, or other precious metals and jewels.

SCHVITZ—From the Yiddish word for "sweat." A "braggart" or "blowhard."

SHESTYORKA—"Little six." Refers to the least valuable playing card in a thirty-six-card deck. *Shestyorka* is a disparaging term for the person who occupies the lowest rung in the prison hierarchy, an errand boy or "bitch."

SHIKSA—Derogatory word for a non-Jewish woman. Yiddish noun derived from the Hebrew term *shekets,* meaning "abomination," "impure," or "object of loathing."

SHMON—Body search in Russian prisons, from the czarist era through the Soviets. Most likely entered Russian criminal slang from the Hebrew word for "eight," *sh'monah,* the hour in the morning when many prisoners were frisked in Russian prisons.

SMENKA—"Switch." In standard Russian, changing clothes. For example, from winter boots to indoor shoes. In the context of the underworld, *smenka* refers to a con in which something of value, a diamond or a gold coin, is switched quickly during a transaction for a fake.

SOOKA—"Bitch." From the Russian for a "female dog."

SPARTAK—One of the most popular sporting clubs in the USSR, and even today, in postcommunist Russia. Spartak was founded in Moscow in 1921 by footballer Nikolai Starostin and by the mid-1920s it came under the sponsorship of the food workers' union. Spartak was the first and the largest All-Union Voluntary Sports Society for workers from various trades and unions. Other popular sports societies of the Soviet era included Dinamo, originally founded by Felix Dzerzhinsky, head of the State Political Directorate (GPU), the Soviet political police and the predecessor to the KGB; Lokomotiv, the clubs of the railway workers; and SKA, traditionally the army clubs.

STARSHIY—Literally "senior." The actual day-to-day term employed by Russians to refer to the head of a Russian organized crime crew in America, as opposed to the anglicized "boss," "godfather," or "don," terms that were *never* used by actual Russian-speaking mobsters.

SUPREME MEASURE—The death penalty in the Soviet Union, execution by firing squad. Abbreviated from "the supreme measure of punishment." See *vyschaya myera nakazaniya* below.

THIEVES IN LAW—See *vory v zakone*.

TREF—A meeting of the *vory v zakone*, usually to decide important financial and internal matters, divide up territory, or settle disputes at the highest "criminal level."

USATY—"Mustached." From *usy* for "moustache."

VLADIMIR LENIN ALL-UNION PIONEER ORGANIZATION—"Young Pioneers" or "Young Pioneer Movement" was a mass youth organization of the Soviet Union that existed from 1922 to 1991 for children ages 9–15 years old. It can be considered analogous to the Boy Scouts in Western countries but far more ideological.

VOLYNA—"Handgun." Pistol or revolver. Possibly from the word *violin*.

VOR—Russian for "thief." In the world of organized crime, the word is an honorary title analogous to an inducted member, or a "made man," in Cosa Nostra.

VOROVSKOY MIR—The "thieves world," refers to the secret criminal society of the *vory v zakone*, with a complex internal set of rules of conduct, generally most evident in the Soviet Union's forced-labor penal system as well as in the prisons of contemporary Russia.

VORY V ZAKONE—Literally "thieves in law." This phrase, which dates back to Soviet labor camps of the 1920s, can best be understood as "thieves following a code" or "thieves with their own sets of laws." *Vory v zakone* are frequently identified by a complex pictoral code of tattoos, most famously the eight-pointed star. It's also common to refer to a *vor v zakone* as having been "crowned" or, in the case of Evsei Agron, to have "lost his crown."

VYSCHAYA MYERA NAKAZANIYA—"The supreme measure of punishment." Under the Soviet Union's penal code, this meant execution by firing squad. Reserved for violent crimes like murder, but as of 1932, theft from the state was punishable by death.

VYZHIVANIYE—"Survival" in Russian.

WITSEC—Acronym of the United States Federal Witness Security Program. More commonly known as the Witness Protection Program, WITSEC was established under Title V of the Organized Crime Control Act of 1970 to aid in the prosecution of organized crime.

YOUNG PIONEERS—See *Vladimir Lenin All-Union Pioneer Organization.*

ZAKROISCHIK—Cutter in a garment factory; a common profession for Jews in cities like Bialystok and Gomel that have large garment-manufacturing industries.

ZHID—Crude anti-Semitic insult for a Jew in Russia. *Zhid* is the Polish word for Jew, whereas the Russian word is *evrei.*

ZHIDOVSKAYA MORDA—An extremely insulting anti-Semitic slur in Russian. *Morda* is a muzzle. Roughly "kike-face."

ZHIGULI—The Lada 2100 ("Zhiguli") was a brand of Soviet car first produced in 1970 in an agreement between Italian automobile manufacture Fiat and the USSR. The Zhiguli was the first and only car available to the majority of Soviet citizens.

ZHIVOGLOT—Can mean a glutton, parasite, ruthless bloodsucker, literally, "one who swallows its prey alive."

ZONA—"Zone." The most common Russian phrase for prison camps.

INDEX